GLOBAL TRENDS
PARADOX OF PROGRESS

A publication of the National Intelligence Council

JANUARY 2017

Printed in the United States of America
ISBN-13: 978-1544779034
ISBN-10: 1544779038

TABLE OF CONTENTS

vi   Letter From the Chairman of the
National Intelligence Council

ix   The Future Summarized

1   The Map of the Future

5   Trends Transforming the Global Landscape

29   Near Future: Tensions Are Rising

45   Three Scenarios for the Distant Future:
Islands, Orbits, Communities

63   What the Scenarios Teach Us: Fostering
Opportunities Through Resilience

70   Methodological Note

72   Glossary

74   Acknowledgements

ANNEXES

85   The Next Five Years by Region

159   Key Global Trends

Letter from the Chairman of the National Intelligence Council

Thinking about the future is vital but hard. Crises keep intruding, making it all but impossible to look beyond daily headlines to what lies over the horizon. In those circumstances, thinking "outside the box," to use the cliché, too often loses out to keeping up with the inbox. That is why every four years the National Intelligence Council (NIC) undertakes a major assessment of the forces and choices shaping the world before us over the next two decades.

This version, the sixth in the series, is titled, "Global Trends: The Paradox of Progress," and we are proud of it. It may look like a report, but it is really an invitation, an invitation to discuss, debate and inquire further about how the future could unfold. Certainly, we do not pretend to have the definitive "answer."

Long-term thinking is critical to framing strategy. The *Global Trends* series pushes us to reexamine key assumptions, expectations, and uncertainties about the future. In a very messy and interconnected world, a longer perspective requires us to ask hard questions about which issues and choices will be most consequential in the decades ahead—even if they don't necessarily generate the biggest headlines. A longer view also is essential because issues like terrorism, cyberattacks, biotechnology, and climate change invoke high stakes and will require sustained collaboration to address.

Peering into the future can be scary and surely is humbling. Events unfold in complex ways for which our brains are not naturally wired. Economic, political, social, technological, and cultural forces collide in dizzying ways, so we can be led to confuse recent, dramatic events with the more important ones. It is tempting, and usually fair, to assume people act "rationally," but leaders, groups, mobs, and masses can behave very differently—and unexpectedly—under similar circumstances. For instance, we had known for decades how brittle most regimes in the Middle East were, yet some erupted in the Arab Spring in 2011 and others did not. Experience teaches us how much history unfolds through cycles and shifts, and still human nature commonly expects tomorrow to be pretty much like today—which is usually the safest bet on the future until it is not. I always remind myself that between Mr. Reagan's "evil empire" speech and the demise of that empire, the Soviet Union, was only a scant decade, a relatively short time even in a human life.

Grasping the future is also complicated by the assumptions we carry around in our heads, often without quite knowing we do. I have been struck recently by the "prosperity presumption" that runs deep in most Americans but is often hardly recognized. We assume that with prosperity come all good things—people are happier, more democratic and less likely to go to war with one another. Yet, then we confront a group like ISIL, which shares none of the presumption.

Given these challenges to thinking about the future, we have engaged broadly and tried to stick to analytic basics rather than seizing any particular worldview. Two years ago, we started with exercises identifying key assumptions and uncertainties—the list of assumptions underlying US foreign policy was stunningly long, many of them half-buried. We conducted research and consulted with numerous experts in and outside the US Government to identify and test trends. We tested early themes and arguments on a blog. We visited more than 35 countries and one territory, soliciting ideas and feedback from over 2,500 people around the world from all walks of life. We developed multiple scenarios to imagine how key uncertainties might result in alternative futures. The NIC then compiled and refined the various streams into what you see here.

This edition of *Global Trends* revolves around a core argument about how the changing nature of power is increasing stress both within countries and between countries, and bearing on vexing transnational issues. The main section lays out the key trends, explores their implications, and offers up three scenarios to help readers imagine how different choices and developments could play out in very different ways over the next several decades. Two annexes lay out more detail. The first lays out five-year forecasts for each region of the world. The second provides more context on the key global trends in train.

The fact that the National Intelligence Council regularly publishes an unclassified assessment of the world surprises some people, but our intent is to encourage open and informed discussions about future risks and opportunities. Moreover, Global Trends is unclassified because those screens of secrets that dominate our daily work are not of much help in peering out beyond a year or two. What is a help is reaching out not just to experts and government officials but also to students, women's groups, entrepreneurs, transparency advocates, and beyond.

Many minds and hands made this project happen. The heavy lifting was done by the NIC's Strategic Futures Group, directed by Dr. Suzanne Fry, with her very talented team: Rich Engel, Phyllis Berry, Heather Brown, Kenneth Dyer, Daniel Flynn, Geanetta Ford, Steven Grube, Terrence Markin, Nicholas Muto, Robert Odell, Rod Schoonover, Thomas Stork, and dozens of Deputy National Intelligence Officers. We recognize as well the thoughtful, careful review by NIC editors, as well as CIA's extremely talented graphic and web designers and production team.

Global Trends represents how the NIC is thinking about the future. It does not represent the official, coordinated view of the US Intelligence Community nor US policy. Longtime readers will note that this edition does not reference a year in the title (the previous edition was *Global Trends* 2030) because we think doing so conveys a false precision. For us, looking over the "long term" spans the next several decades, but we also have made room in this edition to explore the next five years to be more relevant in timeline for a new US administration.

We hope this *Global Trends* stretches your thinking. However pessimistic or optimistic you may be about the years ahead, we believe exploring the key issues and choices facing the world is a worthy endeavor.

Sincerely,

Gregory F Treverton

Gregory Treverton,
Chairman, National Intelligence Council

THE FUTURE SUMMARIZED

We are living a paradox: The achievements of the industrial and information ages are shaping a world to come that is both more dangerous and richer with opportunity than ever before. Whether promise or peril prevails will turn on the choices of humankind.

The progress of the past decades is historic—connecting people, empowering individuals, groups, and states, and lifting a billion people out of poverty in the process. But this same progress also spawned shocks like the Arab Spring, the 2008 Global Financial Crisis, and the global rise of populist, anti-establishment politics. These shocks reveal how fragile the achievements have been, underscoring deep shifts in the global landscape that portend a dark and difficult near future.

The next five years will see rising tensions within and between countries. Global growth will slow, just as increasingly complex global challenges impend. An ever-widening range of states, organizations, and empowered individuals will shape geopolitics. For better and worse, the emerging global landscape is drawing to a close an era of American dominance following the Cold War. So, too, perhaps is the rules-based international order that emerged after World War II. It will be much harder to cooperate internationally and govern in ways publics expect. Veto players will threaten to block collaboration at every turn, while information "echo chambers" will reinforce countless competing realities, undermining shared understandings of world events.

Underlying this crisis in cooperation will be local, national, and international differences about the proper role of government across an array of issues ranging from the economy to the environment, religion, security, and the rights of individuals. Debates over moral boundaries—to whom is owed what—will become more pronounced, while divergence in values and interests among states will threaten international security.

It will be tempting to impose order on this apparent chaos, but that ultimately would be too costly in the short run and would fail in the long. Dominating empowered, proliferating actors in multiple domains would require unacceptable resources in an era of slow growth, fiscal limits, and debt burdens. Doing so domestically would be the end of democracy, resulting in authoritarianism or instability or both. Although material strength will remain essential to geopolitical and state power, the most powerful actors of the future will draw on networks, relationships, and information to compete and cooperate. This is the lesson of great power politics in the 1900s, even if those powers had to learn and relearn it.

The US and Soviet proxy wars, especially in Vietnam and Afghanistan, were a harbinger of the post-Cold War conflicts and today's fights in the Middle East, Africa, and South Asia in which less powerful adversaries deny victory through asymmetric strategies, ideology, and societal tensions. The threat from terrorism will expand in the coming decades as the growing prominence of small groups and individuals use new technologies, ideas, and relationships to their advantage.

Meanwhile, states remain highly relevant. China and Russia will be emboldened, while regional aggressors and nonstate actors will see openings to pursue their interests. Uncertainty about the United States, an inward-looking West, and erosion of norms for conflict prevention and human rights will encourage China and Russia to check US influence. In doing so, their "gray zone" aggression and diverse forms of disruption will stay below the threshold of hot war but bring profound risks of miscalculation. Overconfidence that material strength can manage escalation will increase the risks of interstate conflict to levels not seen since the Cold War. Even if hot war is avoided, the current pattern of "international cooperation where we can get it"—such as on climate change—masks significant differences in values and interests among states and does little to curb assertions of dominance within regions. These trends are leading to a spheres of influence world.

Nor is the picture much better on the home front for many countries. While decades of global integration and advancing technology enriched the richest and lifted that billion out of poverty, mostly in Asia, it also hollowed out Western middle classes and stoked pushback against globalization. Migrant flows are greater now than in the past 70 years, raising the specter of drained welfare coffers and increased competition for jobs, and reinforcing nativist, anti-elite impulses. Slow growth plus technology-induced disruptions in job markets will threaten poverty reduction and drive tensions within countries in the years to come, fueling the very nationalism that contributes to tensions between countries.

Yet this dreary near future is hardly cast in stone. Whether the next five or 20 years are brighter—or darker—will turn on three choices: How will individuals, groups, and governments renegotiate their expectations of one another to create political order in an era of empowered individuals and rapidly changing economies? To what extent will major state powers, as well as individuals and groups, craft new patterns or architectures of international cooperation and competition? To what extent will governments, groups, and individuals prepare now for multifaceted global issues like climate change and transformative technologies?

Three stories or scenarios—"Islands," "Orbits," and "Communities"—explore how trends and choices of note might intersect to create different pathways to the future. These scenarios emphasize alternative responses to near-term volatility—at the national (Islands), regional (Orbits), and sub-state and transnational (Communities) levels.

- *Islands* investigates a restructuring of the global economy that leads to long periods of slow or no growth, challenging both traditional models of economic prosperity and the presumption that globalization will continue to expand. The scenario emphasizes the challenges to governments in meeting societies' demands for both economic and physical security as popular pushback to globalization increases, emerging technologies transform work and trade, and political instability grows. It underscores the choices governments will face in conditions that might tempt some to turn inward, reduce support for multilateral cooperation, and adopt protectionist policies, while others find ways to leverage new sources of economic growth and productivity.

- **Orbits** explores a future of tensions created by competing major powers seeking their own spheres of influence while attempting to maintain stability at home. It examines how the trends of rising nationalism, changing conflict patterns, emerging disruptive technologies, and decreasing global cooperation might combine to increase the risk of interstate conflict. This scenario emphasizes the policy choices ahead for governments that would reinforce stability and peace or further exacerbate tensions. It features a nuclear weapon used in anger, which turns out to concentrate global minds so that it does not happen again.

- **Communities** shows how growing public expectations but diminishing capacity of national governments open space for local governments and private actors, challenging traditional assumptions about what governing means. Information technology remains the key enabler, and companies, advocacy groups, charities, and local governments prove nimbler than national governments in delivering services to sway populations in support of their agendas. Most national governments resist, but others cede some power to emerging networks. Everywhere, from the Middle East to Russia, control is harder.

As the paradox of progress implies, the same trends generating near-term risks also can create opportunities for better outcomes over the long term. If the world were fortunate enough to be able to take advantage of these opportunities, the future would be more benign than our three scenarios suggest. In the emerging global landscape, rife with surprise and discontinuity, the states and organizations most able to exploit such opportunities will be those that are resilient, enabling them to adapt to changing conditions, persevere in the face of unexpected adversity, and take actions to recover quickly. They will invest in infrastructure, knowledge, and relationships that allow them to manage shock—whether economic, environmental, societal, or cyber.

Similarly, the most resilient societies will likely be those that unleash and embrace the full potential of all individuals—whether women and minorities or those battered by recent economic and technological trends. They will be moving with, rather than against, historical currents, making use of the ever-expanding scope of human skill to shape the future. In all societies, even in the bleakest circumstances, there will be those who choose to improve the welfare, happiness, and security of others—employing transformative technologies to do so at scale. While the opposite will be true as well—destructive forces will be empowered as never before—the central puzzle before governments and societies is how to blend individual, collective, and national endowments in a way that yields sustainable security, prosperity, and hope.

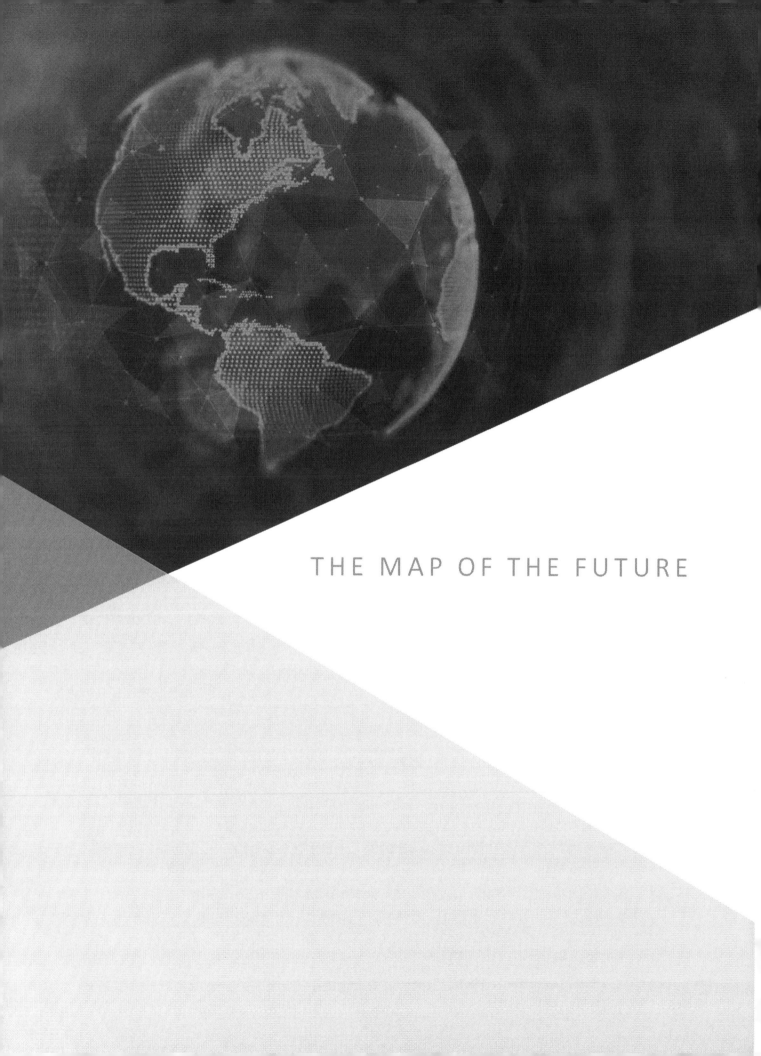

THE MAP OF THE FUTURE

Vietnamese children walking home from school.

THE MAP OF THE FUTURE

Our story of the future begins and ends with a paradox: The same global trends suggesting a dark and difficult near future, despite the progress of recent decades, also bear within them opportunities for choices that yield more hopeful, secure futures. In the pages to come, we use multiple time horizons to help explore the future from different perspectives, to illustrate the risks for sudden discontinuities and deep, slow-moving shifts, and to flag decision points.

We start with an exploration of "Key Trends" that are changing the global landscape and illuminate today's paradox. We discuss as well how these trends are "Changing the Nature of Power, Governance, and Cooperation" as a way to diagnose why and how global dynamics have become more challenging in recent years.

Absent very different personal, political, and business choices, the current trajectory of trends and power dynamics will play out in a "Near-Future of Rising Tensions."

Shifting gears, we explore trajectories for how the trends could unfold over a 20-year horizon through "Three Scenarios for the Distant Future: Islands, Orbits, and Communities." Each scenario identifies decision points that might lead to brighter or darker futures, and develops implications for foreign policy planning assumptions.

Finally, we discuss the lessons these scenarios provide regarding potential opportunities and tradeoffs in creating the future, rather than just responding to it.

Throughout the document, we have placed imagined headlines from the future to highlight the types of discontinuities that could emerge at any point from the convergence of key trends.

TRENDS TRANSFORMING
THE GLOBAL LANDSCAPE

Global Trends and Key Implications Through 2035

The rich are aging, the poor are not. Working-age populations are shrinking in wealthy countries, China, and Russia but growing in developing, poorer countries, particularly in Africa and South Asia, increasing economic, employment, urbanization, and welfare pressures and spurring migration. Training and continuing education will be crucial in developed and developing countries alike.

The global economy is shifting. Weak economic growth will persist in the near term. Major economies will confront shrinking workforces and diminishing productivity gains while recovering from the 2008-09 financial crisis with high debt, weak demand, and doubts about globalization. China will attempt to shift to a consumer-driven economy from its longstanding export and investment focus. Lower growth will threaten poverty reduction in developing countries.

Technology is accelerating progress but causing discontinuities. Rapid technological advancements will increase the pace of change and create new opportunities but will aggravate divisions between winners and losers. Automation and artificial intelligence threaten to change industries faster than economies can adjust, potentially displacing workers and limiting the usual route for poor countries to develop. Biotechnologies such as genome editing will revolutionize medicine and other fields, while sharpening moral differences.

Ideas and Identities are driving a wave of exclusion. Growing global connectivity amid weak growth will increase tensions within and between societies. Populism will increase on the right and the left, threatening liberalism. Some leaders will use nationalism to shore up control. Religious influence will be increasingly consequential and more authoritative than many governments. Nearly all countries will see economic forces boost women's status and leadership roles, but backlash also will occur.

Governing is getting harder. Publics will demand governments deliver security and prosperity, but flat revenues, distrust, polarization, and a growing list of emerging issues will hamper government performance. Technology will expand the range of players who can block or circumvent political action. Managing global issues will become harder as actors multiply—to include NGOs, corporations, and empowered individuals—resulting in more ad hoc, fewer encompassing efforts.

The nature of conflict is changing. The risk of conflict will increase due to diverging interests among major powers, an expanding terror threat, continued instability in weak states, and the spread of lethal, disruptive technologies. Disrupting societies will become more common, with long-range precision weapons, cyber, and robotic systems to target infrastructure from afar, and more accessible technology to create weapons of mass destruction.

Climate change, environment, and health issues will demand attention. A range of global hazards pose imminent and longer-term threats that will require collective action to address—even as cooperation becomes harder. More extreme weather, water and soil stress, and food insecurity will disrupt societies. Sea-level rise, ocean acidification, glacial melt, and pollution will change living patterns. Tensions over climate change will grow. Increased travel and poor health infrastructure will make infectious diseases harder to manage.

The Bottomline

These trends will converge at an unprecedented pace to make governing and cooperation harder and to change the nature of power—fundamentally altering the global landscape. Economic, technological and security trends, especially, will expand the number of states, organizations, and individuals able to act in consequential ways. Within states, political order will remain elusive and tensions high until societies and governments renegotiate their expectations of one another. Between states, the post-Cold War, unipolar moment has passed and the post-1945 rules based international order may be fading too. Some major powers and regional aggressors will seek to assert interests through force but will find results fleeting as they discover traditional, material forms of power less able to secure and sustain outcomes in a context of proliferating veto players.

Franco Lucato / Shutterstock.com

South African school students. Much of the growth in the world's working age population over the next several decades will come from Africa as well as South Asia.

TRENDS TRANSFORMING THE GLOBAL LANDSCAPE

The post-Cold War era is giving way to a new strategic context. Recent and future trends will converge during the next 20 years at an unprecedented pace to increase the number and complexity of issues, with several, like cyber attacks, terrorism, or extreme weather, representing risks for imminent disruption. Demographic shifts will stress labor, welfare, and social stability. The rich world is aging while much of the poorer world is not and is becoming more male to boot. More and more people are living in cities, some of which are increasingly vulnerable to sea-level rise, flooding, and storm surges. So, too, more people are on the move—drawn by visions of a better life or driven by horrors of strife. Competition for good jobs has become global, as technology, especially mass automation, disrupts labor markets. Technology will also further empower individuals and small groups, connecting people like never before. At the same time, values, nationalism, and religion will increasingly separate them.

At the national level, the gap between popular expectations and government performance will grow; indeed democracy itself can no longer be taken for granted. Internationally, the empowering of individuals and small groups will make it harder to organize collective action against major global problems, like climate change. International institutions will be visibly more mismatched to the tasks of the future, especially as they awkwardly embrace newly empowered private individuals and groups.

Meanwhile, the risk of conflict will grow. Warring will be less and less confined to the battlefield, and more aimed at disrupting societies—using cyber weapons from afar or suicide terrorists from within. The silent, chronic threats of air pollution, water shortage, and climate change will become more noticeable, leading more often than in the past to clashes, as diagnoses of and measures to deal with these issues remain divisive around the globe.

The Rich Are Aging, The Poor Are Not

The world's population will be larger, older, and more urban, even as the rate of global population growth slows. The effects on individual countries will vary, however, as the world's major economies age and the developing world remains youthful. The world population is forecasted to jump from roughly 7.3 to 8.8 billion people by 2035. Africa—with fertility rates double those of the rest of the world—and parts of Asia are on course for their working-age populations to soar. This could lead to economic progress or disaster, depending on how well their governments and societies ramp up investment in education, infrastructure, and other key sectors.

Labor and welfare patterns are set to change dramatically, both in rapidly aging countries and chronically young countries. People over 60 are becoming the world's fastest growing age cohort. Successful aging societies will increase elderly, youth, and female workforce participation to offset fewer working-age adults. Median ages will reach highs by 2035 in Japan (52.4), South Korea (49.4), Germany (49.6), and in several other countries. Europe will be hit especially hard, as well as Cuba (48), Russia (43.6), and China (45.7). The United States is aging at a slower rate—reaching a median age of approximately 41 by 2035—and will maintain a growing working-age population.

- **Chronically young populations**—with an average age of 25 years or less— will challenge parts of Africa and Asia, especially Somalia, as well as Afghanistan, Pakistan, Iraq, and Yemen. These states historically have been more prone to violence and instability. Even youthful states, however, will have increasing numbers of elderly to support, adding to their needs for infrastructure and socioeconomic safety nets.

Worldwide, the number of people reaching working age during the coming two decades will decline sharply from the previous two— from 1.20 billion in 1995-2015 to 850 million in 2015-35, according to UN projections. Most of these new workers, however, will be in South Asia and Africa, many of them in economies already struggling to create new jobs in the modern global economy due to inadequate infrastructure, limited education systems, corruption, and lack of opportunity for women.

- Integrating more women into the workforce will be particularly challenging due to longstanding cultural norms, but a study by McKinsey Global Institute assesses that such moves could boost output and productivity. According to the study, global GDP could rise by more than 10 percent by 2025 if roles and relative compensation for women across each region were improved to match the levels of the most-equitable country in that region. McKinsey highlighted improvements in education, financial and digital inclusion, legal protection, and compensation for care work as crucial to gains in gender economic equity—and ultimately beneficial to all workers as well.

More People Are Living In Cities. Demographic trends will boost popular pressure for effective public policy, especially in providing services and infrastructure needed to support increasingly urban populations. Just over half of humanity lives in cities today, a number forecast to rise to two-thirds by 2050. Aging countries that adapt health care, pensions, welfare, employment, and military recruitment systems are likely to successfully weather demographic trends while countries with younger populations would benefit from focusing on education and employment. Immigration and labor policies will remain divisive in the near term,

Estimated Change in Working-Age (15-64) Population 2015-35, Selected Countries

The world's working-age population will grow the most in South Asian and African countries, where education levels are among the lowest—putting them at a disadvantage in the evolving global economy, which will favor higher-skilled workers.

The biggest working-age decreases will be in China and in Europe, where employment opportunities will probably be greatest for skilled laborers and service-sector workers.

Worldwide, low-value-added manufacturing—historically the steppingstone to economic development for poor countries, and a pathway to prosperity for aspiring workers—will tend toward needing ever-fewer unskilled workers as automation, artificial intelligence, and other manufacturing advances take effect.

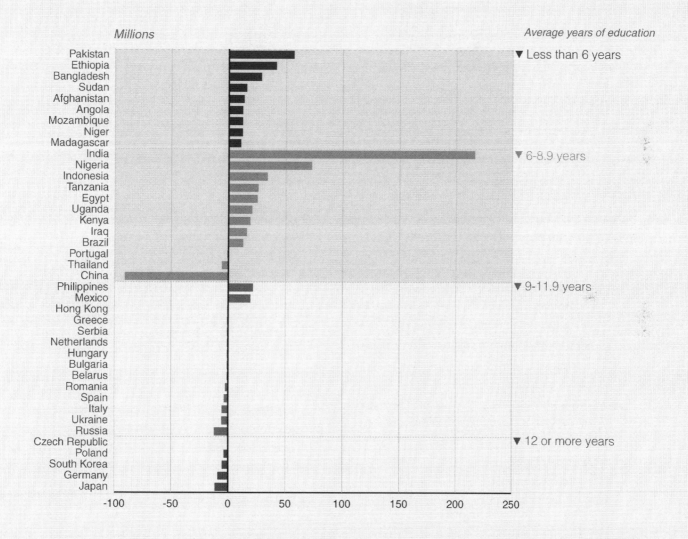

Note: The 40 countries highlighted in this chart are the countries with the largest increases and largest decreases of working-age population, in absolute numbers.
Source: UN population data (median projection).

Global Urban Population Growth Is Propelled by the Growth of Cities of All Sizes

The lion's share of the world's 20-percent population increase between 2015 and 2035 will end up in cities, as inflows of people from rural settings join already-growing city populations. Cities of all sizes will continue to increase in number, led by "megacities" of 10 million or more residents, which will be found on every continent except Australia.

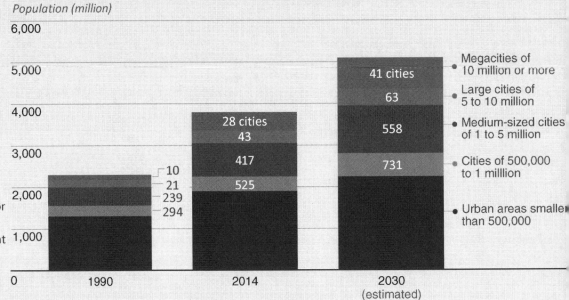

Source: United Nations, Department of Economics and Social Affairs, "World Urbanization Prospects, 2014 Revision."

---

although over time—and with training and education—such policies could address critical labor shortfalls in aging societies.

- Population growth will continue to concentrate in areas vulnerable to sea-level rise, flooding, and storm surges. By 2035, roughly 50 percent more people than in the year 2000 will live in low-elevation coastal zones worldwide, with the number in Asia increasing by more than 150 million and in Africa by 60 million. Many megacities, such as Bangkok, Ho Chi Minh City, Jakarta, and Manila, will continue to sink because of excessive groundwater extraction and natural geologic activity.

More Are On The Move . . . Migration flows will remain high during the next two decades as people seek economic opportunity and flee conflict and worsening environmental conditions. International migrants—or persons who reside outside their countries of birth—and forcibly displaced persons reached the highest absolute levels ever recorded in 2015, with 244 million international migrants and roughly 65 million displaced persons. In short, one in every 112 persons in the world is a refugee, an internally displaced person, or an asylum seeker. Growth in the number of international migrants, refugees, asylum seekers, and internally displaced persons is likely to continue due to major income disparities between areas, persistent conflicts, and festering ethnic and religious tensions. The number of people on the move will remain high or even increase as environmental stresses become more pronounced.

. . . And More Are Male. The recent increase in men compared to women in many countries in the Middle East and in East and South Asia signals countries under stress and the lasting influence of culture. Largely due to sex-selective abortion, female infanticide, and female selective neglect, China and India are already seeing significant numbers of men without

World Population Living in Extreme Poverty, 1820-2015

Extreme poverty is defined as living at a consumption (or income) level below $1.90 per day in real, purchasing-power parity terms (adjusted for price differences between countries and inflation).

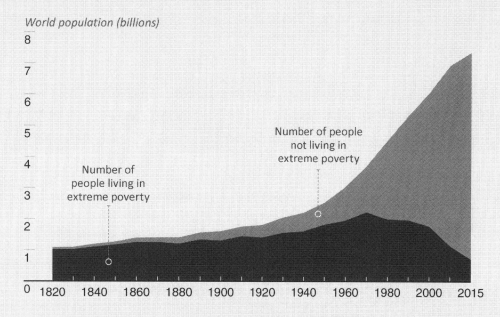

World population (billions)

Number of people living in extreme poverty

Number of people not living in extreme poverty

Source: OurWorldinData.org Max Roser based on World Bank and Bourguignon and Morrisson.

prospects for marriage. Gender imbalances take decades to correct, generating increased crime and violence in the meantime.

The Global Economy Is Shifting

Economies worldwide will shift significantly in the near and distant futures. Wealthy economies will try to halt recent declines in economic growth and maintain lifestyles even as working-age populations shrink and historically strong productivity gains wane. The developing world will seek to maintain its recent progress in eradicating abject poverty and to integrate rapidly growing working-age populations into its economies. Developed and developing alike will be pressed to identify new services, sectors, and occupations to replace manufacturing jobs that automation and other technologies will eliminate—and to educate and train workers to fill them.

Extreme Poverty Is Declining. Economic reforms in China and other countries, largely in Asia, have fueled a historic rise in living standards for nearly a billion people since 1990, cutting the share of the world living in "extreme poverty" (below $2 a day) from 35 to around 10 percent. Two dollars a day hardly makes life easy but does move people beyond surviving day-to-day. Improved living standards, however, lead to changed behaviors while raising expectations and anxieties about the future.

Western Middle Classes Are Squeezed. A global boom in low-cost manufacturing—together with automation driven in part by cost pressures from increased competition—hit US and European middle-class wages and employment hard over the past several decades. At the same time, however, it brought new opportunities to the developing world and dramatically reduced the costs of goods for consumers worldwide.

Stagnant wages are the most dramatic sign of the relentless drive for increased cost-efficiency: real median household incomes in the United States, Germany, Japan, Italy, and France rose by less than 1 percent per year from the mid-1980s through the Global Financial Crisis in 2008, according to the OECD. The post-crisis period has brought little respite, notwithstanding some improvement in the United States in 2015. McKinsey estimated that as of 2014, two-thirds of households in developed economies had real incomes at or below their 2005 levels.

Growth Will Be Weak. During the next five years, the global economy will continue to struggle to resume growth, as the world's major economies slowly recover from the 2008 crisis and work through sharp increases in public-sector debt. Moreover, the global economy also will face political pressures threatening open trade just as China undertakes a massive effort to redirect its economy toward consumption-based growth. As a consequence, most of the world's largest economies are likely to experience, at least in the near term, performance that is sub-par by historical standards. Weak growth will threaten recent gains in reducing poverty.

- China and the European Union (EU)—two of the world's three largest economies—will continue to attempt major, painful changes to bolster longer-term growth. China will be the biggest wildcard, as it attempts to continue raising living standards while shifting away from a state-directed, investment-driven economy to one that is consumer- and service-centered. Meanwhile, the EU is trying to foster stronger economic growth while struggling to manage high debt levels and deep political divisions over the future of the EU project.

- Financial crises, the erosion of the middle class, and greater public awareness of income inequality—all with roots predating the 2008 downturn—have fed sentiment in the West that the costs of trade liberalization outweigh the gains. As a result, the historic, 70-year run of global trade liberalization faces a major backlash, undermining future prospects for further liberalization—and raising the risk of greater protectionism. The world will be closely watching the United States and other traditional supporters of trade for signs of policy retrenchment. Further liberalization of free trade may be limited to more narrow issues or sets of partners.

Imagining a surprise
news headline in 2018 . . .

"Robin Hoodhacker" Paralyzes Online Commerce, Upends Markets

Nov. 19, 2018 – New York

Online commerce ground to a halt a week before the Christmas shopping season started in the United States, Canada, and Europe after numerous attacks by the persona "Robin Hoodhacker." The attacks created chaos by altering online payment accounts by as much as $100,000 in credit or debts—sparking a frenzy of online shopping that has forced retailers to shut down all digital transactions. The disruption sent global financial markets into a free fall before trading was suspended in most exchanges due to uncertainty about how long and widely the hacking would persist.

Changes in Real Income by World Income Percentiles (at Purchasing Power Parity) From 1988 to 2008

The "Elephant Chart," showing real household income changes between 1989 and 2008, shows that the period of the greatest globalization of the world economy—and the rapid growth it fostered in the developing world—brought large income gains to all but the very poorest of the bottom two-thirds of the world's households, and to the world's very wealthiest. The chart—and subsequent variations to it, which show slightly different relative gains between groups but the same broad pattern—suggests that globalization and advanced manufacturing brought relatively little gain to the top third of the world's households apart from the very wealthiest. This segment includes many of the lower-to-middle-income households of the US and other advanced economies.

The data behind the chart only shows changes for each income percentile; individual households in any country could have moved up or down within percentiles and as a result seen substantially larger—or smaller—gains than these global averages.

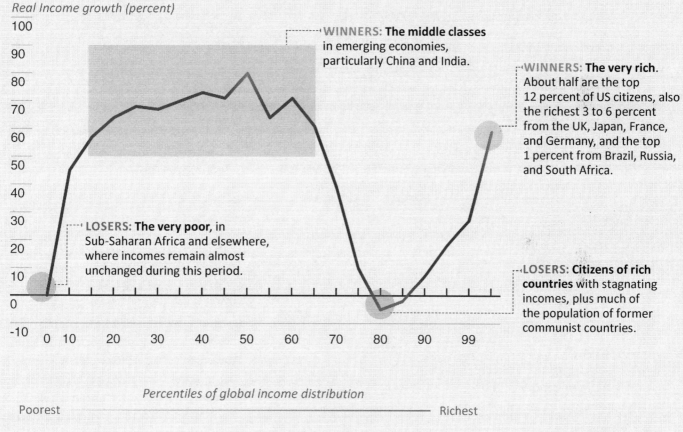

Real Income growth (percent)

WINNERS: **The middle classes** in emerging economies, particularly China and India.

WINNERS: **The very rich.** About half are the top 12 percent of US citizens, also the richest 3 to 6 percent from the UK, Japan, France, and Germany, and the top 1 percent from Brazil, Russia, and South Africa.

LOSERS: **The very poor,** in Sub-Saharan Africa and elsewhere, where incomes remain almost unchanged during this period.

LOSERS: **Citizens of rich countries** with stagnating incomes, plus much of the population of former communist countries.

Percentiles of global income distribution

Poorest — Richest

Source: Branko Milanovic.

Financial Shocks and Economic Doldrums

Debt-fueled economic growth in the United States, Europe, China, and Japan during the past several decades led to real-estate bubbles, unsustainable personal spending, price spikes for oil and other commodities—and, ultimately, in 2008, to massive financial crises in the United States and Europe that undercut economies worldwide. Anxious to stimulate greater growth, some central banks lowered interest rates to near—and even below—zero. They also attempted to boost recovery through quantitative easing, adding more than $11 trillion to the balance sheets of the central banks of China, the EU, Japan, and the United States between 2008 and 2016.

These efforts prevented further defaults of major financial institutions and enabled beleaguered European governments to borrow at low rates. They have not sparked strong economic growth, however, because they have not spurred governments, firms, or individuals to boost spending. Equally important, these efforts have not created incentives for banks to increase lending to support such spending, amid new prudential standards and near-zero or even negative inflation.

Efforts by Beijing, for example, to stoke growth since 2008 have helped maintain oil and raw-materials markets, as well as the producers in Africa, Latin America, and the Middle East who supply them. Nonetheless, these markets have sagged with the realization that China's growth—based largely on investment to boost industrial capacity—is unsustainable.

In this low-rate, low-growth environment, investors have remained skittish. They have vacillated between seeking higher returns in emerging markets and seeking safehavens during periodic scares, providing only unreliable support for potential emerging-economy growth.

Technology Complicates the Long-Term Outlook

Most of the worlds' largest economies will struggle with shrinking working-age populations, but all countries will face the challenge of maintaining employment—and developing well-trained, resilient workers. Automation, artificial intelligence (AI), and other technological innovations threaten the existence of vast swaths of current jobs up and down the socioeconomic ladder, including high-technology manufacturing and even white-collar services.

- Finding new ways to boost productivity in rich countries will become more difficult. The demographic, improved-efficiency, and investment factors behind the post-World War II period of growth are fading. This challenge will be especially relevant as populations in the largest economies age. Advances in technology will help boost productivity in developed and developing countries alike, but improving education, infrastructure, regulations, and management practices will be critical to take full advantage of them.

- As technology increasingly substitutes for labor and puts downward pressure on wages, personal-income-based tax revenues will grow more slowly than economies—or even shrink in real terms.

Fiscal pressure on countries that rely on such taxes will increase, possibly making value-added taxes or other revenue schemes more attractive.

Technological Innovation Accelerates Progress but Leads to Discontinuities

Technology—from the wheel to the silicon chip—has greatly bent the arc of history, but anticipating when, where, and how technology will alter economic, social, political, and security dynamics is a hard game. Some high-impact predictions—such as cold fusion—still have not become realities long after first promised. Other changes have unfolded faster and further than experts imagined. Breakthroughs in recent years in gene editing and manipulation, such as CRISPR,[a] are opening vast new possibilities in biotechnology.

Technology will continue to empower individuals, small groups, corporations, and states, as well as accelerate the pace of change and spawn new complex challenges, discontinuities, and tensions. In particular, the development and deployment of advanced information communication technologies (ICT), AI, new materials and manufacturing capabilities from robotics to automation, advances in biotechnology, and unconventional energy sources will disrupt labor markets; alter health, energy, and transportation systems; and transform economic development. They will also raise fundamental questions about what it means

to be human. Such developments will magnify values differences across societies, impeding progress on international regulations or norms in these areas. Existential risks associated with some of these applications are real, especially in synthetic biology, genome editing, and AI.

ICT are poised to transform a widening array of work practices and the way people live and communicate. The associated technologies will increase efficiencies and alter employment in transportation, engineering, manufacturing, health care and other services. These tools have been around for some time, but will become increasingly mainstream as developers learn to break down more jobs into automated components. Skyrocketing investment in AI, surging sales of industrial and service robotics, and cloud-based platforms operating without local infrastructure will create more opportunities for convergence and more disruption—especially in the near term—to labor markets. The "Internet of Things" (IOT)—where more and more interconnected devices can interact—will create efficiencies but also security risks. The effects of new ICTs on the financial sector, in particular, are likely to be profound. New financial technologies—including digital currencies, applications of "blockchain" technology for transactions, and AI and big data for predictive analytics—will reshape financial services, with potentially substantial impacts on systemic stability and the security of critical financial infrastructure.

Biotechnologies are at an inflection point, where advances in genetic testing and editing—catalyzed by the new methods to manipulate genes—are turning science fiction into reality. The time and cost required to sequence a person's genome has been slashed. Such capabilities open the possibility of much more tailored approaches to enhancing human capabilities, treating diseases, extending longevity, or boosting food production. Given

[a]CRISPR is the acronym for "Clustered Regularly Interspaced Short Palindromic Repeats," which refers to short segments of DNA, the molecule that carries genetic instructions for all living organisms. A few years ago, the discovery was made that one can apply CRISPR with a set of enzymes that accelerate or catalyze chemical reactions in order to modify specific DNA sequences. This capability is revolutionizing biological research, accelerating the rate at which biotech applications are developed to address medical, health, industrial, environmental, and agricultural challenges, while also posing significant ethical and security questions.

that most early techniques will only be available in a few countries, access to these technologies will be limited to those who can afford to travel and pay for the new procedures; divisive political debates over access are likely to ensue.

Further development of advanced materials and manufacturing techniques could speed transformation of key sectors, such as transportation and energy. The global market for nanotechnology has more than doubled in recent years, with applications constantly expanding from electronics to food.

The unconventional energy revolution is increasing the availability of new sources of oil and natural gas, while a wide range of technological advancements on the demand side are breaking the link between economic growth and rising energy utilization. Advancements in solar panels, for example, have drastically reduced the cost of solar electricity to be competitive with the retail price of electricity. With more new energy sources, overall global energy costs will remain low and the global energy system will become increasingly resilient to supply shocks from fossil fuels, to the benefit, in particular, of China, India, and other resource-poor developing countries.

Emerging technologies will require careful parsing to appreciate both the technology and its cumulative effects on human beings, societies, states, and the planet. There is a near-term imperative to establish safety standards and common protocols for emerging ICT, biotechnologies, and new materials. Few organizations—whether governmental, commercial, academic, or religious—have the range of expertise needed to do the parsing, let alone explain it to the rest of us, underscoring the importance of pooling resources to assess and contemplate the challenges ahead.

- Without regulatory standards, the development and deployment of AI—even if less capable than human intellect—is likely to be inherently dangerous to humans, threaten citizens' privacy, and undermine state interests. Further, failure to develop standards for AI in robotics is likely to lead to economic inefficiencies and lost economic opportunities due to non-interoperable systems.

- Biopharmaceutical advances will generate tension over intellectual property rights. If patent rejections, revocations, and compulsory licenses become more widespread, they could threaten innovation of new medicines and undercut the profits of multinational pharmaceutical companies. Governments will have to weigh the economic and social benefits of adopting new biotechnologies—such as genetically engineered (GE) crops—against competing domestic considerations.

Internationally, the ability to set standards and protocols, define ethical limits for research, and protect intellectual property rights will devolve to states with technical leadership. Actions taken in the near-term to preserve technical leadership will be especially critical for technologies that improve human health, change biological systems, and expand information and automation systems. Multilateral engagement early in the development cycle has the potential to reduce international tensions as deployment approaches. This, however, will require a convergence of interests and values—even if narrow and limited. More likely, technical leadership and partnerships alone will be insufficient to avoid tensions as states pursue technologies and regulatory frameworks that work to their benefit.

Ritual of Hindu God Idol Ganesh Immersion at India's Ganges River in 2015.

Ideas and Identities Will Exclude

A more interconnected world will continue to increase—rather than reduce—differences over ideas and identities. Populism will increase over the next two decades should current demographic, economic, and governance trends hold. So, too, will exclusionary national and religious identities, as the interplay between technology and culture accelerates and people seek meaning and security in the context of rapid and disorienting economic, social, and technological change. Political leaders will find appeals to identity useful for mobilizing supporters and consolidating political control. Similarly, identity groups will become more influential. Growing access to information and communication tools will enable them to better organize and mobilize—around political issues, religion, values, economic interests, ethnicity, gender, and lifestyle. The increasingly segregated information and media environment will harden identities—both through algorithms that provide customized searches and personally styled social media, as well as through deliberate shaping efforts by organizations, governments, and thought leaders. Some of these identities will have a transnational character, with groups learning from one another and individuals able to seek inspiration from like-minds a world away.

A key near-term implication of rising identity politics is the erosion of traditions of tolerance and diversity associated with the United States and Western Europe, threatening the global appeal of these ideals. Other key implications include the explicit use of nationalism and threatening characterizations of the West to shore up authoritarian control in China and Russia, and the inflaming of identity conflicts and communal tensions in Africa, the Middle East and South Asia. How New Delhi treats Hindu nationalist tendencies and Israel balances ultra-orthodox religious extremes will be key determinants, for example, of future tensions.

Populism is emerging in the West and in parts of Asia. Characterized by a suspicion and hostility toward elites, mainstream politics, and established institutions, it reflects rejection of the economic effects of globalization and frustration with the responses of political and economic elites to the public's concerns. Both right-wing and left-wing populist parties have been rising across Europe—as leaders of political parties in France, Greece, and the Netherlands, for example, criticize established organizations for failing to protect the livelihood of European residents. South America has had its own waves of populism, as have the Philippines and Thailand.

- Moreover, anti-immigrant and xenophobic sentiment among core democracies of the Western alliance could undermine some of the West's traditional sources of strength in cultivating diverse societies and harnessing global talent.

- Populist leaders and movements—whether on the right or left—may leverage democratic practices to foster popular support for consolidation of power in a strong executive and the slow, steady erosion of civil society, the rule of law, and norms of tolerance.

Nationalist and Some Religious Identities. A close cousin to populism, nationalist appeals will be prominent in China, Russia, Turkey, and other countries where leaders seek to consolidate political control by eliminating domestic political alternatives while painting international relations in existential terms. Similarly, exclusionary religious identities will shape regional and local dynamics in the Middle East and North Africa and threaten to do so in parts of Sub-Saharan Africa between Christian and Muslim communities. In Russia, nation and religion will continue to converge to reinforce political control.

- Religious identity, which may or may not be exclusionary, is likely to remain a potent connection as people seek a greater sense of identity and belonging in times of intense change. Over 80 percent of the world is religiously affiliated and that share

is increasing, due largely to high fertility rates in the developing world, according to a Pew Research Center study on the future of religion. Studies of American politics indicate that religiosity, or the *intensity* of individual expressions of faith, is a better predictor of voter behavior than the particular faith a person follows.

Governing Is Harder and Harder

How governments govern and create political order is in flux and likely to vary even more over the coming decades. Governments will increasingly struggle to meet public demands for security and prosperity. Fiscal limits, political polarization, and weak administrative capacity will complicate their efforts, as well as the changing information environment, the growing stock of issues that publics expect governments to manage, and the proliferation of empowered actors who can block policy formation or implementation. This gap between government performance and public expectations—combined with corruption and elite scandals—will result in growing public distrust and dissatisfaction. It will also increase the likelihood of protests, instability, and wider variations in governance.

- High-profile protests in places like Brazil and Turkey—countries where middle classes have expanded during the past decade—indicate that more prosperous citizens are expecting better, less corrupt governments and society. They are also looking for protection from losing what they have gained. Meanwhile, slower growth, stagnant middle-class wages, and rising inequality in developed countries will continue to drive public demands to improve and protect living standards. This will occur at a time when many governments are constrained by more debt, more intense global economic competition, and swings in financial and commodity markets.

- Greater public access to information about leaders and institutions—combined with stunning elite failures such as the 2008 financial crisis and Petrobras corruption scandal—has undermined public trust in established sources of authority and is driving populist movements worldwide. Moreover, information technology's amplification of individual voices and of distrust of elites has in some countries eroded the influence of political parties, labor unions, and civic groups, potentially leading to a crisis of representation among democracies. Polls suggest that majorities in emerging nations, especially in the Middle East and Latin America, believe government officials "don't care about people like them," while trust in governments has dropped in developed countries as well. Americans demonstrate the lowest levels of trust in government since the first year of measurement in 1958.

- Democracy itself will be more in question, as some studies suggest that North American and Western European youth are less likely to support freedom of speech than their elders. The number of states that mix democratic and autocratic elements is on the rise, a blend that is prone to instability. Freedom House reported that measurements of "freedom" in 2016 declined in almost twice as many countries as it improved—the biggest setback in 10 years.

International institutions will struggle to adapt to a more complex environment but will still have a role to play. They will be most effective when the interests of the major powers align on issues like peacekeeping and humanitarian assistance, where institutions and norms are well in place. Future reforms of international and regional institutions will move slowly, though, because of divergent interests among member states and organizations and the increasing complexity of emerging global issues. Some institutions and member countries will continue to cope on an ad hoc basis, taking steps to partner with nonstate actors and regional organizations and preferring approaches targeting narrowly defined issues.

- *A rise in veto power.* Competing interests among major and aspiring powers will limit formal international action in managing disputes, while divergent interests among states in general will prevent major reforms of the UN Security Council's membership. Many agree on the need to reform the UN Security Council, but prospects for consensus on membership reform are dim.

- *Lagging behind.* Existing institutions are likely to wrestle with nontraditional issues such as genome editing, AI, and human enhancement because technological change will continue to far outpace the ability of states, agencies, and international organizations to set standards, policies, regulations, and norms. Cyber and space also will raise new challenges, especially as private commercial actors play a bigger role in shaping capabilities and norms of use.

- *Multi-stakeholder multilateralism.* Multilateral dynamics will expand as formal international institutions work more closely with companies, civil society organizations, and local governments to address challenges. As experimentation with multi-stakeholder forums grows, new formats for debate will arise, and private sector involvement in governance is likely to increase.

The Nature of Conflict is Changing

The risk of conflict, including interstate conflict, will increase during the next two decades due to evolving interests among major powers, ongoing terrorist threats, continued instability in weak states, and the spread of lethal and disruptive technologies. The decline in the number and intensity of conflicts during the past 20 years appears to be reversing: conflict levels are increasing and battle-related deaths and other human costs of conflict are up sharply since 2011—if not earlier—according to published institutional reports. Furthermore, the character of conflict is changing because of advances in technology, new strategies, and the evolving global geopolitical context—all of which challenge previous conceptions of warfare. More actors will employ a wider range of military and non-military tools, blurring the line between war and peace and undermining old norms of escalation and deterrence.

Future conflicts will increasingly emphasize the disruption of critical infrastructure, societal cohesion, and basic government functions in order to secure psychological and geopolitical advantages, rather than the defeat of enemy forces on the battlefield through traditional military means. Noncombatants will be increasingly targeted, sometimes to pit ethnic, religious, and political groups against one another to disrupt societal cooperation and coexistence within states. Such strategies suggest a trend toward increasingly costly, but less decisive conflicts.

Disruptive Groups. Nonstate and substate groups—including terrorists, insurgents, activists, and criminal gangs—are accessing a broader array of lethal and non-lethal means to advance their interests. Groups like Hizballah and ISIL have gained access to sophisticated weaponry during the last decade, and man-portable anti-tank missiles, surface-to-air missiles, unmanned drones and other precision-guided weapons are likely to be more common. Activist groups like Anonymous are likely to employ increasingly disruptive cyber attacks. These groups have relatively little reason to restrain themselves. Since deterrence is harder, states have had to go on the offense and attack these actors more aggressively, which sometimes feeds the groups' ideological causes.

War From Afar. Meanwhile, both state and nonstate actors will continue to develop a greater capacity for stand-off and remote attacks. Growing development of cyber attacks, precision-guided weapons, robotic systems and unmanned weapons lowers the threshold for initiating conflict because attackers put fewer lives at risk in their attempts to overwhelm defenses. The proliferation of these capabilities will shift warfare from direct clashes of opposing armies to more stand-off and remote operations, especially in the initial phases of conflict.

- A future crisis in which opposing militaries possess long-range, precision-guided conventional weapons risks quick escalation to conflict because both sides would have an incentive to strike before they were attacked.

- In addition, the command, control, and targeting infrastructure, including satellites that provide navigation and targeting information, would probably become targets of attacks for forces seeking to disrupt an enemy's strike capabilities. Russia and China, for example, continue to pursue weapons systems capable of destroying satellites on orbit, which will place US and others' satellites at greater risk in the future.

New WMD Concerns. The threat posed by nuclear and other forms of weapons of mass destruction (WMD) probably will increase in the years ahead due to technology advances and growing asymmetry between forces. Current nuclear weapon states will almost certainly continue to maintain, if not modernize, their nuclear forces out to 2035. Nuclear sabre-rattling by North Korea and uncertainty over Iran's intentions could drive others to pursue nuclear capabilities. The proliferation of advanced technologies, especially biotechnologies, will also lower the threshold for new actors to acquire WMD capabilities. Internal collapse of weak states could also open a path for terrorist WMD use resulting from unauthorized seizures of weapons in failing or failed states that no longer can maintain control of their arsenals or scientific and technical knowledge.

Space

Once the domain only of major powers, space is increasingly democratic. As budgets for national space agencies plateau, private industry will fill the void and pursue serious programs such as space tourism, asteroid mining, and inflatable space habitats. Full realization of their commercial potential, however, is probably decades away.

An increase in space activity brings risks as well, and international action may be necessary to identify and remove the debris most threatening to an expanding global space presence. The immense strategic and commercial value offered by outer space assets ensures that space will increasingly be an arena in which nations vie for access, use, and control. The deployment of antisatellite technologies designed to purposefully disable or destroy satellites could potentially intensify global tensions. A key question will be whether spacefaring countries—in particular China, Russia, and the United States—can agree to a code of conduct for outer space activities.

"Gray Zone" Conflicts. The blurring line between "peacetime" and "wartime" will make it harder for adversaries to rely on traditional calculations of deterrence and escalation in managing conflicts. Strong-arm diplomacy, media manipulation, covert operations, political subversion, and economic coercion are longstanding pressure tactics, but the ease and effectiveness of launching cyber disruptions, disinformation campaigns, and surrogate attacks are heightening tensions and uncertainty. The ability to stay below the threshold for a full-scale war will lead to more persistent economic, political and security competition in the "gray zone" between peacetime and war.

Climate Change Looms

A changing climate, increasing stress on environmental and natural resources, and deepening connection between human and animal health reflect complex systemic risks that will outpace existing approaches. The willingness of individuals, groups, and governments to uphold recent environmental commitments, embrace clean energy technologies, and prepare for unforeseen extreme environmental and ecological events will test the potential for cooperation on global challenges to come.

Climate Change. Changes in the climate will produce more extreme weather events and put greater stress on humans and critical systems , including oceans, freshwater, and biodiversity. These changes, in turn, will have direct and indirect social, economic, political, and security effects. Extreme weather can trigger crop failures, wildfires, energy blackouts, infrastructure breakdown, supply-chain breakdowns, migration, and infectious disease outbreaks. Such events will be more pronounced as people concentrate in climate-vulnerable locations, such as cities, coastal areas, and water-stressed regions. Specific

Projected Average Surface Temperature Change

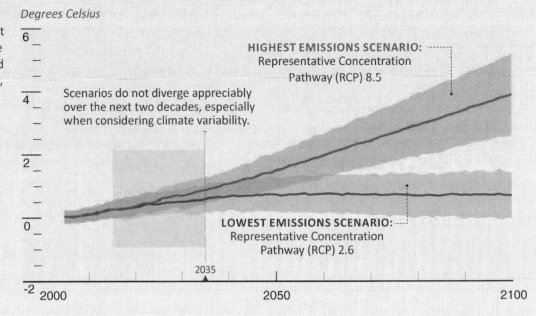

Degrees Celsius

The bold curves represent averages in global surface temperatures determined from computer modeling, but the actual trajectory will have many peaks (higher than average) and valleys (lower than average). The peaks are qualitatively important because they probably represent snapshots of future average climate conditions.

Scenarios do not diverge appreciably over the next two decades, especially when considering climate variability.

HIGHEST EMISSIONS SCENARIO: Representative Concentration Pathway (RCP) 8.5

LOWEST EMISSIONS SCENARIO: Representative Concentration Pathway (RCP) 2.6

Source: Intergovernmental Panel on Climate Change, Fifth Assessment Report, September 2013.

extreme weather events remain difficult to attribute entirely to climate change, but unusual patterns of extreme and record-breaking weather events are likely to become more common, according to the Intergovernmental Panel on Climate Change (IPCC).

Past greenhouse gas emissions already have locked in a significant rise in global mean temperatures for the next 20 years, no matter what greenhouse gas reduction policies are now being implemented. Most scientists expect that climate change will exacerbate current conditions, making hot, dry places hotter and drier, for example.

- Over the longer term, global climatological stresses will change how and where people live, as well as the diseases they face. Such stresses include sea-level rise, ocean acidification, permafrost and glacial melt, air quality degradation, changes in cloud cover, and sustained shifts in temperature and precipitation.

- Current climate models project long-term increases in global average surface temperatures, but climate scientists warn that more sudden, dramatic shifts could be possible, given the complexity of the system and climate history. Such shifts in the climate or climate-linked ecosystems could have dramatic economic and ecological consequences.

Climate change—whether observed or anticipated—will become integral to how people view their world. Many ecological and environmental stresses cut across state borders, complicating the ability of communities and governments to manage their effects. The urgency of the politics will vary due to differences in the intensity and geography of such change. We expect to see increased

Latin America, Africa More Concerned About Climate Change Compared With Other Regions

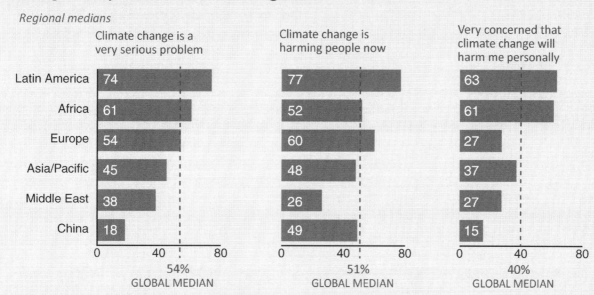

Regional medians

	Climate change is a very serious problem	Climate change is harming people now	Very concerned that climate change will harm me personally
Latin America	74	77	63
Africa	61	52	61
Europe	54	60	27
Asia/Pacific	45	48	37
Middle East	38	26	27
China	18	49	15
GLOBAL MEDIAN	54%	51%	40%

Note: In the United States: 45 percent said "climate change is a very serious problem," 41 percent said "climate change is harming people now," and 30 percent said they were "very concerned that climate change will harm me personally."
Source: Pew Research Center. Spring 2015 Global Attitudes survey. Q32, Q41, and Q42.

popular pressure globally to address these concerns as citizens in the developing world gain awareness and a growing political voice.

- China's experience is a cautionary one for today's developing world, with new members of the middle class expressing greater concern about pollution, water quality, and basic livability. A 2016 Pew poll found that half of Chinese polled were willing to trade economic growth for cleaner air.

Climate change and related natural disasters, policy decisions, and new abatement technologies will create new investment and industry winners and losers, too. One large financial consultant forecasts that developed-country equity markets will see sustained declines in most sectors over the next 35 years due to concerns about climate change. Meanwhile, most of the sectors in developed country equity markets will see investment gains. Agriculture, infrastructure, and real estate are also expected to benefit through 2050. Financial costs from droughts, storms, floods, and wildfires have risen modestly but consistently since at least the 1970s, according to research by development and humanitarian relief agencies worldwide—and are set to increase with more frequent and severe occurrences in the coming decades.

Climate change will drive both geopolitical competition and international cooperation as well. China, poised for global leadership on climate change, would likely keep to its Paris commitments but could weaken its support for monitoring mechanisms and gain favor with developing world emitters like India. Tensions over managing climate change could sharpen significantly if some countries pursue geoengineering technologies in an effort to manipulate large-scale climate conditions. Early

Bangladesh Climate Geoengineering Sparks Protests

April 4, 2033 – Dhaka

Bangladesh became the first country to try to slow climate change by releasing a metric ton of sulfate aerosol into the upper atmosphere from a modified Boeing 797 airplane in the first of six planned flights to reduce the warming effects of solar radiation. The unprecedented move provoked diplomatic warnings by 25 countries and violent public protests at several Bangladeshi Embassies, but government officials in Dhaka claimed its action was "critical to self-defense" after a spate of devastating hurricanes, despite scientists' warnings of major unintended consequences, such as intensified acid rain and depletion of the ozone layer.

research efforts largely live in computer models to explore techniques to alter temperature and rainfall patterns such as injecting aerosols in the stratosphere, chemically brightening marine clouds, and installing space-mirrors in orbit. Other approaches focus on removing carbon dioxide from the atmosphere. Given the lack of international standards or regulations for such activities, any efforts to test or implement large-scale geoengineering techniques would raise tensions over the risks and potential unintended consequences.

Environment and Natural Resources. Nearly all of the Earth's systems are undergoing natural and human-induced stresses outpacing national and international environmental protection efforts. Institutions overseeing single sectors will increasingly struggle to address the complex interdependencies of water, food, energy, land, health, infrastructure, and labor.

- By 2035, outdoor **air pollution** is projected to be the top cause of environmentally related deaths worldwide, absent implementation of new air quality policies. More than 80 percent of urban dwellers are already exposed to air pollution that exceeds safe limits, according to the World Health Organization.

- Half of the world's population will face **water shortages** by 2035, according to the UN. Rising demands from population growth, greater consumption, and agricultural production will outstrip water supplies, which will become less reliable in some regions from groundwater depletion and changing precipitation patterns. More than 30 countries—nearly half of them in the Middle East—will experience extremely high water stress by 2035, increasing economic, social and political tensions.

- ***Melting ice*** in the Arctic and Antarctica will accelerate sea level rise over time. An increasingly navigable Arctic will shorten commercial trading routes and expand access to the region's natural resources in the decades ahead. Glacier melting in the Tibetan Plateau—the source of nearly all of Asia's major rivers—will also have far-reaching consequences.

- More than a third of the world's **soil**, which produces 95 percent of the world's food supply, is currently degraded, and the fraction will probably increase as the global population grows. Soil degradation—the loss of soil productivity due to primarily human-induced changes—is already occurring at rates as much as 40 times faster than new soil formation.

Sharing Water Will Be More Contentious

A growing number of countries will experience water stress—from population growth, urbanization, economic development, climate change, and poor water management—and tensions over shared water resources will rise. Historically, water disputes between states have led to more sharing agreements than violent conflicts, but this pattern will be hard to maintain. Dam construction, industrial water pollution, and neglect or non-acceptance of existing treaty provisions aggravate water tensions, but political and cultural stress often play an even larger role.

Nearly half of the world's 263 international river basins lack cooperative management agreement as well as only a handful of the more than 600 transboundary aquifer systems. Moreover, many existing agreements are not sufficiently adaptive to address emergent issues such as climate change, biodiversity loss, and water quality. Ongoing disputes in key river basins, such as the Mekong, Nile, Amu Darya, Jordan, Indus, and the Brahmaputra, will illustrate how water governance structures adapt in an era of increasingly scarce resources.

- Diversity in the *biosphere* will continue to decline despite ongoing national and international efforts. Climate change will increasingly amplify ongoing habitat loss and degradation, overexploitation, pollution, and invasive alien species—adversely affecting forests, fisheries, and wetlands. Many marine ecosystems, particularly coral reefs, will face critical risks from warming and acidifying oceans.

Health. Human and animal health will increasingly be interconnected. Increasing global connectivity and changing environmental conditions will affect the geographic distribution of pathogens and their hosts, and, in turn, the emergence, transmission, and spread of many human and animal infectious diseases. Unaddressed deficiencies in national and global health systems for disease control will make infectious disease outbreaks more difficult to detect and manage, increasing the potential for epidemics to break out far beyond their points of origin.

- Noncommunicable diseases, however—such as heart disease, stroke, diabetes, and mental illness—will far outpace infectious diseases over the next decades, owing to demographic and cultural factors, including aging, poor nutrition and sanitation, urbanization, and widening inequality.

Converging Trends Will Transform Power and Politics

Together, these global trends will make governing harder while altering what it means to exert power. The number and complexity of issues beyond the scope of any one individual, community, or state to address is increasing—and doing so at a seemingly faster pace than decades ago. Issues once considered long-term will more frequently impose near-term effects. For example, complex, interdependencies like climate change and nefarious or negligent applications of biotechnologies have the potential to degrade and destroy human life. Cyber and information technologies—complex systems on which humans are increasingly dependent—will continue to create new forms of commerce, politics, and conflict with implications that are not immediately understood.

Economic, technological, and security trends are increasing the number of states that can exert geopolitical influence, bringing the unipolar post-Cold War period to a close. The economic progress of the past century has widened the number of states—Brazil, China, India, Indonesia, Iran, Mexico, and Turkey— with material claims to great and middle power status. This opens the door to more actors—and their competing interests and values—seeking to shape international order. Even with profound uncertainties regarding the future of global economic growth, leading forecasters broadly agree that emerging market economies like China and India will contribute a much larger share of global GDP than is currently the case—shifting the focus of the world's economic activity eastward.

Technology and wealth are empowering individuals and small groups to act in ways that states historically monopolized—and fundamentally altering established patterns of governance and conflict. Just as changes in material wealth challenge the international balance of power, empowered but embattled middle classes in wealthy countries are putting extraordinary pressure on once-established state-society relations, specifically on the roles, responsibilities, and relationships that governments and citizens, elites and masses expect of one another. The reduction of poverty, especially in Asia, has expanded the number of individuals and groups who are no longer focused solely on subsistence but instead wield the power of consumption, savings, and political voice—now amplified by the Internet and modern communications.

- The ICT revolution placed in the hands of individuals and small groups the information and the ability to exert worldwide influence—making their actions, interests, and values more consequential than ever before.

- Nonprofits, multinational corporations, religious groups, and a variety of other organizations now have the ability to amass wealth, influence, and a following— enabling them to address welfare and security in ways that may be more effective than those that political authorities wield.

- Similarly, the increasing accessibility of weapon technologies, combined with effective recruiting and communications, has enabled nonstate groups to upend regional orders.

The information environment is fragmenting publics and their countless perceived realities— undermining shared understandings of world events that once facilitated international cooperation. It is also prompting some to question democratic ideals like free speech and the "market place of ideas." When combined with a growing distrust of formal institutions and the proliferation, polarization, and commercialization of traditional and social media outlets, some academics and political observers describe our current era as one of "post-truth" or "post-factual" politics. Nefarious attempts to manipulate publics are relatively easy in such contexts, as recent Russian efforts vis-à-vis both Ukraine and the US presidential election, including manipulation of alleged Wikileaks disclosures, demonstrate.

- Studies have found that information counter to an individual's opinion or prior understanding will not change or challenge views but instead will reinforce the belief that the information is from a biased or hostile source, further polarizing groups.

- Compounding matters, people often turn to leaders or others who think like they do and trust them to interpret the "truth." According to an Edelman Trust Barometer survey, a sizeable trust gap is widening between college-educated consumers of news and the mass population. The international survey reveals that respondents are increasingly reliant on a "person like yourself," who is more trusted than a CEO or government official.

- A Pew study from 2014 showed that the highest percentage of trust for a news agency among the US persons polled was only 54 percent. Alternatively, individuals are gravitating to social media to obtain news and information about world and local events.

The power of individuals and groups to block outcomes will be much easier to wield than the constructive power of forging new policies and alignments or implementing solutions to shared challenges, especially when the credibility of authority and information is in question.

- For democratic governments, this means greater difficulty in setting and communicating a narrative around the common interest. It also complicates implementing policy.

- For political parties, it heralds a further weakening of their traditional role in aggregating and representing interests to the state. Special interest groups have been rising at the expense of political party membership in the United States since the early 1970s, well before the Internet, but information technology and social networking have reinforced that trend.

- For authoritarian-minded leaders and regimes, the impulse to coerce and manipulate information—as well as the technical means to do so—will increase.

The Changing Nature of Power

As global trends converge to make governance and cooperation harder, they are changing the strategic context in ways that make traditional, material forms of power less sufficient for shaping and securing desired outcomes. Material power—typically measured through gross domestic product, military spending, population size, and technology level—has always been, and will continue to be, a prime lever of the state. With such might, powerful states can set agendas and summon cooperation—as with the recent Paris climate accords—and even unilaterally impose outcomes, as Russia's annexation of Crimea attests. Material power does not explain the impact, however, that nonstate actors, like ISIL, have had in shaping the security environment nor the constraints that major state powers have faced in countering such developments. It also does little to compel those who chose the path of non-compliance.

Securing and sustaining outcomes—whether in combating violent extremism, or managing extreme weather—will get harder because of the proliferation of actors who can veto or deny the ability to take action. Growing numbers of state and nonstate actors are deploying new or nontraditional forms of power, such as cyber, networks, and even manipulating the environment, to influence events and create disruption, placing increased constraints on the ability of "materially powerful" states to achieve outcomes at reasonable costs. States and large organizations now confront the increased possibility that those who disagree—whether activists, citizens, investors, or consumers—will exit, withdraw compliance, or protest, sometimes violently. In addition, expanding global connectivity through information and other networks is enabling weaker but well-connected actors to have an outsized impact.

The most powerful actors of the future will be states, groups, and individuals who can leverage material capabilities, relationships, and information in a more rapid, integrated, and adaptive mode than in generations past. They will use material capabilities to create influence and in some instances to secure or deny outcomes. They will demonstrate "power in outcome," however, by mobilizing large-scale constituencies of support, using information to persuade or manipulate societies and states to their causes. The ability to create evocative narratives and ideologies, generate attention, and cultivate trust and credibility will rest in overlapping but not identical interests and values. The most powerful entities will induce states—as well as corporations, social or religious movements, and some individuals—to create webs of cooperation across issues, while exhibiting depth and balance across their material, relational, and informational capabilities. Sustaining outcomes will require a constant tending to relationships.

NEAR FUTURE:
TENSIONS ARE RISING

Greek homeless person sleeping outside a bank in 2015; banks were closed at times during the financial crisis to limit withdrawals.

NEAR FUTURE: TENSIONS ARE RISING

These global trends, challenging governance and changing the nature of power, will drive major consequences over the next five years. They will raise tensions across all regions and types of governments, both within and between countries. These near-term conditions will contribute to the expanding threat from terrorism and leave the future of international order in the balance.

Within countries, tensions are rising because citizens are raising basic questions about what they can expect from their governments in a constantly changing world. Publics are pushing governments to provide peace and prosperity more broadly and reliably at home when what happens abroad is increasingly shaping those conditions.

In turn, these dynamics are increasing tensions between countries—heightening the risk of interstate conflict during the next five years. A hobbled Europe, uncertainty about

America's role in the world, and weakened norms for conflict-prevention and human rights create openings for China and Russia. The combination will also embolden regional and nonstate aggressors—breathing new life into regional rivalries, such as between Riyadh and Tehran, Islamabad and New Delhi, and on the Korean Peninsula. Governance shortfalls also will drive threat perceptions and insecurity in countries such as Pakistan and North Korea.

- Economic interdependence among major powers remains a check on aggressive behavior but might be insufficient in itself to prevent a future conflict. Major and middle powers alike will search for ways to reduce the types of interdependence that leaves them vulnerable to economic coercion and financial sanctions, potentially providing them more freedom of action to aggressively pursue their interests.

Meanwhile, the threat from terrorism is likely to expand as the ability of states, groups, and individuals to impose harm diversifies. The net effect of rising tensions within and between countries—and the growing threat from terrorism—will be greater global disorder and considerable questions about the rules, institutions, and distribution of power in the international system.

Europe. Europe's sharpening tensions and doubts about its future cohesion stem from institutions mismatched to its economic and security challenges. EU institutions set monetary policy for Eurozone states, but state capitals retain fiscal and security responsibilities—leaving poorer members saddled with debt and diminished growth prospects and each state determining its own approach to security. Public frustration with immigration, slow growth, and unemployment will fuel nativism and a preference for national solutions to continental problems.

- *Outlook:* Europe is likely to face additional shocks—banks remain unevenly capitalized and regulated, migration within and into Europe will continue, and Brexit will encourage regional and separatist movements in other European countries. Europe's aging population will undermine economic output, shift consumption toward services—like health care—and away from goods and investment. A shortage of younger workers will reduce tax revenues, fueling debates over immigration to bolster the workforce. The EU's future will hinge on its ability to reform its institutions, create jobs and growth, restore trust in elites, and address public concerns that immigration will radically alter national cultures.

United States. The next five years will test US resilience. As in Europe, tough economic times have brought out societal and class divisions. Stagnant wages and rising income inequality are fueling doubts about global economic integration and the "American Dream" of upward mobility. The share of American men age 25-54 not seeking work is at the highest level since the Great Depression. Median incomes rose by 5 percent in 2015, however, and there are signs of renewal in some communities where real estate is affordable, returns on foreign and domestic investment are high, leveraging of immigrant talent is the norm, and expectations of federal assistance are low, according to contemporary observers.

- *Outlook:* Despite signs of economic improvement, challenges will be significant, with public trust in leaders and institutions sagging, politics highly polarized, and government revenue constrained by modest growth and rising entitlement outlays. Moreover, advances in robotics and artificial intelligence are likely to further disrupt labor markets. Meanwhile, uncertainty is high around the world regarding Washington's global leadership role. The United States has rebounded from troubled times before, however, such as when the period of angst in the 1970s was followed by a stronger economic recovery and global role in the world. Innovation at the state and local level, flexible financial markets, tolerance for risk-taking, and a demographic profile more balanced than most large countries offer upside potential. Finally, America is distinct because it was founded on an inclusive ideal—the pursuit of life, liberty, and happiness for all, however imperfectly realized—rather than a race or ethnicity. This legacy remains a critical advantage for managing divisions.

Central and South America. Although state weakness and drug trafficking have and will continue to beset Central America, South America has been more stable than most regions of the world and has had many democratic advances—including recovery from populist waves from the right and the left. However, government efforts to provide greater economic and social stability are running up against budget and debt constraints. Weakened international demand for commodities has slowed growth. The expectations associated with new entrants to the middle class will strain public coffers, fuel political discontent, and possibly jeopardize the region's significant progress against poverty and inequality. Activist civil society organizations are likely to fuel social tensions by increasing awareness of elite corruption, inadequate infrastructure, and mismanagement. Some incumbents facing possible rejection by their publics are seeking to protect their power, which could lead to a period of intense political competition and democratic backsliding in some countries. Violence is particularly rampant in northern Central America, as gangs and organized criminal groups have undermined basic governance by regimes that lack capacity to provide many basic public goods and services.

- *Outlook:* Central and South America are likely to see more frequent changes in governments that are mismanaging the economy and beleaguered by widespread corruption. Leftist administrations already have lost power in places like Argentina, Guatemala, and Peru and are on the defensive in Venezuela, although new leaders will not have much time to show they can improve conditions. The success or failure of Mexico's high-profile reforms might affect the willingness of other countries in the region to take similar political risks. The OECD accession process may be an opportunity—and incentive— for some countries to improve economic policies in a region with fairly balanced age demographics, significant energy resources, and well-established economic links to Asia, Europe, and the United States.

An Inward West? Among the industrial democracies of North America, Europe, Japan, South Korea, and Australia, leaders will search for ways to restore a sense of middle class wellbeing while some attempt to temper populist and nativist impulses. The result could be a more inwardly focused West than we have experienced in decades, which will seek to avoid costly foreign adventures while experimenting with domestic schemes to address fiscal limits, demographic problems, and wealth concentrations. This inward view will be far more pronounced in the European Union, which is absorbed by questions of EU governance and domestic challenges, than elsewhere.

- The European Union's internal divisions, demographic woes, and moribund economic performance threaten its own status as a global player. For the coming five years at least, the need to restructure European relations in light of the UK's decision to leave the EU will undermine the region's international clout and could weaken transatlantic cooperation, while anti-immigration sentiments among the region's populations will undermine domestic political support for Europe's political leaders.

- Questions about the United States' role in the world center on what the country can afford and what its public will support in backing allies, managing conflict, and overcoming its own divisions. Foreign publics and governments will be watching Washington for signs of compromise and cooperation, focusing especially on global trade, tax reform, workforce preparedness for advanced technologies, race relations, and its openness to experimentation at the state and local levels. Lack of domestic progress would signal a shift toward retrenchment, a weaker middle class, and potentially further global drift into disorder and regional spheres of influence. Yet, America's capital, both human and security, is immense. Much of the world's best talent seeks to live and work in the United States, and domestic and global hope for a competent and constructive foreign policy remain high.

China. China faces a daunting test—with its political stability in the balance. After three decades of historic economic growth and social change, Beijing, amid slower growth and the aftereffects of a debt binge, is transitioning from an investment-driven, export-based economy to one fueled by domestic consumption. Satisfying the demands of its new middle classes for clean air, affordable houses, improved services, and continued opportunities will be essential for the government to maintain legitimacy and political order. President Xi's consolidation of power could threaten an established system of stable succession, while Chinese nationalism—a force Beijing occasionally encourages for support when facing foreign friction—may prove hard to control.

- *Outlook:* Beijing probably has ample resources to prop up growth while efforts to spur private consumption take hold. Nonetheless, the more it "doubles down" on state owned enterprises (SOEs) in the economy, the more it will be at greater risk of financial shocks that cast doubt on its ability to manage the economy. Automation and competition from low-cost producers elsewhere in Asia and even Africa will put pressure on wages for unskilled workers. The country's rapidly

shrinking working-age population will act as a strong headwind to growth.

Russia. Russia's aspires to restore its great power status through nationalism, military modernization, nuclear saber rattling, and foreign engagements abroad. Yet, at home, it faces increasing constraints as its stagnant economy heads into a third consecutive year of recession. Moscow prizes stability and order, offering Russians security at the expense of personal freedoms and pluralism. Moscow's ability to retain a role on the global stage—even through disruption—has also become a source of regime power and popularity at home. Russian nationalism features strongly in this story, with

---

Imagining a surprise
news headline in 2021 . . .

"Gig Workers" Riot in London and New York

September 17, 2021 – London

The Gig Workers Movement (GWM), representing the growing number of independent, temporary workers, organized violent protests and denial of service cyberattacks on major companies in London and New York to protest poor pay, job uncertainty, and a lack of benefits. Movement leaders warned they would stage more disruptive protests unless they received stronger social support for basic food and housing supplemental programs. The cyber-attacks leveraged millions of compromised Internet-connected devices and overwhelmed the targeted companies' information systems.

Prodit.Ph / Shutterstock.com

China's dramatic economic growth has highlighted greater gaps between rich and poor.

President Putin praising Russian culture as the last bulwark of conservative Christian values against the decadence of Europe and the tide of multiculturalism. Putin is personally popular, but approval ratings of 35 percent for the ruling party reflect public impatience with deteriorating quality of life conditions and abuse of power.

- *Outlook:* If the Kremlin's tactics falter, Russia will become vulnerable to domestic instability driven by dissatisfied elites— even as a decline in status suggests more aggressive international action. Russia's demographic picture has improved somewhat since the 1990s but remains bleak. Life expectancy among males is the lowest of the industrial world, and its population will continue to decline. The longer Moscow delays diversifying its economy, the more the government will stoke nationalism and sacrifice personal freedoms and pluralism to maintain control.

An Increasingly Assertive China and Russia. Beijing and Moscow will seek to lock in temporary competitive advantages and to right what they charge are historical wrongs before economic and demographic headwinds further slow their material progress and the West regains its footing. Both China and Russia maintain worldviews in which they are rightfully dominant in their regions and able to shape regional politics and economics to suit their security and material interests. Both have moved aggressively in recent years to exert greater influence in their regions, to contest the US geopolitically, and to force Washington to accept exclusionary regional spheres of influence—a situation that the United States has historically opposed. For example, China views the continuing presence of the US Navy in the Western Pacific, the centrality of US alliances in the region, and US protection of Taiwan as outdated and representative of the continuation of China's "100 years of humiliation."

- Recent Sino-Russian cooperation has been tactical, however, and is likely to return to competition if Beijing jeopardizes

Russian interests in Central Asia and as Beijing enjoys more options for cheap energy supply beyond Russia. Moreover, it is not clear whether there is a mutually acceptable border between what China and Russia consider their natural spheres of influence. Meanwhile, India's growing economic power and profile in the region will further complicate these calculations, as New Delhi navigates relations with Beijing, Moscow, and Washington to protect its own expanding interests.

Imagining a surprise
news headline in 2019 . . .

China Buys Uninhabited Fijian Island To Build Military Base

February 3, 2019 – Beijing

A Chinese development firm—with links to the Chinese Government and People's Liberation Army— today announced that it recently purchased the uninhabited Cobia Island from the Government of Fiji for $850 million. Western security analysts assess that China plans to use the island to build a permanent military base in the South Pacific, 3,150 miles southwest of Hawaii.

Russian assertiveness will harden anti-Russian views in the Baltics and other parts of Europe, escalating the risk of conflict. Russia will seek, and sometimes feign, international cooperation, while openly challenging norms and rules it perceives as counter to its interests and providing support for leaders of fellow "managed democracies" that encourage resistance to American policies and preferences. Moscow has

little stake in the rules of the global economy and can be counted on to take actions that weaken US and European institutional advantages. Moscow will test NATO and European resolve, seeking to undermine Western credibility; it will try to exploit splits between Europe's north and south and east and west, and to drive a wedge between the United States and the EU.

- Similarly, Moscow will become more active in the Middle East and those parts of the world in which it believes it can check US influence. Finally, Russia will remain committed to nuclear weapons as a deterrent and as a counter to stronger conventional military forces, as well as its ticket to superpower status. Russian military doctrine purportedly includes the limited use of nuclear weapons in a situation where Russia's vital interests are at stake to "deescalate" a conflict by demonstrating that continued conventional conflict risks escalating the crisis to a large-scale nuclear exchange.

In **Northeast Asia**, growing tensions around the Korean Peninsula are likely, with the possibility of serious confrontation in the coming years. Kim Jong Un is consolidating his grip on power through a combination of patronage and terror and is doubling down on his nuclear and missile programs, developing long-range missiles that may soon threaten the continental United States. Beijing, Seoul, Tokyo, and Washington have a common incentive to manage security risks in Northeast Asia, but a history of warfare and occupation along with current mutual distrust makes cooperation difficult. Continued North Korean provocations, including additional nuclear and missile tests, might worsen stability in the region and prompt neighboring countries to take actions, sometimes unilaterally, to protect their security interests.

Competing Views on Instability

China and Russia portray global disorder as resulting from a Western plot to push what they see as self-serving American concepts and values of freedom to every corner of the planet. Western governments see instability as an underlying condition worsened by the end of the Cold War and incomplete political and economic development. Concerns over weak and fragile states rose more than a generation ago because of beliefs about the externalities they produce—whether disease, refugees, or terrorists in some instances. The growing interconnectedness of the planet, however, makes isolation from the global periphery an illusion, and the rise of human rights norms makes state violence against a governed population an unacceptable option.

One consequence of post-Cold War disengagement by the United States and the then-USSR, was a loss of external support for strongmen politics, militaries, and security forces who are no longer able to bargain for patronage. Also working against coercive governments are increased demands for responsive and participatory governance by citizens no longer poor due to the unprecedented scale and speed of economic development in the nonindustrial world. Where political and economic development occurred roughly in tandem or quick succession, modernization and individual empowerment have reinforced political stability. Where economic development outpaced or occurred without political changes—such as in much of the Arab world and the rest of Africa and South Asia—instability ensued. China has been a notable exception. The provision of public goods there so far has bolstered political order but a campaign against corruption is now generating increasing uncertainty and popular protests have grown during the past 15 years. Russia is the other major exception—economic growth—largely the result of high energy and commodity prices—helped solve the disorder of the Yeltsin years.

US experience in Iraq and Afghanistan has shown that coercion and infusions of money cannot overcome state weakness. Rather, building a stable political order requires inclusiveness, cooperation among elites, and a state administration that can both control the military and provide public services. This has proved more difficult than expected to provide.

North Korean military parade, 2013.

- Kim is determined to secure international recognition of the North as a nuclear-armed state, for the purposes of security, prestige, and political legitimacy. Unlike his father and grandfather, he has signaled little interest in participating in talks on denuclearization. He codified the North's nuclear status in the party constitution in 2012 and reaffirmed it during the Party Congress in 2016.

- Beijing faces a continuing strategic conundrum about the North. Pyongyang's behavior both undermines China's claim that the US military presence in the region is anachronistic and demonstrates Beijing's lack of influence—or perhaps lack of political will to exert influence—over its neighbor and client. North Korean behavior leads to tightening US alliances, more assertive behavior by US allies, and, on occasion, greater cooperation between those allies themselves—and may lead to a shift in Beijing's approach to North Korea over time.

- The decisions before Seoul and Tokyo are significant as well, with both focused intently on maintaining the US security umbrella while improving their own security capabilities.

Middle East and North Africa. Virtually all of the region's trends are going in the wrong direction. Continuing conflict and absence of political and economic reform threatens poverty reduction, the region's one recent bright spot. Resource dependence and foreign assistance has propped up elites even as it fostered popular dependence on the state by inhibiting markets, employment, and human capital. With oil prices unlikely to recover to levels of the oil boom, most governments will have to limit cash payments and subsidies. Meanwhile, social media has provided new tools for publics to vent frustration. Conservative religious groups—including Muslim Brotherhood affiliates and Shia movements—and ethnically-based organizations like those centered on Kurdish identity are poised to be primary alternatives to ineffective governments in the region. Such groups typically provide social services better than the state and their politics resonate with publics who are generally more conservative and religious than the region's political and economic elites.

- *Outlook:* Left unchecked, current trends will further fragment the region. The influence of extremist Islamist groups is likely to expand, reducing the tolerance for and presence of minorities, setting the stage for additional migration flows. Risks of instability in Arab states such as Egypt, and possibly Saudi Arabia, could tempt rulers to impose control through force—an impulse at odds with countertrends like technology's empowerment of individuals, freer information flows, and poverty reduction. Alternatively, transition to democracy could provide an attractive model, if it delivers greater stability and inclusive prosperity. Progress on poverty reduction, education, and women's empowerment in some parts of the region provides momentum for tapping into the growing number of young people that will be coming of working age.

Geopolitically, growing humanitarian crises and regional conflict in the Middle East and North Africa will threaten to further undermine the credibility of international dispute resolution and human rights norms. Perceptions in the region's capitals that Washington is unreliable have invited competition from Russia, and possibly China, and hedging by Arab states regarding US commitments. These perceptions stem from unenforced redlines in Syria, withheld support for Mubarak and other Arab incumbents in 2011, an alleged tilt toward Iran and away from traditional Sunni allies and Israel, and a sense of neglect because of the US rebalance to Asia.

- Meanwhile, Iran, Israel, and perhaps Turkey are likely to grow in power and influence relative to other states in the region but will remain at odds with each other. Iran's

growing power, nuclear capabilities and aggressive behavior will continue to be a concern for Israel and Gulf Arab states. The sectarian nature of Iranian and Saudi regional competition, which promotes inflammatory rhetoric and allegations of heresy throughout the region, heightens these concerns.

Sub-Saharan Africa. Democratic practices have expanded, civil society groups have proliferated, and public demand for better governance has become more urgent. Still, many African states continue to struggle with "big man" rule, patronage politics, and ethnic favoritism. Many leaders remain focused on political survival rather than reform—with some defying term limits. Global economic headwinds also threaten progress by keeping commodity prices low and foreign investment weak. Even some countries that have made progress toward democracy remain fragile and prone to violence accompanying elections. Tensions between Christian and Muslim groups could escalate into conflict.

- *Outlook:* During the next five years, growing African populations will become more youthful, urban, mobile, and networked, and better educated—and more demanding of a voice. Rapid urbanization will stress infrastructure and increase visibility of elite corruption— fueling public frustration with services or opportunities. Some 75 to 250 million Africans will experience severe water stress, likely leading to mass migration. Nonetheless, Africa will remain a zone of experimentation by governments, corporations, NGOs and individuals seeking to advance development. The progress of the past two decades—including an expanded middle class, increasingly vibrant civil society, and the spread of democratic institutions—suggests upside potential.

South Asia. India will be the world's fastest growing economy during the next five years as China's economy cools and growth elsewhere sputters, but internal tensions over inequality and religion will complicate its expansion. New Delhi, however, will continue to offer smaller South Asian countries a stake in India's economic growth through development assistance and increased connectivity to India's economy, contributing to India's broader effort to assert its role as the predominant regional power. Violent extremism, terrorism, and instability will continue to hang over Afghanistan, Pakistan, and the region's fragile communal relations. The threat of terrorism, from Lashkar-e-Tayyiba (LET), Tehrik-i-Taliban Pakistan (TTP), and al-Qa'ida and its affiliates—as well as ISIL's expansion and sympathy for associated ideology—will remain prominent in the region. Competition for jobs, coupled with discrimination against minorities, may contribute to radicalization of the region's youth, especially given abnormal sex ratios favoring males in several countries.

- *Outlook:* The quality of India's development will depend on addressing widespread poor public health, sanitation, and infrastructure conditions. The rate of malnourished children, for example, is higher in India than in Sub-Saharan Africa. Populism and sectarianism will intensify if Bangladesh, India, and Pakistan fail to provide employment and education for growing urban populations and officials continue to govern principally through identity politics. Human health, food security, infrastructure, and livelihoods will deteriorate from pollution, earthquakes and the effects of climate change, including shifting monsoon patterns and increasing glacier melt. South Asia's openness to the private sector, community groups, and NGOs, however, should position it well for an era of empowered individuals, especially if governments curb their support for chauvinistic groups that divide societies.

Imagining a surprise
news headline in 2032 . . .

IMF Says African Economic Growth Rate Surpasses Asia

February 11, 2032 – Washington, DC

The International Monetary Fund (IMF) said Africa's economic growth rate last year topped 5 percent, surpassing Asia for the first time as numerous improvements converged to spur regional development. The availability of cheaper solar power panels and home batteries have revolutionized energy in the region over the last decade; advances in GMOs and desalination technology stabilized food production; growing financial services, digital payments, and peer-to-peer social funding boosted commerce; and widespread use of 3D printing increased local manufacturing that harnessed Africa's growing workforce.

In **South Asia**, Pakistan will feel compelled to address India's economic and conventional military capabilities through asymmetric means. Pakistan will seek to enhance its nuclear deterrent against India by expanding its nuclear arsenal and delivery means, including pursuing "battlefield nuclear weapons" and sea-based options. India, by contrast, will focus its attention on both Islamabad and Beijing—seeking military partnerships with Europe, Japan, the United States, and others—to boost its conventional capabilities while striving for escalation dominance vis-a-vis Pakistan.

- At-sea deployments of nuclear weapons by India, Pakistan, and perhaps China, would increasingly nuclearize the Indian Ocean

In Emerging Economies, Incomes Are Rising Faster, and at a Greater Scale, Than at Any Point in History

India and China doubled per capita income much faster than much smaller emerging economies in the past.

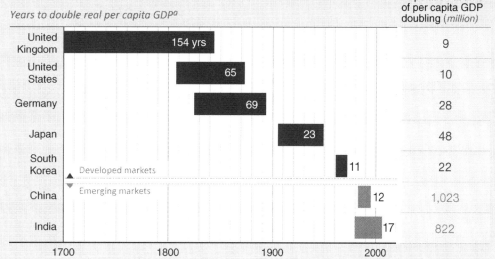

Years to double real per capita GDP[a]

	Years to double	Population at time of per capita GDP doubling (*million*)
United Kingdom	154 yrs	9
United States	65	10
Germany	69	28
Japan	23	48
South Korea	11	22
China	12	1,023
India	17	822

Developed markets ▲
Emerging markets ▼

1700   1800   1900   2000

[a]From $1,300 to $2,600 per year at purchasing power parity.
Source: Groningen Growth and Development Center, The Maddison-Project database, Groningen, Netherlands, 2013. http://www.ggdc.net/maddison/maddison-project/home.htm, 2013 version.

during the next two decades. The presence of multiple nuclear powers with uncertain doctrine for managing at sea incidents between nuclear-armed vessels increases the risk of miscalculation and inadvertent escalation. Nuclear mating requirements for naval-based delivery vehicles remove a safety valve that until now has kept nuclear weapons stored separately from missiles in South Asia.

Growing Terrorism Threat

The terrorism threat is likely to increase as the means and the motivations of states, groups, and individuals to impose harm diversify. Prolonged conflicts and the information age allow terrorists to recruit and operate on a large scale, demonstrating the evolving nature of the threat. Terrorism kills fewer people globally than crime or disease, but the potential for new capabilities reaching the hands of individuals bent on apocalyptic destruction is all too real. This ultimate low-probability, high-impact event underscores the imperative of international cooperation and state attention to the issue.

Terrorists will continue to justify their violence by their own interpretations of religion, but several underlying drivers are also in play. Within countries, the breakdown of state structures in much of the Middle East continues to create space for extremists. The ongoing proxy war between Iran and Saudi Arabia also is fueling Shia-Sunni sectarianism—with some militant groups further fracturing over religious differences. In addition, perceptions of "Western hegemony," remains a potent rallying cry for some groups, mobilized around striking the "far enemy."

- Although the location of religiously driven terrorism will fluctuate, the rise of violent religious nationalism and the schism between Shia and Sunni are likely to worsen in the short term and may not abate by 2035. The combination of powerful ideologies like Salafi-jihadism, whether ISIL's or al-Qa'ida's, in a region undergoing vast and rapid political change against the backdrop of generations of autocratic government and economic disparities creates the nexus in which violence becomes more likely. Militant Christianity and Islam in central Africa, militant Buddhism in Burma, and violent Hindutva in India will all continue to fuel terror and conflict.

- Extremists will exploit anger and link perceived injustices with the common identity of deepening religious affiliation in some parts of the world. Religion will become a more important source of meaning and continuity because of increasing information connectedness, the extent of state weakness in much of the developing world, and the rise of alienation due to the dislocation from traditional work in the developed world. Rapid change and conditions of political and economic uncertainty, if not insecurity, will encourage many people to embrace ideologies and identities for meaning and continuity.

- Advances in information technologies—whether with the printing press and Gutenberg Bible in the 15th century or with the invention of the World Wide Web in 1989—allow religious content to spread widely, in part because religions are ideas that transcend borders and are often more influential in daily lives than state authority. The vast majority of believers will be peaceful, but those with extreme views will find likeminded followers and vulnerable recruits through information technologies. Most world religions—including Christianity, Islam, and Judaism, Buddhism, and Hinduism—have exclusionary aspects of doctrine that can be exploited in this way.

Beyond religion, psychological and social factors will drive individual participation in terrorism, as well as help terrorist groups attract recruits and resources and maintain cohesion.

- *Some level of alienation,* whether being disconnected from the sociocultural mainstream, unable to participate in the political process, or lacking economic benefits from society.

- *Ethnic and kinship bonds*—peer, social or familial networks—as well as a desire for adventure, fame, and belonging.

- *"Denationalizing,"* that is, the loss of connection with their community of origin, of young immigrants in European cities, combined with lack of opportunity or effective incentive to take on a new European identity.

- *Ethnic and religious tensions* (beyond today's hotspots), as between Malays and Thais in Thailand, Muslims and Buddhists in Burma, and Christians and Muslims in Nigeria.

Technology will be a double-edged sword. On the one hand, it will facilitate terrorist communications, recruitment, logistics, and lethality. On the other, it will provide authorities with more sophisticated techniques to identify and characterize threats—if their publics allow them. Technology will continue to enable nonstate actors to mask their activity and identity. The use of cyber tools to take down electrical systems, for instance, has potential mass disruption effects, some with lethal consequences. Communications technology also will be key to nonstate actors' ability to recruit new members, finance operations,

A man lights a candle in front of the restaurant "Le Carillon" in tribute to victims of the Nov. 13, 2015 terrorist attack in Paris at the Bataclan.

and disseminate messages. Advancements in technology will also lower technological barriers to high-impact, low-likelihood terrorist WMD scenarios, and enable the proliferation of lethal, conventional weaponry to terrorist groups.

- Technology will further decentralize the threat—from an organized and controlled al-Qa'ida to a fragmented jihadist militancy, for example. This trend will pose challenges to counterterrorism efforts and change the nature of future terrorist plots and strategies.

Future International Order in the Balance

The post-World War II international order that enabled today's political, economic, and security structures and institutions is in question as power diffuses globally, shuffling seats at the "table" of international decision making. Today, aspiring powers seek to adjust the rules of the game and international context in ways favorable to their

---

Imagining a surprise
news headline in 2019 . . .

Mexico Outlaws Private Drones After Latest Assassination Attempt

May 13, 2019 – Mexico City

The Mexican Government today announced it was a crime for private citizens to own drones after the fifth "drone-bomb" assassination attempt by drug cartels against senior government officials in less than three months, the latest targeting the new Minister of Interior.

---

interests. This dynamic complicates reform of international institutions such as the UN Security Council or the Bretton-Woods institutions, and brings into question whether civil, political, and human rights—hallmarks of liberal values and US leadership since 1945—will continue to be so. Norms that were thought to be settled will be increasingly threatened if current trends hold, and consensus to build new norms may be elusive—particularly as Russia, China, and other actors such as ISIL seek to shape regions and international norms in their favor. A few features of the evolving international order are clear:

- Geopolitical competition is on the rise as China and Russia seek to exert more sway over their neighboring regions and promote an order in which US influence does not dominate.

- Although states and organizations will continue to shape citizen expectations about the future order, citizen and subnational concerns will increasingly press states to the point that international and domestic politics will not be separable.

- This will result in the near term in waning commitments to existing security concepts and human rights among some states, even as some individuals and small groups advocate for such ideas through new and legacy platforms, venues, and institutions.

- Authoritarian regimes are likely to increasingly reinterpret and manipulate human rights norms. This will probably lead to decreasing consensus in the international arena on the extraterritorial obligations of states, such as when to apply concepts such as the Responsibility to Protect— which could have negative consequences for domestic civil societies and the resolution of humanitarian conflicts.

- The norms and practices emerging around climate change—and their influence on international and state development policies—are the most likely candidates for fostering a 21st century set of common principles. Majorities in 40 countries polled by Pew say climate change is a serious problem, with a median of 54 percent globally saying it is a very serious problem.

The near-term likelihood of international competition leading to greater global disorder and uncertainty will remain elevated as long as a la carte internationalism persists. As dominant states limit cooperation to a subset of global issues while aggressively asserting their interests in regional matters, international norms and institutions are likely to erode and the international system to fragment toward contested regional spheres of influence.

THREE SCENARIOS
FOR THE
DISTANT FUTURE

ISLANDS

ORBITS

COMMUNITIES

THREE SCENARIOS FOR THE DISTANT FUTURE: ISLANDS, ORBITS, AND COMMUNITIES

Thinking about the future beyond the next five years involves so many contingencies that it is helpful to consider how selected trends, choices, and uncertainties might play out over multiple pathways—as told through a set of short stories, commonly known as scenarios. While no single scenario can describe the entirety of future global developments, scenarios can portray how the foremost issues and trends might characterize the future, much like the terms "Cold War" and "Gilded Age" defined the dominant themes of past eras. For us, the three primary uncertainties shaping the next 20 years revolve around:

(1) **Dynamics within countries.** How governments and publics renegotiate their expectations of one another and create political order in an era of heightened change, marked by empowered individuals and a rapidly changing economy;

(2) **Dynamics between countries.** How the major powers, along with select groups and individuals, work out patterns of competition and cooperation; and

(3) **Long-term, short-term tradeoffs.** To what extent will states and other actors prepare in the near-term for complex global issues like climate change and transformative technologies.

The three scenarios—"Islands," "Orbits," and "Communities"—explore how critical trends and choices might intersect to create different paths to the future. These scenarios postulate alternative responses to near-term volatility—at the national (Islands), regional (Orbits), and substate and transnational (Communities) levels. The scenarios also consider alternative US responses to these trends—for instance, ranking US domestic and economic issues over foreign relations, engaging globally to defend US interests overseas, or adjusting governing practices to take advantage of the proliferation of influential actors. While no single outcome is preordained, the following scenarios characterize the types of issues that will confront policymakers in the years ahead.

Methodology of Scenario Analysis

Good scenarios are far more art than science. The stories need to be grounded enough to feel plausible, while imaginative enough to challenge our assumptions—because the world regularly twists and turns in surprising ways. None of these outcomes, however, are predetermined. The choices people make—individually and collectively, whether by intent or chance—will remain the biggest variables driving the course of events. Many more scenarios could have been generated from the trends we discuss in this report, but we hope the scenarios we have crafted stimulate thinking and discussion about the future.

- Thinking creatively about the future is often difficult because of the tendency for the recent past and current events to prejudice assessments. Developing alternative scenarios helps to challenge unstated assumptions about the future, revealing new possibilities and choices that are otherwise difficult to discern.

- Our scenarios, and the challenges and opportunities they represent, are not necessarily mutually exclusive. The future will probably include elements from each, but at different levels of intensity or in different regions of the world. For example, the future described in the "Islands" scenario might prompt some states to react to increasing economic instability and the inward focus of the West by taking actions to secure their own interests, moving the future in the direction of our "Orbits" scenario. Alternatively, the inability of national governments to effectively manage economic and technological changes might generate a greater role for local governments and private actors, creating the conditions for the "Communities" scenario to emerge.

- We encourage readers to use these scenarios to challenge their current planning assumptions and to begin a strategic conversation about preparing for the challenges and opportunities that might lie ahead. The scenarios should be reevaluated as new developments emerge.

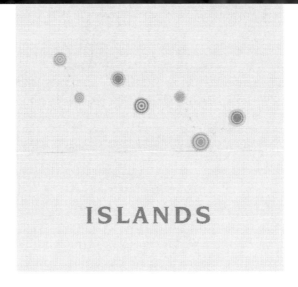

ISLANDS

This scenario investigates the issues surrounding a restructuring of the global economy that leads to long periods of slow or no growth, challenging the assumption that traditional models of economic prosperity and expanding globalization will continue in the future. The scenario emphasizes the difficulties for governance in meeting future societal demands for economic and physical security as popular pushback to globalization increases, emerging technologies transform work and trade, and political instability grows. This scenario underscores the choices governments will face in adjusting to changing economic and technological conditions that might lead some to turn inward, reduce support for multilateral cooperation, and adopt protectionist policies and others to find ways to leverage new sources of economic growth and productivity. Here is an economist reflecting on the 20 years since the 2008 global financial crisis:

The past 20 years of coping with downsides of globalization, financial volatility, and increasing inequality has transformed the global environment. Mounting public debt, aging populations, and decreased capital investment exacerbated downward pressures on developed economies. Public and business demands for protection from market swings, disruptive technologies, disease outbreaks, and terrorism drove many countries to turn inward. Political instability increased as public frustration rose in countries that failed to manage change. Many governments struggled to maintain services to their populace, as tax revenues failed to keep pace with growing obligations. The segments of populations that had obtained "middle class" status prior to the financial crisis were most at risk and many fell back into moderate levels of poverty. Globalization slowed as governments adopted protectionist policies in response to domestic pressures. Most economists identify the following developments as key factors slowing global economic growth and accelerating the reversal of much of the globalization trends of the previous decades:

- **The rise of inequality as wealth** became more concentrated fed tensions within societies and led to popular pushback against globalization.

- **The spread of artificial intelligence** and automation technologies disrupted more industries than economists expected.

This trend sparked a backlash from large numbers of displaced workers, creating a political constituency that forced some governments to stop participating in global trade institutions and agreements they had previously committed to support.

- **Trade patterns shifted** as governments favored employing regional trading blocs and bilateral trade agreements over comprehensive global arrangements. The wide adoption of new technologies, such as additive manufacturing (3-D printing), often provided local producers a competitive advantage vis-à-vis foreign suppliers reducing global trade in manufactured goods.

- **Slower global economic growth** depressed energy prices and placed additional pressures on the energy-dependent economies of Russia, the Middle East and South America while also increasing competition among energy producers.

- **China and India remained stuck in the "middle income trap,"** suffering stagnant economic growth, wages, and living standards, because they were unable to generate sufficient domestic demand to drive higher economic growth when foreign trade flagged.

- **Domestic and economic challenges drove the United States and Europe to focus inward.** The United States and the EU adopted protectionist policies to preserve domestic industries. European economies suffered because of declining exports and underdeveloped service industries. Germany and France found enough common ground to hold together the Euro Zone; however, renewed fiscal stimulus did little to reinvigorate economic growth in the periphery states of Europe,

and insufficient willingness to ease labor restrictions undermined EU member states' ability to maintain or boost their international competitiveness.

- **Rising intellectual property theft and cyber attacks** drove some governments to introduce stringent controls that hampered information sharing and cooperation across the Internet.

- **Changing climate conditions** challenged the capacity of many governments to cope, especially in the Middle East and Africa, where extended droughts reduced food and water supplies and high temperatures suppressed the ability of people to work outdoors. Large numbers of displaced persons from the region often found they had no place to go as a series of dramatic terrorist attacks in Western countries drove those governments to adopt stringent security policies that restricted immigration.

- **The global pandemic of 2023** dramatically reduced global travel in an effort to contain the spread of the disease, contributing to the slowing of global trade and decreased productivity.

The combination of these events led to a more defensive, segmented world as anxious states sought to metaphorically and physically "wall" themselves off from external challenges, becoming "islands" in a sea of volatility. International cooperation on global issues, such as terrorism, failing states, migration, and climate change eroded, forcing more isolated countries to fend for themselves. Furthermore, declining defense budgets and preoccupying domestic concerns drove the West to spurn military force when its vital interests were not threatened. This led to an atrophying US alliance system. Instability increased in parts of Africa, the Middle East, and South Asia.

Economic challenges still exist 20 years after the 2008 financial crisis, but several developments indicate we are now entering a new era of economic growth and prosperity. Technology advances, such as, artificial intelligence, machine learning, additive manufacturing, and automation—although disruptive to traditional job markets—have the potential to boost economic efficiency and productivity, leading to new areas of activity and economic growth for a broad range of countries. The realization that the most creative and innovative solutions are often achieved through man-machine cooperation rather than through machines alone is helping to reverse earlier job losses, although providing opportunities for individual displaced workers through training has not been universally successful.

Furthermore, the slowing of globalization and trade is sparking a new generation of experimentation, innovation, and entrepreneurship at local levels. The increasing costs of food imports as countries have imposed carbon taxes have also spurred local agriculture production. These developments are most prominent in societies that provide access to online education resources as well as scientific and technical knowledge that is shared among communities of like-minded entrepreneurs and hobby-technologists. Some governments, however, are ill prepared to handle the security aspects raised by the proliferation of new technologies, which also has resulted in the rise of tech-enabled criminal gangs and terrorist groups and new methods for circumventing government controls.

Developments in biotechnologies and health care also are leading to new industries and improved productivity, as greater access to care is creating healthier workforces. Expanding working-age populations through better health care has the potential to provide an economic boost to countries with aging populations. A proliferation of robotics and artificial intelligence in basic medicine and diagnostics is also helping to make affordable care more widely available and has reduced the cost burden of caring for aging citizens on cash-strapped governments.

Improving economic growth will continue to depend on new technologies, local innovation and entrepreneurship. There remains an acute need for government programs to cushion future economic disruptions and ensure the welfare of those in society who are least able to adapt. Addressing these issues, however, requires overcoming the political polarization that has prevented many governments from achieving the necessary budget compromises. Continued government support for these endeavors through the reinvigorated trading of technologies, expertise, and resources also might help bridge the economic gaps that exist within and between countries.

Islands Implications

This scenario explores the ramifications if governments fail to manage the changes in global economic conditions that have led to increasing inequality, lower growth rates in developed economies, job displacements, and societal divisions. The scenario highlights the need for the rich countries to address the negative byproducts of past economic policies and to manage the tensions between populism and inclusion. The most successful states will be those with governments that encourage research and innovation; promote information sharing; maintain high-quality education and lifelong learning in science, technology, engineering and mathematics; provide job retraining; and adopt tax, immigration, and security policies to attract and retain high-tech talent. Such developments would encourage greater experimentation, innovation, and entrepreneurship to help boost domestic manufacturing and create employment.

Alternatively, states that choose to place controls on access to information, fail to honor intellectual property rights, and discourage the import of high-tech talent will likely be excluded from the economic benefits offered by emerging technology advances. Security will be another key issue as these developments also create challenges in the forms of technology-enabled terrorist attacks and criminal activity.

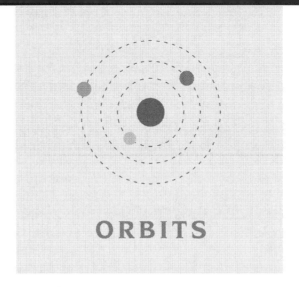

ORBITS

This scenario explores a future of tensions created by competing major powers seeking their own spheres of influence while attempting to maintain stability at home. It examines how the trends of rising nationalism, changing conflict patterns, emerging disruptive technologies, and decreasing global cooperation might converge to increase the risk of interstate conflict. This scenario emphasizes policy choices that would reinforce stability and peace or exacerbate tensions. These choices are explored through the memoirs of a National Security Advisor reflecting on his assessment of the international environment near the end of President Smith's second term in office in 2032:

Over the course of the Smith presidency, I witnessed a number of developments giving me hope that the next President will find the world in a much better place. It was not that long ago, however, that increasing geopolitical tensions led to the brink of interstate conflict.

It was the combination of competing values among rival states, military build-ups, rising nationalism, and domestic insecurity that created an era of increased geopolitical competition among the major powers. In the early 2020s, polarizing politics and fiscal burdens constrained US engagement on the world stage, prompting foreign assessments that the United States was moving toward a prolonged period of retrenchment. China and Russia, in particular, viewed this time as an opportunity to seek greater influence over neighboring countries within their respective regional economic, political and security orbits. Iran also attempted to take advantage of instability in the Middle East to expand its influence in the region.

By the mid-2020s, these developments led to the international system devolving toward contested regional spheres. The powers at the center of the spheres attempted to assert their right to privileged economic, political, and security influence within their regions. China increasingly used its economic and military power to influence the behavior of neighboring states and to force concessions from foreign business seeking access to its markets. India, Japan, and other states adopted more assertive independent foreign policies to counter Chinese encroachment on their interests, increasing regional tensions in East and South Asia. Russia also asserted itself more forcefully in Central Asia to keep that region under Moscow's influence and to counter China's growing presence.

Regional tensions increased as China undertook extensive engineering projects to change local environmental conditions, such as diverting major rivers to the detriment of neighboring states. As environmental conditions in China continued to degrade, Beijing considered more ambitious geoengineering projects, such as injecting tons of sulfate aerosols into the atmosphere to lower temperatures. These efforts ignited an international debate over the ethics of a single state taking action that affected the global ecosystem, prompting some countries to threaten China with punitive actions if Beijing unilaterally pursued climate modification.

When President Smith came to power eight years ago, there was a general consensus among national security experts that while geopolitical competition was intensifying, both economic and political interests would stop states from direct military conflict. This seemed to be the case as China, Iran, and Russia separately eschewed direct military conflict in favor of lower levels of competition—diplomatic and economic coercion, propaganda, cyber intrusions, proxies, and indirect applications of military power—blurring the distinction between peace and war. The most frequent victim was "the truth" as propaganda from these states—distributed through a variety of social, commercial, and official outlets—distorted, misrepresented, and shaped information about what was really happening. The culmination of these actions, however, undermined international norms about sovereignty and peaceful resolutions of disputes and perpetuated perceptions of US disengagement.

The President decided early in his first term that the United States could no longer stand by and allow these developments to continue unabated. He moved to shore up US alliances and increasingly employed US military forces in exercising international norms such as freedom of navigation operations. Efforts, however, by China, Iran, and Russia to prepare for traditional military conflicts—by deploying greater numbers of advanced weapons such as long-range, precision-guided, strike systems to threaten rival military forces operating in their regional sphere— intensified global perceptions of increasing security competition between these countries and the United States and its allies. We did not fully realize at the time, however, that Beijing, Moscow, and Tehran were increasingly nervous about their standing at home due to economic stress and social tensions, leading them to believe they could not compromise on external challenges to their interests for fear of appearing weak. The collision between a Chinese underwater autonomous vehicle and a Japanese Coast Guard ship patrolling off the Senkaku islands, the cyber attacks against European financial centers attributed to Russian hackers, and the Iranian threat to employ its increasingly accurate ballistic missiles to strike Saudi energy and desalination facilities were a few of the flashpoints that narrowly missed escalating into broader conflict.

It took a mushroom cloud in a desert in South Asia to shake us from our complacency. I remember how the crisis between India and Pakistan started: the Second Indus Waters Treaty was abandoned by both sides, followed shortly by a series of explosions in New Delhi that the Indian Government quickly attributed to Pakistan-based extremist groups. Islamabad denied involvement, but both sides began mobilizing their military forces. After a few confusing days of cyber attacks that disrupted the ability of both sides to understand what was happening, the situation escalated quickly. According to a subsequent investigation, artificial intelligence systems supporting the military decision makers made the crisis worse by misinterpreting signals meant to deter instead as signs of aggressive intent. The result was the first use of a nuclear weapon in a conflict since 1945.

With China's help, the United States quickly moved to defuse the crisis—we were lucky. The conflict barely missed escalating to a full nuclear exchange. President Smith shared the Nobel Peace Prize with the President of China that year. More importantly, however, the Indo-Pakistani war of 2028 reminded all the major powers of the dangerous game we were playing. A series of confidence-building measures and arms control agreements with China and Russia followed, placing limits on the most unstable escalatory weapon capabilities. Putin's successor also made great strides in repairing Russia's relations with Europe to the benefit of the Russian economy. These experiences allowed the United States and the other major powers to build a foundation of trust that enabled cooperation on other security issues, such as instability in North Korea and the Middle East.

The next US President will have to deal with a world where geopolitical competition still exists, but where the major powers learned, for self-preservation, to cooperate with each other in areas of mutual interest. If not for the shock we all felt by the close call in South Asia, the choices President Smith and others might have made could have led to a very different outcome.

Orbits Implications

This scenario examines how increasing geopolitical competition could raise the risk of interstate conflict and threaten the rules-based international order. It highlights the importance of reassuring allies and preventing "gray-zone" conflicts from undermining international norms and from escalating into a war between major powers. Furthermore, the deployment of new capabilities, such as hypersonic weapons, autonomous systems, counterspace weapons, and cyber operations, introduces new—and not well understood—escalation dynamics that increase the risk of miscalculation.

Growing geopolitical tensions that produce destabilizing events and increase the dangers for all involved might provide incentive for rivals to find common ground and negotiate confidence-building measures to reduce risks. For example, the prospect of a "close call"—in which a major military conflict is barely averted or a large natural disaster illustrating the negative global impact of climate change—might compel nations to work together for self-preservation, leading to a more stable international order. Such an outcome, however, is not assured, highlighting the importance of managing increasing geopolitical competition in ways that reduce the risk of miscalculation and escalation while leaving open the possibility for greater cooperation on issues of shared risk.

COMMUNITIES

This scenario explores the issues that arise as the enormity of future economic and governance challenges test the capacity of national governments to cope, creating space for local governments and private actors and thus questioning assumptions about the future of governance. This scenario emphasizes the trends associated with the changing nature of power and advances in ICT that are enabling a broader array of influential actors and identifies how such trends might lead to choices that create both opportunities and hurdles for future governance. It is written from the perspective of a future mayor of a large Canadian city in 2035, reflecting on the changes she has witnessed during the previous two decades:

The increasing role in governing of groups beneath and across national governments seems inevitable in retrospect. National governments simply proved less adept at managing some public needs in a rapidly changing environment than local governments, which were better attuned to increasingly powerful societal groups and commercial entities. In addition, as public trust in national government leaders and institutions continued to erode, more critical public services were privatized. Point-to-point commercial transactions that did not rely on government intermediaries became more common, and people grew increasingly comfortable working through nongovernmental channels. This further diminished governments' ability to provide oversight—and to generate revenue through fees and taxes.

While critical state functions such as foreign policy, military operations, and homeland defense remained the province of national governments, local populations increasingly relied on local authorities, social movements, or religious organizations to provide a growing array of education, financial, commercial, legal, and security services. At the same time, businesses gained far-reaching influence through increasingly sophisticated marketing, product differentiation, and incentive programs to build intense customer loyalty that transcended borders. The involvement of private-sector companies in the lives of their employees grew as these companies expanded services, such as education, health care, and housing, they provided to their employees. Large, multinational corporations increasingly assumed a role in providing public goods and funding global research.

People increasingly defined their relationships and identities through evolving and interconnected groups outside of national government channels. Information and communication technologies are now key to defining relationships and identities based on shared ideas, ideologies, employment, and histories, rather than nationality. Furthermore, advances in biotechnologies led to class distinctions in some countries between those who could afford human modifications from those who were not artificially "enhanced."

As the ability to control and manipulate information became a key source of influence, companies, advocacy groups, charities, and local governments were often more adept than national governments in exerting the power of ideas and tapping into emotions to sway populations to support their agenda. In some cases, governments willingly ceded some of their power to these networks of social and commercial "communities" in the hopes of defusing political divisions and public frustration—and of providing local services that national governments were unable to offer. In other cases, subnational entities, and alliances between them, asserted greater authority in defiance of national institutions.

In the Middle East, a "lost generation" of dissatisfied Arab youths, whose foundational experiences had been shaped by violence, insecurity, displacement, and lack of economic and educational opportunities—especially for women—emerged through information networks to challenge the traditional centralized governing structures. Arab youth in many countries demanded more services and political reforms to allow them to have greater say in the policies of their governments. Further, there was broad societal rejection of the violent religious extremism of the terrorist groups that emerged on the world stage in the early part of the 21st Century. Once started, these movements quickly spread throughout the region.

The experience of the Middle East repeated elsewhere, but not always with the same results. For example, amid a rocky leadership succession, Moscow found maintaining central control harder and harder as Russians banded together to protest rampant government corruption and the power of the oligarchs, and to urge local economic and political reform. Some regimes successfully engineered power-sharing arrangements with local authorities and some leveraged the resources of transnational foundations and charitable organizations to meet the needs of their societies. Others resorted to force to quell internal protests and employed advanced information technologies to identify and silence dissidents. China's Communist Party initially took this approach but was forced to adjust its strategy and make compromises as retaining power through force alone became increasingly difficult. Other governments succumbed to internal pressures and fragmented along ethnic, religious, and tribal lines.

What resulted was messy. Governance globally evolved through a trial and error to address changing public needs and demands. The more agile and open states, like the United States, adapted their governing approach to public engagement and policymaking by harnessing the power of subnational and nonstate actors, increasing the importance of cities and other forms of local governance. City leaders, like myself, increasingly worked with our counterparts from around the world, with the encouragement of our national governments, to share information and resources and to develop new approaches to common problems, such as climate change, education, and poverty reduction.

Adjusting to this new style of governing was easier for Canada, the United States and other liberal democracies that had a tradition of strong, local public and private sector leadership, in contrast to countries with centralized governments. Authoritarian regimes that resisted the increasing diffusion of power and tried to limit and control the activities of nongovernmental organizations, for example, continued to experience widespread popular movements that sapped their authority. In the worst cases, extremists, criminal gangs, and warlords flourished in areas where national government lost control of parts of its territory.

Over time, commercial and religious organizations, as well as civil society groups and local governments, became multi-stakeholder coalitions of various sorts—some including national governments. These new approaches to solving global challenges gradually coalesced around common values, including human rights. States, city and civic leaders, and commercial and civil society organizations now routinely participate in regional and interregional processes and issue-based networks to create alternative venues for driving positive change. Social movements, religious organizations, local governments, and publics propel the political agendas of national governments. Removed from its old "Cold War" context, the term "Free World" now defines the networked group of state, substate, and nonstate entities that work cooperatively to promote respect for individual freedoms, human rights, political reform, environmentally sustainable policies, free trade, and information transparency.

Communities Implications

This scenario examines issues associated with the future of governing. In it, governments will need policies and processes for encouraging public-private partnerships with a wide-range of actors—city leaders, non-governmental organizations, and civil societies—to address emerging challenges. Large multinational corporations and charitable foundations, in particular, might increasingly complement the work of governments in providing research, education, training, health care, and information services to needy societies.

While states will remain the primary providers of national security and other elements of "hard power," their ability to leverage communities of local, private, and transnational actors would enhance their "soft power" attributes and resilience. Liberal democracies that encourage decentralized governance and private-public partnerships will be best suited to operate in this world. In these societies, technology will enable interactions between the public and government in new ways, such as collective decision making. Other governments, however, might not fare as well, leading to a variety of outcomes, including increased authoritarianism and state failure.

WHAT THE SCENARIOS
TEACH US: FOSTERING
OPPORTUNITIES
THROUGH RESILIENCE

Anton Foltin / Shutterstock.com

Diverse plants adapt to a desert climate.

WHAT THE SCENARIOS SUGGEST: FOSTERING OPPORTUNITIES THROUGH RESILIENCE

Examining the trends across the three scenarios makes vivid that the world will become more volatile in the years ahead. States, institutions, and societies will be under pressure from above and below the level of the nation-state to adapt to systemic challenges— and to act sooner rather than later. From above, climate change, technology standards and protocols, and transnational terrorism will require multilateral cooperation. From below, the inability of government to meet the expectations of their citizens, inequality, and identity politics will increase the risk of instability. Responding effectively to these challenges will require not only sufficient resources and capacity but also political will. Moreover, the extent of these challenges might overwhelm the capacity of individual states and international institutions to resolve problems on their own, suggesting a greater role for a wide range of public and private actors.

The scenarios also highlight, however, that the very same trends heightening risks in the near term can enable better outcomes over the longer term if the proliferation of power and players builds resilience to manage greater disruptions and uncertainty. In a world where surprises hit harder and more frequently, the most successful actors will be those that are resilient, enabling them to better adapt to changing conditions, persevere in the face of adversity, and act quickly to recover after mistakes.

Although resilience increases in importance in a more chaotic world, traditional calculations of state power rarely factor in a state's resilience. The sudden collapse of the Soviet Union and the breakdown of state authority in the aftermath of the "Arab Spring" suggest that states can be fragile in ways that conventional measures of power do not capture.

- For example, by traditional measures of power, such as GDP, military spending, and population size, China's share of global power is increasing. China, however, also exhibits several characteristics, such as a centralized government, political corruption, and an economy overly reliant on investment and net exports for growth—which suggest vulnerability to future shocks.

- Alternatively, the United States exhibits many of the factors associated with resilience, including decentralized governance, a diversified economy, inclusive society, large land mass, biodiversity, secure energy supplies, and global military power projection capabilities and alliances.

The governments, organizations, and individuals that are most capable of identifying opportunities and working cooperatively to act upon them will be most successful, but the window for forging new patterns of cooperation is narrowing. The collective action challenge is becoming more pronounced as global challenges grow. The near-term choices of individuals, organizations, and states will shape how the current governability and cooperation crisis is addressed, or whether an extended period of ad hoc, uncoordinated responses to uncertainty and volatility will intensify tensions within, between, and among states. Alliance management, improvement of national governance and international institutions, and openness to mobilizing a wide range of commercial, religious, civil, and advocacy organizations at all levels of government will be key to sustaining positive outcomes.

Issues that lead to shared vulnerabilities and the need for global approaches—such as climate change and expanding terrorist threats—might induce states to increase their **resiliency, particularly if cooperation were limited.** These issues might also push states to find far greater utility in international institutions and other transnational forums to develop solutions and coordinate actions. In turn, such developments might prompt a new era of global engagement that includes states along with local governments, companies, and civil society groups working cooperatively to deal with existential challenges facing humanity.

- Two high-profile UN initiatives—the "Sustainable Development Agenda" and the "Framework Convention on Climate Change"—set broad strategic goals to be pursued through cooperation between governments and public-private partnerships. Such efforts allow parties to refine the programs over time and enable corporations and civil society groups to play a role in forging international norms and global governance arrangements.

- Increasing resilience at the institution level could also occur through the employment of dedicated strategic planning cells, exercises, technologies, and processes that would accelerate responses during crises.

- The election of future UN Secretaries General also will provide opportunities to pivot the strategic direction of the UN's system of agencies and to rethink priorities in light of emerging challenges as senior leadership and appointments change.

The downsides of globalization that drive some governments to adopt protectionist and nationalist policies might also create opportunities to increase resilience and innovation at local levels. The slowing of globalization and trade and the advent of additive manufacturing (3-D printing) technologies might lead to increased emphasis on near-by services, improving the self-reliance of local societies and groups. These developments might set

Assessing State Resilience

Measuring a state's resilience is likely to be a better determinant of success in coping with future chaos and disruption than traditional measures of material power alone. Tomorrow's successful states will probably be those that invest in infrastructure, knowledge, and relationships resilient to shock—whether economic, environmental, societal, or cyber.

Factors enhancing the resiliency of states, according to existing research, include:

- **Governance:** Governments capable of providing goods and services, promoting political inclusiveness, enforcing the rule of law, and earning the trust of their populace will be better positioned to absorb shocks and rally their population in response.

- **Economics:** States with diversified economies, manageable government debt and adequate financial reserves, robust private sectors, and adaptable and innovate workforces will be more resilient.

- **Social System:** A prepared, integrated, and orderly society is likely to be cohesive and resilient in the face of unexpected change and have a high tolerance for coping with adversity.

- **Infrastructure:** The robustness of a state's critical infrastructure, including diversified sources of energy and secure and redundant communication, information, health, and financial networks, will lessen a state's vulnerability to both natural disasters and intentional attempts to create disruption through cyber and other forms of attack.

- **Security:** States with a high military capacity, capable and trusted domestic law enforcement and emergency responders, good civil-military relations, and robust alliances will more likely be able to defend against unexpected attacks and restore domestic order following a disruptive shock.

- **Geography and the Environment:** States that have a large land mass, high levels of biodiversity, and good quality air, food, soil, and water will be more resilient to natural disasters.

the stage for a new wave of entrepreneurship and manufacturing that provides economic benefits to local communities. Governments and academic institutions, historically the source for science discoveries that enable private sector development, could encourage local developments that boost additional productivity and innovation by expanding public access to science and technology education and resources and by providing basic research.

Initiatives to provide continuous workforce education, enable a mobile and secure workforce, and preserve technology leadership in multiple disciplines will enhance the resilience of states to potentially disruptive advances in technology, such as automation, data analytics, artificial intelligence, and biotechnologies. Such resilience would mitigate the near-term risk to jobs and markets and allow the technologies to produce greater economic efficiency and productivity over time.

- Public-private continuing education would assist workforces in affordably adapting to changing job markets and potentially diffuse populist sentiment that elites disregard the average worker. Such initiatives, akin to the German apprenticeship model, could involve collaboration between governments, private industry, and education institutions—private or public—to train new or newly arrived workers, recently displaced employees, and the long-term unemployed.

- Academic institutions could develop curricula through consultation with would-be employers on necessary skills, creating pools of workers fully prepared to make use of new and evolving industries—commonly cited as a constraint on hiring for many high-tech businesses. These efforts could help academic institutions

remain current and relevant, as well as reduce the long-term need for public assistance for idled workers.

Such programs, which could encourage corporate participation through tax incentives or wage subsidies for new hires, would particularly benefit developed industrialized countries experiencing rapid technology adoption, global labor competition and shrinking, but highly educated, working-age populations. Such initiatives might also protect intellectual property rights, provide incentives for new-industry start-ups to locate in sponsoring communities, and preserve national leadership in defining technology protocols and standards.

Transparency enabled by communication technology will build resilience by enhancing citizens' visibility into government processes, supporting anti-corruption measures, and moderating divisive impulses. The creation of media and technology organizations that provide objective reporting and support transparent fact-checking would be a step toward building a foundation for enhanced trust in government and institutions. Coupled with education on critical thinking skills, increased transparent communication could reduce fear and broaden citizens' understanding of different perspectives. With greater trust, historically disengaged populations such as minorities could seize on the opportunity for greater inclusion and a more free exchange of ideas.

Generating resiliency in currently troubled societies, such as those in the Middle East, also requires reducing the forces promoting extremism. Nascent indications of popular frustration in the Middle East with the abuses of extremism couched as "Islamic" might propel local populations to reject extremist ideologies and instead push for new political reforms. Across the Middle East and North Africa, extremists who claim Islamic affiliation are inspiring some to disaffiliate themselves with Islamists, openly or in private. For example, Ennahda, Tunisia's ruling political party, recently announced its intention to no longer identify as Islamist but rather as Muslim democrats, citing, in part, sensitivity to the connotations of the label.

Investments in data, methods, modeling, and surveillance of critical human and natural-support systems—such as infrastructure, energy, water, and air quality—could spark emergent technologies in sustainability, increasing community and environmental resilience. The likely widespread private-sector demand for mitigation technologies and services will drive some countries and corporations to dominate this new market early. The profitability of such developments could in turn offset the need for a natural disaster or other crisis to change the politics of this issue. Programs that simultaneously strengthen short-term crisis response capacity and the long-term development of climate-resilient and adaptive systems would minimize potential economic losses from ongoing demographic and environmental pressures. Beneficiaries would span construction, energy, mining, agriculture, insurance, finance, and R&D sectors and have local to international impact.

The most resilient societies will also be those that unleash the full potential of individuals—including women and minorities—to create and cooperate. Such societies will be moving with, rather than against, historical currents, drawing upon the ever-expanding scope of human agency and skill to shape the future. In all societies, even in the bleakest circumstances, there will be those who choose to improve the welfare, happiness, and security of others—and who will use transformative technologies to do so at scale. The opposite will be true as well—destructive forces will be empowered as never before. The central choice before governments and societies is how to blend individual, collective, and national endowments in a way that yields sustainable security, prosperity, and hope.

METHODOLOGICAL NOTE

As with every *Global Trends*, the National Intelligence Council (NIC) seeks to innovate its approach, employ rigorous foresight methods, learn from ever more diverse perspectives, and maximize its policy relevance. We built on this tradition for the current and sixth *Global Trends* report by introducing several new elements to our analytic process.

- We examined regional trends first and aggregated those assessments up to identify broader global dynamics.

- We assessed emerging trends and their implications in two timeframes: a near-term, five-year look that focused on issues confronting the next US administration and a long-term, 20-year projection to support US strategic planning. This is why we have dropped the year from the title.

- We developed a new concept for thinking about geopolitical "power," moving away from past methods that overemphasized state-based material power, such as Gross Domestic Product and military spending, to consider also nonmaterial aspects of power, such as ideas and relationships, and the rise of consequential corporations, social movements, and individuals.

- We made extensive use of analytic simulations—employing teams of experts to represent key international actors—to explore the future trajectories for regions of the world, the international order, the security environment, and the global economy.

- We considered the potential for discontinuities in all regions and topic areas, developing an appreciation for the types of discontinuities likely to represent fundamental shifts from the status quo. These are highlighted in the text as fictional news articles from the future.

Early on, we reviewed enduring, bipartisan US planning assumptions since 1945 to identify those most and least likely to be in tension with the emerging strategic context. These exercises helped us prioritize issues, countries, and people to visit, and manage the scope of research. Ultimately, our two-year exploration of the key trends and uncertainties took us to more than 35 countries and meetings with more than 2,500 individuals—helping us understand the trends and uncertainties as they are lived today and the likely choices elites and non-elites will make in the face of such conditions in the future. Visits with senior officials and strategists worldwide informed our understanding of the evolving strategic intent and national interests of major powers. We met and corresponded with hundreds of natural and social scientists, thought leaders, religious figures, business and industry representatives, diplomats, development experts, and women, youth, and civil society organizations around the world. We supplemented this research by soliciting feedback on our preliminary analysis through social media, at events like the South by Southwest Interactive Festival, and through traditional workshops and individual reviews of drafts.

Like previous *Global Trends* reports, we developed multiple scenarios to describe how the key uncertainties and emerging trends might combine to produce alternative futures. The scenarios also explore the key choices, which governments, organizations, and individuals might make in response to emerging trends that might realign current trajectories leading to opportunities to shape better futures.

Ultimately, we offer "Global Trends: Paradox of Progress" as a framework for understanding the world's complexity and its potential for sharp, imminent discontinuities. The project reflects our own assessment of the trends and implications as professional analysts who do our best to "call them as we see them." The judgments do not represent official US Government policy, or the coordinated position of the US intelligence community. We offer them humbly, fully recognizing the audacity of the task and that we will have made errors—all of which are ours alone. We believe, however, that sharing with the world our assessment of the near and more distant futures provides a starting point for a shared understanding of the risks and opportunities to come.

GLOSSARY

Climate encompasses the averages, variability, and other statistics of weather over several decades or longer, while **weather** reflects short-term conditions of the atmosphere in a particular region. Weather includes very hot or cold or rainy days, while extreme weather events include extended droughts, floods, heatwaves, coldwaves, and intense tropical storms.

Climate change reflects nonrandom change in climate measured over several decades or longer.

Climate variability reflects the way that climate fluctuates above or below long-term average values.

We use the terms **developed and developing countries** to differentiate between states that are broadly industrialized with relatively high per capita incomes and those where industrialization and wealth are more limited. For the purpose of this study, "developing countries" are those included in the IMF's "emerging markets and developing countries" group, defined as all countries besides the advanced economies of the United States, Canada, Western Europe, Japan, South Korea, Australia, and New Zealand. Although the World Bank now uses more precise terms to characterize economic

development and more organizations are likely to do so, we retain the traditional terms, given their widespread conventional use, including by the United Nations and business entities.

Globalization is the process of interaction and integration among the world's people, companies, and governments, driven by the movement of trade, capital, people, ideas, and information across borders.

We follow World Bank researchers in defining **governance** as "the traditions and institutions by which authority in a country is exercised." This includes "the process by which governments are selected, monitored, and replaced; the capacity of the government to effectively formulate and implement sound policies; and the respect of citizens and the state for the institutions that govern economic and social interactions among them."

Internally displaced person (IDP) is a person or groups of persons who have been forced or obliged to flee or to leave their homes or places of habitual residence as a result of or in order to avoid the effects of armed conflict, situations of generalized violence, violations of human rights, or natural or manmade disasters, and who have not crossed an internationally recognized national border.

International system refers to the distribution of power and interactions among states as well the suite of institutions, rules, and norms that guide these interactions. The term **international order** is often used to characterize the nature of these interactions, typically associated with specific types of order such as the rules-based international order created after 1945.

Islamist describes a movement or approach dedicated to increasing the role of Islam in politics and sometimes other aspects of public life, and may or may not be violent.

Major economies are the world's largest developed economies—the G7 member states: the United States, Japan, Germany, the UK, France, Italy, and Canada, plus China. These are not the "largest economies," because Brazil and India have surpassed Canada and Italy in nominal terms, and several additional countries— Russia, Indonesia, Mexico, South Korea, and Saudi Arabia—supplant some G7 members in purchasing power parity terms. Nonetheless, we have used this grouping to reflect a balance of national economic size and per-capita wealth, as well as shared demographic challenges.

A **migrant** is any person who is moving or has moved across an international border or within a state away from his/her habitual places of residence, regardless of 1) the person's legal status; 2) whether the movement is voluntary or involuntary; 3) the causes driving the movement are; or 4) duration of stay.

Migration is the movement of a person or a group of persons, either across an international border or within a state. Migration is a population movement, encompassing any kind of movement of people, whatever its length, composition, and causes. It includes refugees, displaced persons, economic migrants, and persons moving for other purposes, including family reunification.

Nationalism is an ideology based on the premise that an individual's loyalty and devotion to the nation surpass other individual or group interests A **nation** is a large body of people united by common descent, history, culture, or language, living in a particular state or territory. A nation may or may not be a state.

Nativism is the promotion of the interests of native-born or established inhabitants against those of newcomers or immigrants and may also be expressed as an emphasis on traditional or local customs as opposed to outside influences.

Populism is a political program that champions the common person, usually in contrast to elites. Populist appeals can be from the political left, right, or combine elements of both. Populism can designate democratic and authoritarian movements and typically promotes a direct relationship between the people and political leadership.

A **refugee** is a person who, according to the 1951 UN Refugee Convention, "owing to a well-founded fear of persecution for reasons of race, religion, nationality, membership of a particular social group, or political opinions, is outside the country of his or her nationality and is unable or, owing to such fear, is unwilling to avail him or herself of the protection of that country."

ACKNOWLEDGEMENTS

The process of creating Global Trends is as important as the final report. The NIC learns from individuals and organizations around the world while coincidentally fostering strategic, future-focused discussions across cultures and interests. Our two year process began in 2014 and took us to 36 countries and territories—allowing us to build up from roughly 2,500 local and diverse perspectives to a global view.

On each trip, we met with people from all walks of life in major cities and often smaller towns. We sought perspectives from the worlds of business, philanthropy, science, technology, arts, humanities, and international affairs. We met with religious men and women, people of deep formal learning and those schooled in practical matters. Our visits with students and youth were especially valuable—challenging us to see what could be. Without fail, our interlocutors were generous with their insights and time, even when delivering difficult messages. "A-ha!" moments were plentiful, helping us make connections across regions and topics. A few interlocutors, no doubt, sought to shape the views of official Washington but most shared with us their expectations of the future, whether locally or internationally. Importantly, virtually all saw themselves in some way responsible for the world to come—driving home our key finding that the choices and actions of individuals matter more now than ever.

Although we can thank only a few individuals and organizations by name, we owe everyone we met a debt of gratitude. We appreciate as well the support of the Department of State and its Embassy country teams who facilitated many of these engagements.

Africa. In Angola, civil society and government organizations shared insights on urbanization and poverty reduction and helped us understand how Luanda, Africa's fourth largest city, is preparing for the future. A very brief visit to Botswana spotlighted key opportunities to build on past governance successes. In Congo, we appreciated discussions with civil society, government, and traditional leaders. In Senegal, we benefitted from discussions on religion, technology, and youth at think tanks. Meetings elsewhere on the continent helped us explore the region's demographic and economic potential as well as recent dynamics in technology, energy, and identity politics.

Asia and the Pacific. In Australia, the Office of National Assessments, Australia National University's Futures Hub at the National Security Institute, Lowy Institute, and Commonwealth Scientific and Industrial Research Organisation arranged workshops and provided critical feedback throughout. Our time in Burma was spent with numerous civil society and government organizations on interfaith, political reform, and conflict resolution issues. In China, repeat visits to China Institutes of Contemporary International Relations and Peking University were especially helpful—as were sessions with the China Institute for International Strategic Studies, Nanjing University, National Defense University, Fudon University, Renmin University, and the Chinese Executive Leadership Academy at Pudong. In Indonesia, we gained valuable insights from meetings with students, environmentalists, business figures, provincial officials, human rights activists, and religious leaders as well as from the Centre for Strategic and International Studies, the Institute for Policy Analysis of Conflict, and other think tanks. In Japan, we thank the Japan Institute for International Affairs, Tokyo Foundation, Institute for Energy and Economics, and the Asian Development Bank Institute, among others. In Singapore, the Prime Minister's Strategy Office, the S. Rajaratnam School of International Studies, and the National University of Singapore East Asian Institute were especially helpful on geopolitics and foresight methodologies. In South Korea, we were treated to an event organized by ASAN and learned much as well from the WTO Law Center, EWHA Women's University, Seoul National University, and Hankuk University of Foreign Studies. We thank especially Australia's Rory Medcalf and Andrew Shearer, China's Cui Liru and Da Wei, Shingo Yamagami in Japan, and Singapore's Peter Ho for helping us better understand Asia's changing dynamics and their global implications.

Europe. We thank our fellow travelers in strategic and futures assessment, including the UK's Cabinet Office, Joint Intelligence Organization, and the Defense Concepts and Doctrine Centre in the Ministry of Defense, the Blavatnik School of Government and the Oxford Martin School at the University of Oxford, and foresight programs with the European Union, NATO, and the OECD. We thank as well for their support, world-class insights, and generosity in hosting or arranging meetings on our behalf: Thomas Bagger, director of the German Foreign Ministry's policy planning staff, and his British counterpart, Peter Hill; Paolo Ciocca, Deputy Director-General of Italy's Department of Intelligence for Security; and former Swedish Prime Minister Carl Bildt, Hans-Christian Hagman of the foreign ministry, and Lars Hedstrom of the Swedish Defense College. We are extremely grateful to Professor Monica Toft who organized a two-day workshop at the University of Oxford on the future of religion and provided significant contributions to the final report on demography and security dynamics. Oxford scenario planning expert Angela Wilkinson provided early and critical feedback on methods and drafts—as well as the courage to make needed course corrections. US Ambassador to the Holy See Kenneth Hackett arranged two utterly unforgettable meetings with leaders of the Vatican's Secretariat of State as well as religious men and women working in Africa, Europe, the Middle East, and Pakistan. A similar meeting in Istanbul with leaders of minority religious communities in Turkey and the Levant made indelible impressions. We benefited from the remarkable convening power of Wilton Park in the UK and its indefatigable Richard Burge and Julia Purcell. Important contributions came from Chatham House, the International Institute for Strategic Studies, and think tanks in Italy, Spain, and Turkey. Finally, meetings with leading policy planners and senior officials from Germany, Denmark, Finland, France, Italy, the Netherlands, Spain, Sweden, Switzerland, Russia, the United Kingdom, and the European Union and UN agencies—and often in Washington too—helped draw insights across issue sets.

Middle East and North Africa. Discussions with senior officials and civil society leaders in Israel, Jordan, Tunisia, the United Arab Emirates, and the West Bank underscored new and old sources of insecurity as well as promise. We are extremely grateful as well to the many thought leaders, journalists, and others who have shared their experiences and perspectives online and otherwise in the public record. In Tunisia, we thank the US diplomatic missions to both Tunis and Tripoli for their insights and arranging meetings with civil society, government, and regional affairs experts as well as numerous women's rights, labor, political party, human rights, and regional security representatives.

South Asia. In Bangladesh, meetings with city planners and NGO's underscored the importance of individual contributions to local welfare while think tank discussions informed our views on religion, regional trade potential, and climate change. We thank Daniel Twining of the German Marshall Fund for organizing a terrific week of meetings in Delhi and Mumbai with, among others: the Observer Research Foundation, the Vivekenanda International Foundation, faculty and students at Jawaharlal Nehru University, Brookings India, Gateway House, the Public Health Foundation of India, Tata Industries, the Indian Ministry of Finance, PRS Legislative Research, and TeamLease, one of India's largest private employers. We appreciate as well insightful exchanges with traders on the Bombay Stock Exchange, journalists, and Hindu and Muslim civil society leaders.

Americas. We are grateful to US diplomats in Brazil, Chile, Mexico, and Peru for organizing a robust program of meetings, with friends old and new. In Brasilia, Sao Paulo, and Rio de Janeiro, we met with academics, government officials, and thought leaders, including many leading academics, futurist Sylvio Kelsen Coelho, Carlos Eduardo Lins da Silva of Sao Paolo Research Foundation (FAPSEP), Ricardo Sennes of Prospectiva, and Rubens Ricupero of the Fundacao Armando Alvares Penteado. In Chile, we are grateful for the time and insights of Foreign Minister Heraldo Muñoz, the participants of an international affairs roundtable organized by the Ministry's strategic planning staff, as well as Senator Hernan Larrain and Valor Minero's Alvaro Garcia Hurtado. We thank Sergio Bitar, director the Global Trends and Future Scenarios Project for the Inter-American Dialogue, for organizing a dinner with leading strategic minds, including Carlos Ominami Fundacion Chile 21 and Senator Guido Girardi Lavin, founder of the Chilean Congressional initiative Challenges of the Future. In Mexico, we thank former Foreign Secretary Jorge Castaneda, Alejandro Hope, Transparency International and other rule of law groups, Ilena Jinich Meckler and Instituto Tecnológico Autónomo de México (ITAM) students for a remarkable roundtable, CIDE's Jorge Chabat, and the US Embassy for hosting a roundtable of leading economists. In addition, we benefited from Mexico's Center for Research for Development (CIDAC) hosting a workshop on the future of the region with experts convened from throughout Central and North America. In Peru, we are grateful for time with Foreign Minister Ricardo Luna, Transparency International's Jose Ugaz, thought leaders like Roberto Abusada of the Instituto Peruano de Economia, and representatives of industry, media, and academia. An extraordinary session with futurist Francisco Sagasti capped our time in Lima.

In Canada, we thank the International Assessment Secretariat at the Privy Council Office and the Canadian Security Intelligence Service for their consistent support and facilitating important exchanges with Canadian leaders and thinkers—allowing us to road-test key findings in the final drafting stages.

In the United States, we thank the Director of National Intelligence James Clapper and Deputy Director Stephanie O'Sullivan for their constant encouragement and commitment to strategic analysis, transparency, and diversifying the perspectives that inform our work. We benefitted from close access to sitting and former National Security Council and Departments of State and Defense leadership, policy planners, and net assessors who helped us maximize the policy relevance of Global Trends. We recognize especially Undersecretary of State for Political Affairs Thomas Shannon and staff, Directors of Policy Planning Jonathan Finer and David McKean, NSC Senior Director for Strategic Planning Salman Ahmed, and Director of the Office of Net Assessments at the Department of Defense James Baker. Always helpful counsel, good humor, and steadfast support came from current NIC Chairman Greg Treverton and Vice Chair Beth Sanner as well as former Chairmen Chris Kojm, Tom Fingar, and Joe Nye and Vice Chairs Joseph Gartin, David Gordon, and Ellen Laipson. David, along with colleagues at Eurasia Group and Brookings' Thomas Wright, went above and beyond in assisting with end-game geopolitical and economic analysis and filling gaps where needed. Mathew Burrows, former NIC Counselor and principal author of Global Trends 2030, 2025, and 2020 provided critical hand-over guidance and continued to support GT with demographic analysis. Similarly, Richard Cincotta, Banning Garrett and Barry Hughes provided important lessons learned and contacts from prior GTs.

Three remarkable thinkers—science fiction author David Brin, retired CIA leader Carmen Medina, and Professor Steve Weber of UC-Berkeley—helped us hone our thinking early and engage ever-more diverse audiences at the South by Southwest Interactive Festival in Austin, TX. Duke University's Peter Feaver and University of Texas at Austin's Will Inboden took the lead in leading a team of scholars in identifying enduring US planning assumptions since 1945. Professor John Ikenberry of Princeton University organized workshops on key themes, engaged with the report on its own terms, and provided critical feedback and support throughout, as did fellow scholars: Robert Art, Dale Copeland, Daniel Drezner, Martha Finnemore, Harold James, Robert Jervis, Jonathan Kirchner, Charles Kupchan, Jeff Legro, Mike Mastanduno, Kate McNamara, John Mearsheimer, Rajan Menon, John Owen, Barry Posen, Randy Schweller, Jack Snyder, William Wohlforth, and Ali Wyne. We thank as well Georgetown's Casimir Yost, former director of the NIC's Strategic Futures Group, for taking the lead in crafting the US futures, and Bruce Jones for involving the NIC in Brookings workshops on multilateralism. Mark Sable reviewed multiple drafts, providing extremely helpful suggestions regarding style, voice and argumentation.

Similarly, we are grateful for workshops hosted by Deborah Avant at the Sié Chéou-Kang Center for International Security and Diplomacy at the University of Denver, Sumit Ganguly at Indiana University, Steven Krasner at Stanford University, and Steve Weber at UC Berkeley. Author Karen Armstrong, Texas A&M's Valerie Hudson, University of London's Eric Kauffman, Kathleen Kuehnast of the US Institute of Peace, and Hamid Khan of the University of South Carolina, among others, were instrumental in helping the NIC address gender and religious issues. Nick Evans and team at Strategic Business Insights provided extensive and sophisticated support on key technologies and their implications. We thank as well New York Congressman Steve Israel for convening a discussion at Baruch College. Our thinking improved as well with critical feedback from experts or audiences at the Atlantic Council, American Enterprise Institute, Brookings, the Carnegie Endowment for International Peace, Columbia University, the Council on Foreign

Relations, Center for Strategic and International Studies, Georgetown University, George Washington University, Harvard University, the Heritage Foundation, Illinois State University, Penn State University, the Research Triangle of North Carolina consortium, the Stimson Center, Southern Methodist University and the World Affairs Council of Dallas, Stanford University, University of Texas at Austin, Texas A&M University, and the National Laboratories at Oak Ridge, Livermore, and Sandia.

Global Trends: Paradox of Progress would not have happened without the expert and can-do support of Hannah Johnson and colleagues at SAIC and Leidos, who helped us convene workshops, analytic simulations, and scenario exercises. Similarly, we benefitted from conference support from Jim Harris, Greg Brown and many others at Centra Technologies and the Bureau of Intelligence and Research at the Department of State. Commissioned studies from the Atlantic Council, the Economist Intelligence Unit, Eurasia Group, Institute for the Future, RAND, Stimson Center, and Strategic Business Insights provided current baseline assessments in the key functional areas. Additionally, we are grateful for the many contributions from colleagues, associates, and the public at large to our Tumblr website and to us directly. We thank Dr. Jeffrey Herbst and the Newseum for partnering with the NIC for the public launch of Global Trends: Paradox of Progress.

Finally, we would like to individually recognize and thank for their contributions:

Clement Adibe, Bill Anderson, Anders Agerskov, Mark Bessinger, Richard Betts, Andrew Bishop, Phillip Bobbitt, Hayley Boesky, Hal Brands, Esther Brimmer, Shlomo Brom, Sarah Chayes, Erica Chenoweth, Gregory Chin, Ed Chow, Jack C. Chow, Thomas Christensen, Sean Cleary, Peter Clement, Keith Darden, James Dator, Jacquelyn Deal, Larry Diamond, Karen Donfried, Eric Edelman, Eran Etzion, Nick Evans, Darryl Faber, Mark Fitzpatrick, Jack Goldstone, Lawrence Gostin, Paul Heer, Francis Hoffman, Peter Huybers, Kim Jae-On, Joseph Jaworski, Kerri-Ann Jones, Rebecca Katz, John Kelmelis, Cho Khong, Andrew Krepinevich, David Laitin, Hardin Lang, Doutje Letting, Michael Levi, Marc Levy, Peter Lewis, Edward Luck, Anu Madgavkar, Elizabeth Malone, Thomas Mahnken, Katherine Marshall, Monty Marshall, Wojciech Maliszewski, Jessica Mathews, Michael McElroy, Walter Russell Mead, Suerie Moon, Anne Marie Murphy, Kathleen Newland, John Parachini, Jonathan Paris, Tom Parris, Stewart Patrick, Minxin Pei, Robert Putnam, Ebrhahim Rahbari, Kumar Ramakrishna, Eugene Rumer, Tomas Ries, Paul Salem, Miriam Sapiro, Derek Scissors, Lee Schwartz, Peter Schwartz, Jim Shinn, Anne Marie Slaughter, Constanze Stelzenmüller, Teija Tiilikainen, Avi Tiomkin, Ashley Tellis, Ivan Arreguin-Toft, Andrew Trabulsi, Ben Valentino, Kristel Van Der Eist, Peter Wallensteen, Stephen Watts, Judith Williams, Kevin Young, Amy Zegart, and Suisheng Zhao.

GLOBAL TRENDS ANNEXES

TABLE OF CONTENTS

.

GLOBAL TRENDS ANNEXES

83   Introduction

85   The Next Five Years by Region

    89   East and Southeast Asia

    101   South Asia

    107   Middle East and North Africa

    115   Sub-Saharan Africa

    123   Russia and Eurasia

    129   Europe

    135   North America

    143   South America

    149   The Arctic and Antarctica

    155   Space

159   Key Global Trends

    161   People

    169   How People Live

    175   How People Create and Innovate

    183   How People Prosper

    191   How People Think

    201   How People Govern

    215   How People Fight

    223   Terrorism

Introduction

The Global Trends project encompasses wide-ranging research and engagement across a variety of regions and topics. These multiple inputs are designed to serve as building blocks, helping us to generate larger insights for assessing strategic risks and opportunities for the world over the next 20 years. This annex includes two important foundational elements to the Global Trends report:

- The first section, "The Next Five Years," represents a systematic overview of trends across each region of the world, focusing on the first-order effects of the changes we see underway over a five-year time horizon.

- The second section, "Key Global Trends," explores these first-order effects over a 20-year time horizon organized around issues—such as demographics, economics, governance and security—rather than by geographic region.

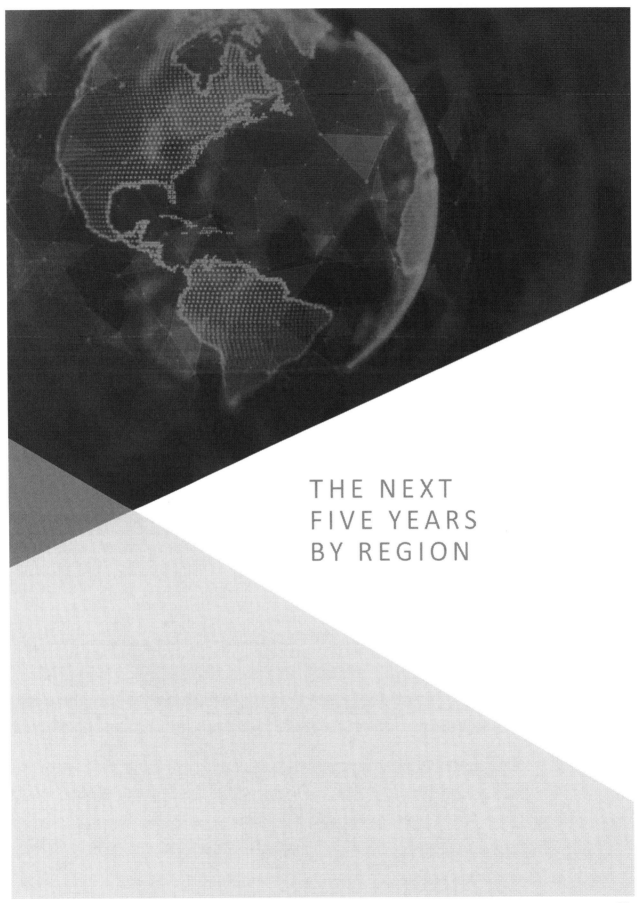

THE NEXT
FIVE YEARS
BY REGION

The Next Five Years by Region

Continued instability and significant political, economic, social, and environmental adjustments will mark the next five years worldwide. Although important differences will distinguish the world's regions, all will experience urbanization; migration; and stresses related to environmental, ecological, technological, and climate changes. Many societies will not succeed completely in efforts to lock in the development achievements of the past two decades—especially for the new members of their middle classes—highlighting governance shortfalls for rich and poor countries alike. Advanced information technology will amplify differences over inequality, globalization, politics, and corruption, while perceived humiliation and injustice will spur protests and violent mobilization. Structural shifts in the world's economies—from technology and finance that create wealth without creating jobs to growing debt that burdens future growth—will fuel these changes. Discontent will drive many societies to populist, nativist, or nationalist leaders; others may soberly reevaluate what citizens owe one another when facing unsustainable costs. Fragmentation of regions and states is possible—even likely—if multiple centers of geopolitical power emerge.

- **Economic stress.** The most significant global economic uncertainty of the next five years will be China's growth: how successfully Beijing maintains economic growth and foreign investment, and how effectively—even whether—it manages an overdue transition from an export- and investment-driven economy to one based on consumer-led growth. China's economy expanded from 2 percent of global GDP in 1995 to 14 percent in 2015, and it has been the greatest source of global growth for several years; a sharp economic deceleration in China would undermine growth elsewhere and slow worldwide progress on poverty reduction. During such a slump, many governments would face increasing public pressure for reforms that promote employment and inclusive growth, changes that might threaten their control and ability to provide benefits to political supporters.

- **Political stress.** Few governments are poised to make such political and economic reforms, and many states simply lack the capacity to address the challenges they face. In the Middle East and North Africa, such shortcomings will combine with societal and geopolitical forces to produce— or prolong—turmoil and violence. In the developed West, public disillusion will find expression in populist or reformist voices that seek to address wealth and power imbalances. In East and South Asia and Latin America, dissatisfaction with corruption, crime, and environmental, health, and urban stresses will continue to stoke activism and demands for government response.

- **Societal stress.** Societal confrontation and polarization—often rooted in religion, traditional culture, or opposition to homogenizing globalization—will become more prominent in a world of ever-improving communications. The new technologies are also likely to continue fueling political polarization and increasing the influence of extreme or fringe groups by improving their presence and reach. Militant extremist and terrorist groups will continue to have a transnational presence, still fragmented but sharing ideas and resources with organizations in Africa, the Arab world, and South and Southeast Asia. The spread of existing or emergent infectious diseases will remain a risk for all nations and regions, but particularly for governments that lack the capacity to prepare for such a crisis.

- **Geopolitical stress.** Major-power competition and the risk of conflict will intensify in the next five years, reflecting a fraying of the current international system and the ambitions of China and Russia for greater status and influence. States and nonstate actors alike will wield new and nontraditional forms of power, such as cyber capability and social networks, to shape outcomes and create disruption. The emergence of multiple, rival power centers is possible in the next five years if regional aggression and flouting of international norms go unchecked.

- **Environmental stress.** Scientists report that 2016 was the hottest year recorded since the instrumental record began in 1880, and 16 of the 17 hottest years have occurred since 2000. Although predicting temperature trends over short intervals is difficult because of internal climate variability, the baseline global temperature clearly will be higher over the next five years. This warming has implications for storms and rainfall, melting ice, rising sea level, and the general conditions under which people live. The impact of the change will be especially acute for the substantial share of the world population concentrated in climate-vulnerable areas, such as coastal cities and urban centers with strained water resources.

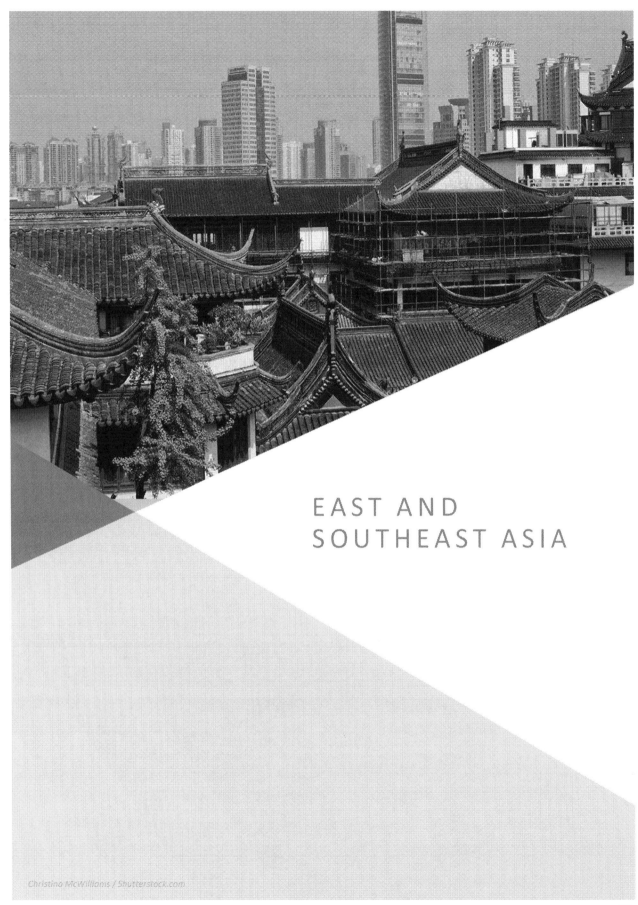

EAST AND
SOUTHEAST ASIA

East and Southeast Asia

East and Southeast Asia—the world's most ethno-culturally diverse region and the most likely to grow in economic importance—will remain center stage for both economic cooperation and geopolitical competition in the near future. For China, many factors are increasing political uncertainty: a slowing economy; Beijing's attempt to advance its primacy in Asia; a shrinking labor force as a result of population aging; and President Xi's concentration of power. This uncertainty casts a shadow over the peace and prosperity of the region, since China is deeply integrated into the global economy and anchors the region economically but also selectively embraces and seeks to shape international norms and rules to advance its interests. China's assertions of sovereignty on issues such as the South China Sea are provoking reactions among its neighbors and stirring nationalist sentiment at home that could reduce Beijing's room for maneuver. The interplay between security competition, regime stability, and economic cooperation will color most regional interactions, with middle powers and smaller states alike seeking assurances against Chinese assertiveness that will not sacrifice economic opportunities with China; the risk of a less-robust Chinese economy is a further complication. The actions of the United States and Japan vis-à-vis China, as well as those of emerging powers like India and Indonesia, will also shape the assessment of risks and opportunities by countries in the region.

- The region's many longstanding **territorial and maritime disputes** are unlikely to be resolved in the next five years and will instead keep tension simmering, prompt requests for US assistance, and complicate the maturation of regional institutions and coping mechanisms, such as the Association of Southeast Asian Nations (ASEAN). A further escalation of tension around any of Asia's fault lines probably would undermine economic confidence, slowing investment and regional economic cooperation

- Beijing may judge that **China** has a closing "window of strategic opportunity" to secure greater influence in the region before stronger pushback against its rise develops as a result of increased US strategic attention to the region, the evolution of Japan's defense policy, Taiwan's new leadership and growing sense of a separate identity, North Korea's nuclear program, and China's own mounting economic challenges. Foreign views of China probably will vary with Beijing's readiness to abide by widely accepted international rules.

- Increasingly self-reliant **Japan** will take on more international engagement—potentially increasing its involvement in regional and global security affairs and becoming a stronger partner of the United States—initially by building on its robust economic relations, especially in Southeast Asia. The growing uncertainty in East Asia—driven primarily by China's growing power and assertiveness—is prompting Tokyo to ease postwar constraints on its security policies and build capacity for a policy of collective self-defense.

- **India** is likely to insert itself further into East and Southeast Asian economic and security matters, especially if its relationship with Japan continues to strengthen. China's ambitions and disregard for India's interests fuel New Delhi's inclination—along with Japan and the United States—to balance and hedge. Although rising Western concern about free trade is limiting the options, a Trans-Pacific Partnership (TPP)-like agreement that included India could turn India into an economic wildcard, potentially deepening its economic integration with the United States and other major Pacific economies, helping to propel domestic economic reform and growth, and bolstering India's ability to take a more assertive regional economic role.

- **Indonesia** has the world's largest Muslim population and some of the world's greatest biodiversity, and it could take on a global role by anchoring Islam's response to the influence of globalized terrorist networks or by leading stewardship of the world's remaining primary forests, even as it continues to grapple with the challenge of effectively governing a far-flung archipelago. Burning in Indonesian forests contributes to global carbon emissions as well as air pollution and rising death rates from bronchial disease across Southeast Asia. In **Malaysia**, shifts in racial and religious policies in the democratic, majority Malay Muslim country could have implications for the region's democratization and social stability trends and could help boost global counter-radicalization efforts. Malaysia and Indonesia, like other Muslim states, face the influence of increasingly intolerant Salafist Islam on traditional Sufi Islamic practices, fueling tension in their multiethnic and multireligious societies. **Thailand** and the **Philippines** are struggling with governance issues resulting in emerging preferences for strongman rule.

- Major **economic shifts**, **demographic changes**, and **urban stresses**—driven by ongoing migration to cities—are likely to become more significant in Asian countries in the next five years and will demand political responses. Aging populations will add to the demands on Asian healthcare systems to confront chronic diseases, adding to governments' funding needs. Economic inequality could boost public dissatisfaction in China and elsewhere in the region, particularly as firms face greater pressure from low-cost competitors in the region and elsewhere. Beijing will face pressure to meet the aspirations and demands of its growing middle and affluent classes or to manage their disappointment.

- **Climate change**—through severe weather, storm surges, sea level rise, and flooding—disproportionately affects East and Southeast Asian countries, whose populations cluster in coastal zones. Ongoing stress will reduce resilience to even modest weather events. According to Pew polling, publics in China, Malaysia, and the Philippines consider climate change their top existential threat, and publics in Indonesia, Japan, and South Korea include climate change in their top three threats. Fears about water security and food security are also among the region's environmental concerns, with recent drought conditions in Cambodia, Laos, and Thailand, and highlighting these risks. Cooperation on water issues will be crucial in a heavily populated region, with disputes over water flows among Burma, Cambodia, China, and Laos, adding to the list of regional disputes.

- In **public health**, several countries in the region are considered hotspots for the emergence of influenza virus of pandemic potential. The highly pathogenic avian virus H5N1 is endemic in poultry in China, Indonesia, and Vietnam, and has a high mortality rate in humans. The highly pathogenic virus H7N9 is also circulating in Chinese poultry, and an increased number of human cases have been seen since 2013.

Geopolitical Relevance of Region in Next Five Years: Whither China. All countries in the region have much riding on China's economic and political prospects. The next few years will test whether Beijing can continue to raise living standards and expand the number of economic beneficiaries while making structural changes in its economy, shifting it from export-driven to consumer- and service-driven and becoming a more-balanced player in global trade rather than an ever-greater consumer of raw materials. In addition to trade and commercial ties, China now figures strongly in the development plans of countries across the region; most East Asian publics—and many in South Asia, Central Asia, and Europe—look favorably on Chinese investment, providing Beijing a way to boost its foreign influence. However, any shortfall in Beijing's delivery on its promises of economic partnership—as embodied in the

Asian Infrastructure Investment Bank (AIIB) and the One Belt, One Road projects—might sour foreign populations on Chinese engagement and hurt China's global reputation as well as its efforts to develop its interior and western regions as new export markets.

Beijing's greatest political test lies in whether it can satisfy an ever-more-empowered and engaged public, which expects accountable government, social mobility, and continued growth, without risking social instability or Chinese Communist Party (CPP) control. Beijing's recent increased use of surveillance and other advanced communications technologies and its ongoing human rights crackdown reflect a doubling down on social control and a continued rejection of pluralism and of any political alternatives to the CCP.

- **Religious and ethnic tension** will also test Beijing's ability to accommodate and tolerate what it historically has viewed as a threat to its authority. China's already substantial Muslim and Christian populations are projected to grow further in the next two decades. The government closely monitors and restricts Muslim affairs in Xinjiang Province, exacerbating residents' resentment toward Beijing, and the tens of thousands of Christians who worship in underground "house churches" also face frequent government persecution. Tibet, where population growth is the fastest in China, could be the scene of unrest similar to that of the past.

- **Public health issues** will come to bear during the next few years. China's rising income levels are shifting living patterns toward Western standards of consumption, leading to higher rates of chronic diseases such as obesity, heart disease, and cancer. With millions more people engaging in unhealthy habits—and the rapid aging of the country's general population—the anticipated rise of noncommunicable diseases will strain the capacity of China's national health system, as well as the ability of the government to invest in health infrastructure and train sufficient personnel.

- **Environmental problems** will worsen. In many regions, Beijing faces challenges in providing water of sufficient quantity and quality to its citizens. Degradation of agriculturally significant resources and major industrial contamination have worsened air quality in many cities; environmental protests have occurred when these conditions have become locally intolerable. Cancer and other environmentally-induced illnesses are severe enough in some regions that no advanced methods are necessary to diagnose the situation.

These tests will occur in a period of slowing economic growth, structural transformation of the Chinese economy, and bills from debt-fueled building at home and abroad since the 2008-09 global financial crisis. At the same time, the Chinese leadership is increasingly centralizing power and prosecuting an anticorruption campaign that—while popular with the public—has alienated a segment of the wealthiest Chinese. This domestic backdrop will help shape whether China's growing influence in Asia and the world brings renewed vigor and effectiveness to the international system or results in systemic economic shocks and a heightened risk of regional conflict.

- Success in meeting these challenges may have repercussions in **China's approach to its East Asian neighbors**. A smooth and deft economic transition and a more unified leadership would bolster Beijing's confidence in its dealings with Japan, the Philippines, and Vietnam. Just as they are likely to defend their territorial sovereignty, foreign corporations, universities, and individuals will complicate China's adjustment by seeking protection against cyber and intellectual property theft, regulatory harassment, and market manipulation.

- Beijing will also gain **international influence and respect** if its new multilateral investment initiatives succeed in boosting employment and livelihoods at home and abroad. Multilateral investment could also threaten China's influence abroad, however, particularly if coziness with corrupt regimes in Africa gives rise to the kind of popular resentment that the United States has faced in the Middle East.

- Similarly, Beijing could benefit by playing a leadership role in helping the region **manage greenhouse gas emissions and build resilience** to sea level rise, pollution, extreme weather, and biodiversity loss. Environmental issues will remain key quality of life concerns and pathways to civil society activism across the region, opportunities for governments' responsiveness, and innovation.

- As the ethnic Russian population in the Far East plummets and eastern Russian cities stand largely empty, it would be natural for Chinese interest and appetites to turn northward, potentially increasing friction in the area. Large numbers of Chinese have already been filtering into the region on a variety of pretexts, visas, and business interests.

- Whether Beijing wields its ties with Islamabad and Pyongyang more effectively against protracted threats in Afghanistan and North Korea's nuclear program will have a significant impact on peace and stability in South and Northeast Asia.

Other Considerations: Partnership Management. Partnership and alliance management will be the primary East Asian task for the United States, with free trade agreements such as the Trans-Pacific Partnership (TPP) offering the potential to help the region diversify away from overdependence on China. However, many TPP participants—as well as business elites, working publics, and political leaders in some Asian countries—see more opportunity than threat in China and are uncertain about the US approach and commitment to the TPP. China's size, level of development, and particular needs, including resources and high-end capital goods, make it an economic prospect for other countries in the region as a market, investment source, and production location in ways and degrees that the United States cannot necessarily match.

- **US allies** and partners also remain uncertain about the future of the US "rebalance" to the region, given Washington's domestic and other international preoccupations and potential resource constraints.

- In **Northeast Asia**, Beijing, Tokyo, and Seoul will remain economically interdependent, even while they improve their individual security capabilities. They will need to manage security risks resolutely and avoid security-dilemma dynamics and the reciprocal escalation that can occur when defensive measures are interpreted offensively.

- Political posturing and longstanding historical issues are likely to hinder a deepening of **Japan-South Korea** security relations in the next five years despite some progress. South Korean frustration with China's reluctance to rein in North Korea will drive Seoul toward cooperation with Tokyo and Washington, even while Seoul continues to view China as a crucial partner for tourism, trade, and investment. Meanwhile, Japan will continue to pursue active diplomatic and security engagement in the region and beyond. Japan's economy, while stagnating in aggregate terms, remains the third largest in the world, and—despite the declining population—continues to provide material advances for most of its aging population.

In **Southeast Asia**, growing economic interdependence will be the backdrop to great-power rivalry, internal strife, religious radicalization, and domestic political uncertainty, including struggles between democratization and authoritarianism. Some combination of these could threaten the open, stable, and developing regional community with stagnation, authoritarianism, and instability, but such outcomes remain unlikely. Nationalism will remain a powerful force but is unlikely to disrupt the region's growing economic integration by itself.

- **India, Indonesia,** and **Vietnam** will become far more prominent players in Asia than in the past several decades, in part due to their own development achievements, rapidly growing trade relationships, and favorable demographic profiles relative to many of their competitors. The blueprint for economic integration in the region will be the ASEAN economic community and its goals of trade liberalization, harmonization, and improved customs procedures; trade in services; investment and capital market liberalization; and infrastructure connectivity.

- **Security challenges** will motivate continued buildup and potential use of military instruments in the region. With economic growth at or near current levels, countries around the region will boost military spending, partly for domestic reasons and partly to hedge against China and uncertainties about US attention to the region. The maritime disputes in the East and South China Seas will continue, and ASEAN countries will spend greater resources cracking down on Islamic radicalism.

- **Governance deficiencies** affect authoritarian as well as democratic regimes in the region, and both will continue to find it a struggle to implement policies, address corruption, and manage often problematic relationships between national-level policymakers and local officials in charge of executing policy. How well governments provide public goods and meet rising demand for better standards of living will strongly influence levels of stability in the region.

Thinking About a Rebalanced China

"Rebalancing" China from an investment-driven and export-led economy to one that relies more on domestic consumers will require years of adjustment, with far-reaching consequences for day-to-day life in China as well as for its economic partners around the world. Beijing has long stimulated growth with unusually high investment in infrastructure and equipment—much of which has been underutilized or ineffective—as part of a now-unsustainable model that nevertheless will be hard to replace soon with consumption-led growth.

- In 2015, China's investment amounted to more than 40 percent of its GDP, well beyond the 30-percent average among other developing Asian economies and little changed from recent peaks. Such high investment spending is otherwise unprecedented among major economies during peacetime.

- Even with real investment growth at only 1 percent per year—something that last happened in 1990, the year after the Tiananmen Square crisis—bringing China's consumption-investment balance in line with those of its Asian peers would take a full decade of private and government consumption growing at 8 percent yearly .

Even if Beijing succeeds in rebalancing, the change would disrupt longstanding patterns in China's domestic economy.

- Greater private consumption would expand opportunities for private firms, which are more responsive to consumer demand than state-owned companies, but it would increase pressure on Beijing to make long-avoided improvements in the rule of law and intellectual property rights protections and to develop private consumer finance.

- Equally important, reducing the role of China's heavy-industry-oriented, state-owned enterprises (SOEs) in the economy would weaken one of the government's main levers of economic control, something Beijing has shown little willingness to do in recent years.

- Private consumption has lagged in China because of high individual saving rates, which are unlikely to shift unless Beijing strengthens social safety net programs, particularly healthcare and retirement benefits. However, such increases would compete against spending on military modernization and domestic security.

A rebalanced Chinese economy certainly would remain a major player in the world economy and be better positioned for long-term growth, but it would also be a substantially different trade partner, both in the region and in the wider world.

- With less focus on infrastructure and heavy industry, China's imports could be expected to include fewer capital goods—such as machinery and manufacturing equipment—and a smaller share of raw materials, like iron ore and copper, which are more intensely used in investment goods than in consumption goods. These accounted for nearly $800 billion, or 47 percent of China's total imports in 2015, with Germany, Japan, and raw-materials exporters worldwide among the largest suppliers.

Thinking About a Rebalanced China *(continued)*

- A more-developed consumer sector would almost certainly mean greater imports of consumer goods, food, and agricultural products, categories that in 2015 accounted for only about $90 billion, or less than 6 percent of China's imports. Worldwide, excluding China, the leading exporters of these goods are led by the United States and Germany (for consumer goods) and the United States and the Netherlands (for food and agricultural products); these most-competitive exporters probably would see the greatest gains from strong Chinese demand growth. Even if a more-consumption-directed Chinese economy could meet much of its own needs, demand for such goods would increase worldwide, benefiting producers in China and elsewhere alike.

- Rebalancing's effect on China's imports of intermediate goods—parts used for production and assembly of goods for export or domestic use—is less clear. A substantial share of the consumer goods China now produces would probably appeal to a rapidly growing domestic consumer sector, although the country's low-value-added production would face increasing competition from other countries, including elsewhere in East Asia, as well as South Asia and even Africa.

Beijing has ample resources to help smooth the transition, using government and directed SOE spending to prop up growth while efforts to spur private consumption take hold, and might even be able continue dragging its feet for the full five years. But the transition—and the imbalance that has forced it—will become more costly and disruptive the longer it is put off; the coming years, even with growth already flagging, probably will be Beijing's best window of opportunity.

- In the next 20 years, China's median age will increase from 37 to nearly 46 and will continue to rise rapidly thereafter, as its workforce-age population actually declines. China's retirement ages were set in the early 1950s, when life expectancy was very low, and open discussion of changing these arrangements is underway, but rising healthcare costs for the aging population will add an additional burden.

CHINA

2035 Population Projection:

1,408,316,000

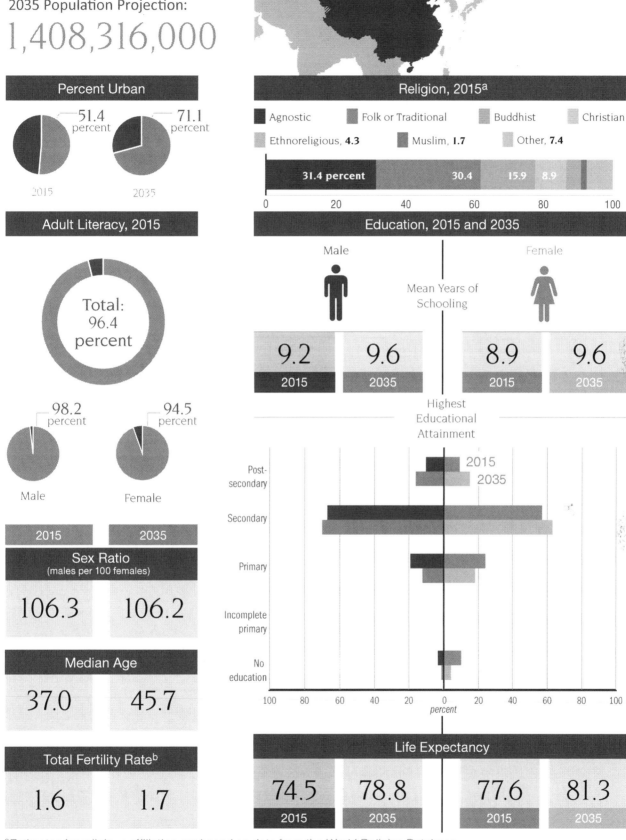

Percent Urban

51.4 percent
2015

71.1 percent
2035

Adult Literacy, 2015

Total: 96.4 percent

98.2 percent
Male

94.5 percent
Female

2015	2035

Sex Ratio
(males per 100 females)

106.3	106.2

Median Age

37.0	45.7

Total Fertility Rate[b]

1.6	1.7

Religion, 2015[a]

- Agnostic
- Folk or Traditional
- Buddhist
- Christian
- Ethnoreligious, **4.3**
- Muslim, **1.7**
- Other, **7.4**

31.4 percent	30.4	15.9	8.9

0 20 40 60 80 100

Education, 2015 and 2035

Male

Female

Mean Years of Schooling

9.2	9.6
2015	2035

8.9	9.6
2015	2035

Highest Educational Attainment

2015
2035

Post-secondary
Secondary
Primary
Incomplete primary
No education

100 80 60 40 20 0 20 40 60 80 100
percent

Life Expectancy

74.5	78.8
2015	2035

77.6	81.3
2015	2035

[a]Estimates for religious affiliation are based on data from the World Religion Database and are rounded to the nearest one-tenth of a percent.
[b]Total Fertility Rate is the projected average number of children born to a woman if she lives to the end of her childbearing years.
Note: Demographic data is presented for countries estimated to have the largest population in each region in 2035.

INDONESIA

2035 Population Projection:

304,847,000

Percent Urban

53.7 percent — 2015

65.2 percent — 2035

Adult Literacy, 2015

Total: 95.4 percent

97.1 percent — Male

93.8 percent — Female

2015	2035
Sex Ratio (males per 100 females)	
101.4	99.8

Median Age	
28.4	33.2

Total Fertility Rate[b]	
2.4	2.0

Religion, 2015[a]

Muslim Christian Ethnoreligious, **2.3** Hindu, **1.6** Other, **4.7**

79.3 percent **12.1**

0 20 40 60 80 100

Education, 2015 and 2035

Male

Female

Mean Years of Schooling

10.3	11.6
2015	2035

10.4	11.7
2015	2035

Highest Educational Attainment

2015
2035

Post-secondary
Secondary
Primary
Incomplete primary
No education

100 80 60 40 20 0 20 40 60 80 100
percent

Life Expectancy

67.0	69.8
2015	2035

71.2	74.7
2015	2035

[a]Estimates for religious affiliation are based on data from the World Religion Database and are rounded to the nearest one-tenth of a percent.
[b]Total Fertility Rate is the projected average number of children born to a woman if she lives to the end of her childbearing years.
Note: Demographic data is presented for countries estimated to have the largest population in each region in 2035.

SOUTH ASIA

South Asia

Tremendous internal and external changes will shape security and political stability in South Asia in the next five years as the planned drawdown of international forces in Afghanistan; the deepening relationship between the United States and India; China's westward-facing development objectives under its One Belt, One Road initiative; and inroads by the Islamic State in Iraq and the Levant (ISIL) and other terrorist groups all have their impact. South Asia also will face continuing challenges from political turmoil—particularly Pakistan's struggle to maintain stability—as well as violent extremism, sectarian divisions, governance shortfalls, terrorism, identity politics, mounting environmental concerns, weak health systems, gender inequality, and demographic pressures.

These factors almost certainly will prolong the delays of economic integration and political reforms that the region needs to capitalize on development gains of the past several decades.

- Governments across the region will find it hard to meet **growing public expectations,** given the urgent environmental and urban stresses already under way. Creating conditions that would help more individual- and community-level initiatives to thrive and address corruption would probably encourage progress.

- Geopolitically, the region's greatest hope is India's ability to use its **economic and human potential** to drive regional trade and development. At the same time, Afghanistan's uncertain prospects, extremism and violence in Pakistan, and the ever-present risk of war between India and Pakistan probably represent the greatest challenge to unlocking the region's potential.

Geopolitical Relevance of Region in Next Five Years: Competition. Despite persistent problems like violent extremism and tension between its two nuclear powers, India and Pakistan, the region's global relevance is changing, as Iran opens up economically after sanctions relief and China turns its focus westward. India is also an increasingly important factor in the region as geopolitical forces begin to reshape its importance to Asia, and the United States and India will grow closer than ever in their history. New Delhi will be a victim of its own success as India's growing prosperity complicates its environmental challenges. For example, providing electricity to 300 million citizens who now lack it will substantially increase India's carbon footprint and boost pollution if done with coal- or gas-fired plants.

New Delhi will reinforce its cooperation in regional trade and infrastructure investment with Bangladesh, Burma, Iran, Nepal, and Sri Lanka. Such cooperation could encourage stability and prosperity across much of the region, particularly if India enlists the support of political parties in the region.

- **Insecurity on the Afghan-Pakistan border**—political turmoil, resilient insurgencies, and poor border security—along with Afghanistan's conflict and the presence of violent extremist groups will be the primary drivers of regional instability. More than 30 violent extremist groups threaten regional stability, and drugs will remain an important revenue source for nonstate actors, including jihadi groups, in Afghanistan. The threat of terrorism from groups such as Lashkar-e-Tayyiba, Tehrik-i-Taliban Pakistan, and al-Qa'ida and its affiliates—as well as ISIL expansion and sympathy for associated ideology—will remain key drivers of insecurity in the region.

- Much of South Asia will see a **massive increase in youth population,** escalating demands for education and employment. According to one estimate, India alone will need to create as many as 10 million jobs per year in coming decades to accommodate people newly of working age in the labor force Insufficient opportunity as a result of inadequate resources, coupled with social discrimination, could contribute to the radicalization of a segment of the region's youth. Additionally, widespread prenatal sex selection is helping to make the country's youth cohort disproportionately male, with potential major consequences for social stability, as numerous social scientists emphasize the correlation between prospectless young men and violence.

- Moreover, **Pakistan**, unable to match India's economic prowess, will seek other methods to maintain even a semblance of balance. It will seek to maintain a diverse set of foreign partners, from which it can draw economic and security assistance, and to develop a credible nuclear deterrent by expanding its nuclear arsenal and delivery means, including "battlefield" nuclear weapons and sea-based options. In its efforts to curtail militancy, Islamabad will also face multiple internal security threats, as well as a gradual degradation of equipment used in these operations, declining financial resources, and a debate over changes needed to reduce the space for extremism. While violent extremism is unlikely to present an existential threat to Pakistan during this period, it will have negative implications for regional stability.

Other Considerations: Environment, Health, and Urbanization. South Asia's poorly governed countries are ill prepared for the range of ongoing and near-term challenges that will result from continued urbanization. The region is increasingly urban, with a megacity developing that will stretch from New Delhi to Islamabad with only terrain—and political boundary-imposed breaks. The subcontinent may come to have three of the world's 10 biggest cities and 10 of its top 50. Merely providing services for such burgeoning populations would be a major challenge for any country and may overwhelm resource strapped governments in South Asia, but urban areas of this size also create new social, political, environmental, and health vulnerabilities, for instance creating openings for new political movements and encouraging support for religious organizations as disparate groups come into contact,.

- **Pollution** almost inevitably increases with urbanization at South Asia's stage of development, creating atmospheric conditions that damage human health and crops and add to the economic costs of city living. South Asia already has 15 of the world's 25 most polluted cities, and more than 20 cities in India alone have air quality worse than Beijing's. Decisions regarding waste management will also significantly affect the quality of urban life; dense populations living in close proximity with limited services can intensify health challenges and extend the spread of infectious diseases.

- Although megacities often contribute to national economic growth, they also spawn **sharp contrasts between rich and poor** and facilitate the forging of new identities, ideologies, and movements. South Asia's cities are home to the largest slums in the world, and growing awareness of the economic inequality they exemplify could lead to social unrest. As migrants from poorer regions move to areas with more opportunities, competition for education, employment, housing, or resources may stoke existing ethnic hatred, as has been the case in parts of India.

- Newly urbanized populations tend to be **more religious**, as well. In Pakistan and Bangladesh, the pressures of urban life may bolster political Islamic movements: the oldest and most deeply rooted Islamist group in both nations. Jamaat-e Islami, is a largely urban organization. Hindutva, or Hindu nationalism, is likewise a predominantly urban phenomenon in India: the most radical Hindutva political party, Shiv Sena, has governed India's commercial center

Mumbai for much of the past four decades. India is projected to surpass Indonesia as having the world's largest Muslim population in 2050, raising questions about stability in the face of sectarian mistrust. The perceived threat of terrorism and the idea that Hindus are losing their identity in their homeland have contributed to the growing support for Hindutva, sometimes with violent manifestations and terrorism. India's largest political party, the Bharatiya Janata Party, increasingly is leading the government to incorporate Hindutva into policy, sparking increased tension in the current sizable Muslim minority as well as with Muslim-majority Pakistan and Bangladesh.

Climate change almost certainly will affect South Asia in the form of higher temperatures that damage human health and food security. Increased greenhouse gas concentrations and localized aerosol pollution both have the capacity to alter patterns of precipitation. Almost half the world's population lives in areas affected by South Asia's monsoons, and even slight deviations from normal in the timing and intensity of monsoons can have major repercussions for regional agriculture. Agricultural production, water availability, and hydroelectric power generation and grid stability would be substantially reduced by delayed monsoon onset. Conversely, increases in precipitation over some areas, including Bangladesh, could exacerbate flooding and have consequences for emigration.

- **Climate change** could lead to a faster-than-expected melting of the glaciers in the Pamir Knot, which feed the northern rivers of Pakistan and India. Tropical storm surges on top of even a modest sea level rise could reduce the already-sparse landmass of Bangladesh, spoiling freshwater resources and pushing people into India and Burma, exacerbating ethnic and regional conflicts.

- India and Pakistan are also vulnerable to a variety of **extreme weather events**. Major examples include massive floods that devastated Pakistan in 2010, unpredictable monsoons that decreased food security, and heatwaves in 2015 that killed over 1,000 in Pakistan and 2,500 in India. A shift in the monsoon patterns that amplified those seen in recent years—when "100 year floods" have been increasingly frequent—could overwhelm Pakistan's dams, already straining to contain floodwaters from deforested mountains and ravines. Meanwhile, public awareness of the long term risks of sea-level rise will grow as the Maldives and other Pacific Islands gradually disappear.

- **Changing precipitation patterns** could alter water ecosystems in ways that foster spikes in dangerous waterborne or water-linked illnesses such as malaria, cholera, and polio. Storm surges and flooding can expose millions to sewage-and otherwise contaminated waters and myriad diseases, making investments in more modern and resilient water systems vital for public health and safety.

INDIA

2035 Population Projection:

1,585,350,000

Percent Urban

32.7 percent
2015

42.1 percent
2035

Adult Literacy, 2015

Total: **72.2** percent

80.9 percent
Male

63.0 percent
Female

2015	2035
Sex Ratio (males per 100 females)	
107.6	106.6
Median Age	
26.6	32.8
Total Fertility Rate[b]	
2.4	2.0

Religion, 2015[a]

■ Hindu ■ Muslim ■ Christian. **4.7** ■ Ethnoreligious, **4.0** ■ Other, **4.4**

72.5 percent | **14.4**

0   20   40   60   80   100

Education, 2015 and 2035

Male

Female

Mean Years of Schooling

8.7	9.9		7.4	9.5
2015	2035		2015	2035

Highest Educational Attainment

2015
2035

Post-secondary

Secondary

Primary

Incomplete primary

No education

100 80 60 40 20 0 20 40 60 80 100
percent

Life Expectancy

66.9	71.7		69.8	75.3
2015	2035		2015	2035

[a]Estimates for religious affiliation are based on data from the World Religion Database and are rounded to the nearest one-tenth of a percent.
[b]Total Fertility Rate is the projected average number of children born to a woman if she lives to the end of her childbearing years.
Note: Demographic data is presented for countries estimated to have the largest population in each region in 2035.

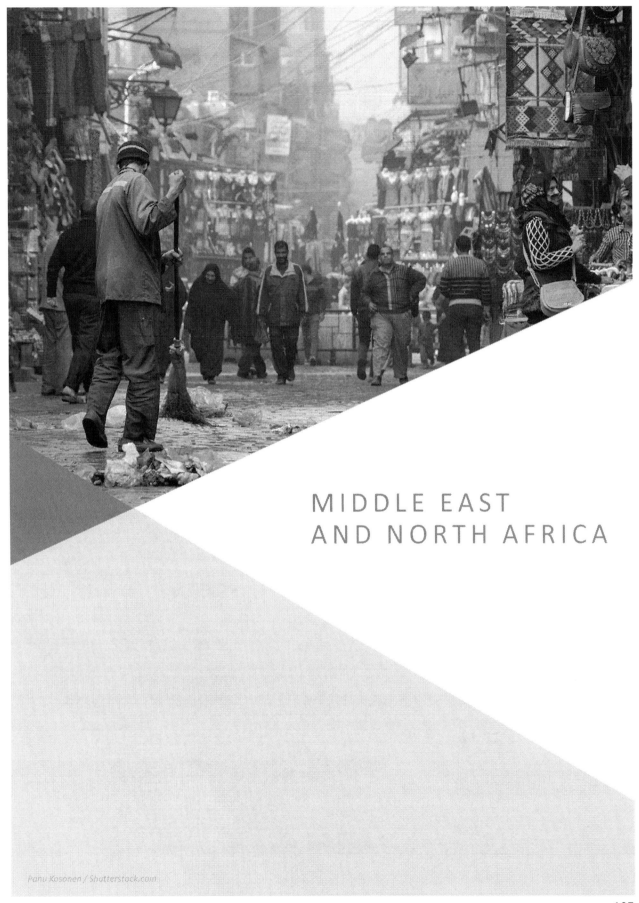

MIDDLE EAST
AND NORTH AFRICA

Middle East and North Africa

Political upheaval will characterize the next five years in the Middle East and North Africa, as populations demand more from entrenched elites and civil and proxy wars are likely to continue in a number of failed states. Contests among religious and political forces are likely as low energy prices weaken institutions. Such contests are likely to include security competition among Iran, Saudi Arabia, Turkey, Israel, and perhaps Egypt, and could involve China, Russia, and the United States. The endemic leadership and elite disconnect from the masses will almost certainly persist for many countries in the region through the period. Socioeconomic and popular challenges will worsen and tension rooted in the region's legacies of authoritarian rule, repression, and dependency could stoke calls by subnational groups, particularly the Kurds, for greater representation.

- The central challenge for the region is to boost growth and create political conditions and economic opportunities to **engage its young working-age residents**. If this is not done in ways that recognize the potential of people and are consistent with traditional beliefs, however, the absence of justice and respect will continue to foster despair and maltreatment of others. In extreme cases, the absence of dignity can contribute to religious radicalization, often in tandem with the rise of secularism, which the Arab world experiences through globalization, Western foreign policies, and social media that conservative religious believers find offensive.

The turmoil of recent years has interrupted what had been a period of significant progress in poverty reduction and individual empowerment. Extreme poverty in the region has declined gradually since 1987, with the greatest progress in Algeria, Jordan, Morocco, and Egypt. The share of the population living below the poverty line in Egypt, for example, declined from 12 percent in 1981 to only 2 percent in 2005, although upheaval undoubtedly has halted—or even reversed—this progress in the most affected countries. Similarly, Iran since 1979 has reduced poverty and expanded its middle class and literacy rates. Absent outside assistance, countries that have been less volatile but have large refugee populations, particularly Lebanon and Jordan, probably also will see this improving trend begin to reverse as refugees strain already limited economic resources and continue to overwhelm health care systems. Meanwhile, low oil prices are squeezing the budgets and economies of the Gulf countries, limiting their ability to bail out strategically critical countries like Egypt or to offer aid to others.

- The region has not been conducive to much self-generated growth, with revolutionary and counterrevolutionary dynamics in Egypt; civil wars in Iraq, Libya, Syria, and Yemen; and the persistent Israeli-Palestinian conflict—all of which have undercut any efforts to provide meaningful political and economic opportunity.

- The usual tool in the region for managing public discontent—subsidies and other cash payouts, funded by hydrocarbons and foreign assistance—is faltering with oil prices well below pre-2014 levels and unlikely to recover. After nearly a decade of capital surpluses—at least some of which found its way to non-oil states through aid—and strong investment and remittance flows, the region will see a distinct capital shortfall. The richer oil states of the Gulf Cooperation Council (GCC) will draw on their reserves to sustain domestic spending but will have less to share. Middle-level producers like Algeria and Iraq will struggle to continue buying social peace, increasing the risk they will resort to crackdowns on dissent. Egypt, Jordan, Lebanon, and Tunisia will see less Gulf largesse, worsening the economic conditions and increasing the risk of instability in these countries. The non-Arab, non-oil states of Israel and Turkey could escape these pressures, but neither has a large enough economy nor sufficient regional ties to be a major source of regional growth.

In the next five years, states' failures to meet popular demands for security, education, and employment will continue to provide fertile ground for **violent radicalization**. Support for illiberal religious and sectarian elements could expand in popularity, reducing historic tolerance of minority groups and preparing the ground for a violent push to create a more homogenous region. Alternatively, the actions of extremists still could discredit radicalism and encourage more citizens to rally around state institutions.

- Civil conflict and lower oil revenue are stressing governance structures in the region, resulting in a **decline in overall governance** and service provision. Prolonged periods of conflict are also taking a toll on institutions: from 2004 to 2014—with civil war and regime change in Iraq, Syria, Yemen, and Libya—regional states' scores on the World Bank's Governance Indicators declined in the key areas of voice and accountability, political stability and absence of violence, government effectiveness, the rule of law, and control of corruption.

- In light of these **shortcomings of central governance**, individuals and tribes are likely to play a larger role in political debate, organizing and mobilizing at a subnational level. The creation of local and municipal councils in the war-torn states of Syria and Libya may exemplify this trend.

Geopolitical Relevance of Region in Next Five Years: Contagion and Competition. Progress toward a regional security framework is likely to be limited at best, with large-scale violence, civil wars, authority vacuums, and humanitarian crises persisting for many years. Similarly, the region will be shaped by state and nonstate actors who seek political and strategic advantage for their own versions of religion but also work to manipulate the views and behavior of wider circles of believers.

- The **intensity of violence** in the Levant and the Arabian Peninsula threatens to further fragment the region—creating distinct political and economic conditions in the Gulf, Levant, and Maghreb regions—and to spread contagion well into Sub-Saharan Africa, Europe, and Central, East, and South Asia via transnational radical Islamist ideas and movements.

- The area is especially **vulnerable to water stresses** and local, national, and transnational tension over access to water resources. Even the wealthiest countries in the region, which use desalinization plants for water supplies, face existential vulnerabilities if those plants are compromised.

The region's ills are unlikely to be contained, ensuring that growing humanitarian crises and civilian victimization will continue to undermine international conflict and human rights norms. Heavy touting of these norms by the West without sufficient backing or material support further weakens the West in the eyes of Arab publics. Perceptions in the region's capitals that the United States is not a reliable partner—whether due to the US pivot to Asia or Washington's decision not to support Mubarak and other Arab incumbents in 2011—has opened the door to geopolitical competition with Russia and possibly China and to hedging by Arab states regarding commitments to Washington. Amid persistent conflict, refugee flows will persist—although some may be forced to seek destinations other than increasingly inhospitable Europe.

Iran, Israel, Saudi Arabia, and possibly Turkey may remain powerful and influential relative to states in the region that are grappling with instability but they will be at odds with each other on a variety of issues, and several face looming domestic challenges that are likely to affect their regional aspirations. Iran's growing power, nuclear capabilities, and aggressive behavior will remain a concern for Israel, Saudi Arabia, and some other GCC states. These concerns are exacerbated by the sectarian nature of Iranian and Saudi regional competition, with dehumanizing rhetoric and allegations of heresy fanning the conflict throughout the region.

- Risks of instability in Arab states such as **Egypt, Algeria, and Saudi Arabia** will almost certainly grow in the long term, especially if the price of oil remains low. Riyadh is embarking on some economic reforms and much smaller social and political reforms. These efforts are significant and could increase job creation for Saudi youth but could also come too late to satisfy popular expectations. Moreover, the reforms are aimed at developing a Saudi Arabia that can compete with emerging Asian and African exporters as a low-cost option, or with developed countries in services, and will prove exceedingly difficult to meet. Lack of clarity about a Saudi transition after King Salman will also contribute to uncertainty about the prospects for the reform effort.

- **Global demand for the region's energy resources**—especially from Asian states—will continue to ensure international interest and engagement in the region, but external powers will lack the will or capability to "fix" the region's numerous problems, and some will be drawn into its fights, probably protracting current and future conflicts.

- **Israel, Saudi Arabia, and some other GCC states are concerned** that Iran will use funds from the Joint Comprehensive Plan of Action (JCPOA) to increase regional activities that will further erode regional stability. In the long term, these states also will be sensitive to Iran's behavior as restrictions on Iranian nuclear activity are lifted under the JCPOA process. Tension between Iran and regional states will increase if Tehran uses its greater financial and military resources to aggressively assert its interests in the region or if Iran's neighbors fear Tehran seeks to resume nuclear weapons work.

- The **return of great-power politics** to the region, with renewed Russian engagement, will be another powerful force affecting future dynamics. Since coming to power in 2000, Russian President Putin has sought to project power into the region; Moscow's military and intelligence support for Damascus may suggest overtures to other former Soviet allies, such as Iraq and Egypt, could be on the horizon.

Other Considerations. Demographic and economic pressure, as manifested in the "Arab Spring" uprisings, probably will remain unresolved and could worsen if protracted turmoil fuels a major brain drain. Youth unemployment—certain to remain a challenge for years as a result of the region's demographic profile—and the absence of economic diversification will further hinder economic growth, improved living standards, and integration into the global economy for most countries in the region. Land and water resources, already critically tight, are likely to get worse with urbanization, population growth, and climate change. Better management and sanctions relief have spurred Iranian economic growth, but whether economic improvement will help bring about political reform is less clear.

- An **emerging lost generation of conflict-scarred children** without access to education or adequate healthcare probably will create new populations vulnerable to radicalization. Continued instability is likely to make conditions for women throughout the region even worse, judging by the increased harassment and victimization experienced in recent years. Specifically, weak economic growth and concern about employment can fuel the growth of identity-based extremism. Arab youth questioned in the eighth annual Burson-Marsteller survey in 2016 overwhelmingly rejected the rise of the so-called Islamic State but simultaneously noted that a lack of jobs and opportunities was the top recruitment driver for the group.

- In light of these dynamics, **reinvigorated interest in the fate of the West Bank and Gaza** could emerge as a galvanizing force among Arab populations. Recent events—including the civil war in Syria and the rise of the Islamic State—that have dominated the media are also prompting additional Palestinian refugee movement and concern about shortfalls in financial support for the Palestinian people. Palestinian studies suggest Gaza residents still need $3.9 billion for reconstruction and recovery support as a result of the Hamas-Israel conflict in 2014. Their needs are of interest to the rest of the region's Arab populations: In a poll conducted in 2011 by the Arab Centre for Research and Policy Studies, over 80 percent of more than 16,000 respondents across the Arab world noted that the Palestinian question was the cause of all Arabs, not of the Palestinians only.

Risks for **environmental crises**, such as drought, extreme temperatures, and pollution will also remain high. Land and water resources are already critically tight and are likely to get worse with urbanization and the effects of climate change.

- **In Yemen, conflict zones, high water prices, and damaged infrastructure** have aggravated already grim water problems, leaving 80 percent of the population without access to reliable fresh-water sources. Without adequate infrastructure, water stored for domestic use can become contaminated and expand the breeding habitats for mosquitos, malaria, dengue fever, and cholera.

- In **Jordan**, the influx of refugees from **Syria** has forced the government to pump more extensively from declining aquifers. **Egypt** will face emergent water challenges from upstream development on the Nile, particularly as Ethiopia begins filling the reservoir of the Grand Ethiopian Renaissance Dam.

- Urban air pollution in the region remains among the worst in the world, particularly in **Iran** and **Saudi Arabia**.

Public health issues in the region will also be critical. Egypt is one of the countries in which the highly pathogenic avian influenza virus is now endemic in poultry and presents a risk to humans. Since 2012, Saudi Arabia has been handling an outbreak of the Middle East respiratory syndrome (MERS-coronavirus) and there is ongoing concern that the virus could mutate and become increasingly contagious. A more widespread outbreak could contribute to instability if handled poorly.

Nevertheless, despite these pressures, a low-probability, more beneficial scenario for the region might emerge if oil markets tighten and prices begin to rise. Leaders in Iran and Saudi Arabia would feel less pressure to focus on a zero-sum competition for oil market share, which could result in a lowering of their sectarian rhetoric. Better bilateral relations could defuse their proxy wars and help stabilize the region, potentially helping create the conditions for grassroots movements to offer a compelling and constructive alternative to authoritarianism or ISIL and Islamic extremism. A genuine public dialogue and economic development that is consistent with religious and other cultural norms could channel the frustrations that underlay the Arab uprisings of 2011.

EGYPT

2035 Population Projection:

125,589,000

Percent Urban

43.1 percent
2015

48.9 percent
2035

Adult Literacy, 2015

Total: **75.8** percent

83.6 percent
Male

68.1 percent
Female

2015	2035
Sex Ratio (males per 100 females)	
102.1	101.8
Median Age	
24.7	27.2
Total Fertility Rate[b]	
3.3	2.6

Religion, 2015[a]

■ Muslim ■ Christian ■ Agnostic, **0.6** ■ Atheist, **0.1**

90.9 percent | 8.4

0   20   40   60   80   100

Education, 2015 and 2035

Male

Female

Mean Years of Schooling

Male		Female	
11.1	12.7	11.0	12.8
2015	2035	2015	2035

Highest Educational Attainment

2015
2035

Post-secondary
Secondary
Primary
Incomplete primary
No education

100 80 60 40 20 0 20 40 60 80 100
percent

Life Expectancy

69.2	72.5	73.6	77.1
2015	2035	2015	2035

[a]Estimates for religious affiliation are based on data from the World Religion Database and are rounded to the nearest one-tenth of a percent.
[b]Total Fertility Rate is the projected average number of children born to a woman if she lives to the end of her childbearing years.
Note: Demographic data is presented for countries estimated to have the largest population in each region in 2035.

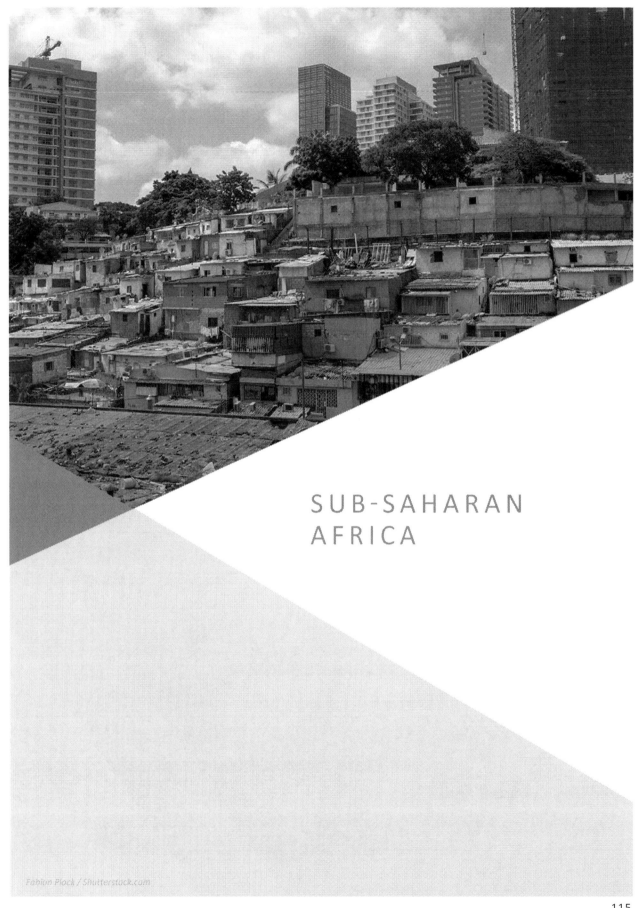

SUB-SAHARAN
AFRICA

Sub-Saharan Africa

In the next five years, Sub-Saharan Africa will become more populous, youthful, urban, mobile, educated, and networked. Projected rates of population growth for the region are the world's highest and, with no likely imminent changes to the longstanding gender inequality issues that are largely driving high fertility, the sheer scale of the population increase will strain food and water resources, health care capacity, education, and urban infrastructure. These conditions will also generate increased migration outflows where economic growth is insufficient to support the population. As a result, a young, urban, and networked population will become the engine of economic and political dynamism, despite the waning of the geopolitical and economic trends that fueled the region's strong performance in the past decade. At the same time, a growing population of educated and urban youth will strengthen existing trends of religious affiliation and of protests fueled by dissatisfaction with corruption, rising inflation, high unemployment, and poor government performance. In such conditions, complex security problems will mount, ethnic tension escalate, and religious extremism, particularly radical Islam and fundamentalist Christianity, will spread even further.

The region is likely to suffer from insufficient economic growth and job creation, putting a premium on good governance and further overwhelming the abilities of most governments, very few of which have implemented policies and have infrastructure—or the educated workforces—to secure "demographic dividend" economic growth by adding productive new workers. Chinese demand for commodities—a windfall for African exporters in recent years—will moderate as China's economy cools, and aid flows may decline as developed countries' economies remain weak and growing humanitarian needs elsewhere compete for donors.

- **Mass mobilization, urbanization, and religious affiliation.** Given the expansion of democracy—there are more democratically elected governments in Africa today than since decolonization in the early 1960s—African publics will increasingly use protests and political action to shape government policy and drive societal change. Nevertheless, some experts warn that democracy has stalled or even reversed; the majority of these young democracies remain weak, and corrupt and badly fractured states—including the latest addition, South Sudan. The process of democratic deepening in the medium and longer term will rely on the success of a growing number of assertive civil society organizations in challenging election results, unpopular economic policies, overzealous security agencies, human rights abuses, and unwanted constitutional amendments. In this regard, Africa's growing urban populations become crucial to democratization because the vast majority of civil society organization members will live in cities.

- Rapid urbanization is also likely to stress marginal infrastructure, however, and this will combine with the increased visibility of corruption to fuel public frustration with governments' failures to provide services. First-generation city dwellers tend to be more religious than subsequent generations, and urbanization will boost religious affiliation, possibly giving rise to religion-based conflict. Urbanization can also boost public participation in governance, potentially raising tension between political groups or serving as an engine of nation building that helps blend Africa's mosaic of ethnicities and religions. These divergent possibilities highlight the importance of sustaining African-driven good-governance efforts through regional and subregional institutions such as the African Union, the Economic Community of West African States, the East African Community, and the South African Development Community.

Complex Security Threats. Although significant efforts have been made to confront willful destruction by groups such as al Shabab, Boko Haram, ISIL, Ansar al Shari'a, and Al Qa'ida in the Lands of the Islamic Maghreb, African governments will continue to grapple with the asymmetric threats posed by rebels and extremist groups. Many national and regional militaries almost certainly will lack funding, personnel, and training to deal with such challenges, especially because rebels and terrorists can acquire weapons and other resources easily from international networks across the many porous African borders. Africans will continue to contribute troops to international and regional peacekeeping, but some of these well-intentioned operations are ad hoc mechanisms being used to address complex security threats, facing an uphill task under mandates that blur peacekeeping, stabilization, counterinsurgency, counterterrorism, atrocity prevention, and state building. Some troop contributing countries probably will continue to rely on multilateral peacekeeping missions to train and fund their militaries, but recent acknowledgment that peacekeeping forces sometimes commit atrocities themselves may undermine some multilateral engagement.

- **Radicalization.** Most of Sub-Saharan Africa will continue to reject violent and radical ideologies, but those who embrace such movements are increasingly capable of disruption and widespread messaging, in part through use of social media. Radical groups, with their promises of purposeful opposition to the government and cash rewards, will appeal to some of the disenfranchised. For example, Christian militias have driven tens of thousands of Muslims to flee their homes in the Central African Republic as opposition groups vie for power. The quality of state responses to these challenges will be crucial. Military and extrajudicial responses—as seen in West and East Africa—will only complicate and heighten the trend. Better results are likely from deescalatory measures, improved state capacity in intelligence gathering and analysis, judicial transparency, political decentralization, community policing and development, and youth engagement and employment initiatives that would drastically reduce extremist groups' recruiting pools.

- **Slowing Demand.** Many of Africa's economies will remain vulnerable to swings in global commodity prices and Chinese and Western demand. Most African commodity exporters are not sufficiently diversified to withstand a rout in commodity prices, although some African countries that are not commodity producers instead benefit from low prices. After 15 years of unprecedented growth rates, African economic growth slowed to 3.8 percent in 2015, largely because of weakening Chinese and other demand for commodities such as copper, oil, and gas. Nigeria and Angola—the region's biggest oil exporters and accounting together for roughly a fifth of Africa's population—were hard-hit and could take years to develop non-oil revenue sources. That effort would probably force both governments to cut spending, potentially including education and other programs needed to prepare their large youth populations for employment in the modern global economy.

- **Environmental, ecological, and health risks.** Africa's mosaic of savannahs, forests, grasslands, deserts, and freshwater resources, its millions of people and countless ecosystems face severe threats from natural as well as human-induced environmental change. Many of these challenges transcend national borders and individual states' capacities and require coordinated multinational action, but the troubled states involved probably will not view environmental and human health issues as their most-pressing priorities.

- **Pressures from populations and grazing livestock and loss of arable land**, coupled with recurrent droughts and floods, will drive further degradation of soil fertility and vegetation cover in the region. Desertification threatens Sub-Saharan Africa more than any other region in the world, and deforestation—progressing in the region at twice the world rate—adversely affects habitats, soil health, and water quality, particularly in Central Africa. An estimated 75 to 250 million people in Africa will face severe water stress, which will likely lead to migration. Uncontrolled burning, wood and charcoal cooking, industrialization, and widespread use of leaded gasoline contribute to greatly polluted air, while waste management is uniformly poor across the continent.

- Despite great strides in raising global public awareness of the **critical human threats to wildlife**—particularly elephants and rhinos—huge profits for criminals continue to drive poaching and illicit trafficking and nudge them closer to extinction. The rich fisheries off the West African coasts are being rapidly depleted by commercial and illegal fishers. Intensifying pig and poultry farming contributes to emergent zoonotic diseases that pose economic and health risks to Africans and in some cases to the rest of the world.

The political effects of these trends will vary considerably across the 49 countries, with some moving towards decentralization while others experiment with Rwanda-style centralization and authoritarianism. Most leaders will remain transactional and focused on political survival rather than political or economic reform. The generational transition in politics that many African countries will undergo in the next five years will be a telling indicator of future security and stability, with those that maintain the status quo risking instability and those that let power pass to the next generation probably better equipped to manage the technology- and development-induced changes to come. These transitions are also likely to play into ethnic divisions, heightening the possibilities for conflict.

- **Investment in human capital—especially for women and youth**—and in institutions that foster human development and innovation will be critical to the region's future prospects. The expansion of the region's middle class, the dramatic improvement in life expectancy in the past two decades, the vibrancy of civil society, the spread of democratic institutions and a democratic ethos, and the decline in the incidence of HIV/AIDS all point to the many positive possibilities that exist in Africa.

Geopolitical Relevance of Region in Next Five Years: Competition in Governance. In the next five years, Sub-Saharan Africa will remain a zone of experimentation and influence for governments, corporations, nongovernmental organizations (NGOs), and individuals seeking to improve Africa's development conditions and eventual access to its markets. Most African countries will focus on internal issues as they struggle to consolidate gains of the past 15 years and to resist the geopolitical and economic headwinds that threaten them. The flow of economic migrants out of Africa will increase if job prospects remain insufficient amid slowed global growth rates and as rural environmental stresses and rapid population growth swell urban populations. Security and counterterrorism activity will increase in the region in the near term as militant Islam and Christian extremism continue to spread into regional enclaves and even some cities.

The region may well become an arena of geopolitical and resource competition as political elites make different governance choices. Increasing religious affiliation in many parts of Africa may encourage pushback on some liberal norms and institutions, reflecting current misgivings about international liberalism and resentment of the West for imposing its morality on Africa.

- The **weakness of formal political institutions** in many African states suggests that vacillation between democratic and authoritarian politics will persist, particularly as international engagement wanes, risking large-scale political instability. US and Western retrenchment from Africa will be of particular concern in light of the relative expansion of China's influence, but China's role in the region remains uncertain. Economic strength and interest in African resources have made China an important source of funding for infrastructure, and significant commercial investments by Chinese companies contributed to Beijing's clout in the region, but the recent cooling of Chinese demand for raw materials—and Chinese firms' poor reputation as employers—may dilute this influence. Russia has not been a significant player in Africa since the collapse of the Soviet Union and is unlikely to have the capacity or desire to engage in a significant way. European policy is likely to be limited by economic constraints but could find increased aid a cost-effective way to help abate the flow of migrants.

- The **international human rights agenda** in Africa will almost certainly weaken, with realist calculations offsetting normative impulses in Europe and North America. African leaders will continue to see the International Criminal Court as biased against Africans and may be more assertive in rejecting the Court.

- Electricity generation and technologies that leapfrog brick-and-mortar infrastructure—such as 3D printing, which could obviate the need for many large-scale manufacturing plants—hold the promise of significant economic benefits and will attract significant public and private interest. Investment in basic infrastructure will be critical to economic growth, and the potential returns to well-managed infrastructure investments are high, given Africa's strong growth potential compared to other regions. An environment of low yields elsewhere could make Africa attractive for foreign investors, potentially improving economic and political fortunes across the continent.

Other Considerations. Africa's population will be the world's fastest growing in the next five years. Fertility rates have declined slower than many demographers anticipated, decreasing from 5.54 children per woman in 1995 to 4.56 in 2015. The overall drop may reflect the relative success of the UN Millennium Development Goals, especially in the areas of women's health and education. The central regions of Africa will remain among the world's most-youthful and the most at risk for violence and instability if opportunity and governance are insufficient.

- **Development conditions**, which have improved significantly in the past 15 years, probably will stall or even deteriorate if the continent fails to reduce corruption and to develop capacities for political and microeconomic policymaking in its difficult geopolitical and economic environment. Issues related to persistent poverty are the most pressing problem for Sub-Saharan Africa. Life expectancy at birth in Africa is 60 years, a significant improvement from two decades ago but still the world's lowest. Lack of access to clean water, sanitation, and health infrastructure increases the risk of rapidly spreading communicable diseases that range from intestinal parasites to Ebola. Despite substantial gains in mitigating the impact of HIV/AIDS made with international aid, 19 million Africans still live with the virus, more than in any other region. Beyond HIV/AIDS, other indicators highlight the continent's continued public-health fragility. Maternal mortality rates have declined recently but remain high, and health outcomes for children under five years are even worse: in 2015 alone, 5.9 million children under age five died, a rate of almost 16,000 per day; 83 percent of those deaths were caused by infections, neonatal complications, or nutritional status.

- The **progress made against HIV/AIDS** and the eventual containment of the 2014 West Africa Ebola breakout spotlight the potential for further health gains in through partnerships between African states and the international community. Sub-Saharan Africa has become the world's central health strategy proving ground, with major aid agencies concentrating their efforts against many disease fronts. The operational footprint of these initiatives spans dozens of national governments and numerous international agencies and NGOs and affects millions of Africans. Managing and implementing these operational networks will be a prime test of responsible, effective governance for African governments and their development partners.

- **Africa will drive the global pace of rural-to-urban migration.** Some African cities have tried to limit movement to metropolitan areas, citing concern about infrastructure and capacity, but others recognize the potential benefits of urbanization, and the trend will continue largely unabated. For example, Accra, Ibadan, and Lagos have formed an urban development corridor to link commerce in those three cities, creating opportunities for growth that, in turn, can generate jobs. By 2020, Lagos (14 million people) and Kinshasa (12 million) will be larger and more congested than Cairo. In many African countries, even what are now small trading centers will grow into cities. Nigeria, for example, will soon have 100 cities of more than 200,000 inhabitants.

NIGERIA

2035 Population Projection:

293,965,000

Percent Urban

47.8 percent
2015

60.8 percent
2035

Adult Literacy, 2015

Total: **59.6** percent

69.2 percent
Male

49.7 percent
Female

2015 | 2035

Sex Ratio
(males per 100 females)

103.8 | 104.4

Median Age

17.9 | 20.0

Total Fertility Rate[b]

5.6 | 4.3

Religion, 2015[a]

- Christian
- Muslim
- Ethnoreligious
- Agnostic, **0.3**

46.2 percent | 45.9 | 7.6

0   20   40   60   80   100

Education, 2015 and 2035

Male

Female

Mean Years of Schooling

| 7.6 | 11.1 |
| 2015 | 2035 |

| 7.3 | 10.9 |
| 2015 | 2035 |

Highest Educational Attainment

2015
2035

Post-secondary
Secondary
Primary
Incomplete primary
No education

100 80 60 40 20   0   20 40 60 80 100
percent

Life Expectancy

| 52.7 | 58.2 |
| 2015 | 2035 |

| 53.4 | 59.6 |
| 2015 | 2035 |

[a]Estimates for religious affiliation are based on data from the World Religion Database and are rounded to the nearest one-tenth of a percent.
[b]Total Fertility Rate is the projected average number of children born to a woman if she lives to the end of her childbearing years.
Note: Demographic data is presented for countries estimated to have the largest population in each region in 2035.

RUSSIA
AND EURASIA

Russia and Eurasia

The next five years will see the Russian leadership continue its effort to restore Russia's great-power status through military modernization, foreign engagements that seek to extend Russian influence and limit Western influence, nuclear saber rattling, and increased nationalism. Moscow remains insecure in its worldview and will move when it believes it needs to protect Russia's national interests—as in Ukraine in 2014—or to bolster its influence further afield, as in Syria. Such efforts have enabled President Putin to maintain popular support at home despite difficult economic conditions and sanctions, and he will continue to rely on coercive measures and information control to quash public dissent. Moscow will also continue to use anti-Western rhetoric—and a nationalist ideology that evokes the imperial and moral strength of the Russian people—to manage domestic vulnerability and advance its interests.

The Kremlin's ideology, policies, and structures—and its control of the economy—enjoy elite and popular support, notwithstanding significant repression of civil society and minorities.

- This **amalgam of authoritarianism, corruption, and nationalism** represents an alternative to Western liberalism that many of the world's remaining autocrats and revisionists find appealing. In Moscow's view, liberalism is synonymous with disorder and moral decay, and pro-democracy movements and electoral experiments are Western plots to weaken traditional bulwarks of order and the Russian state. To counter Western attempts to weaken and isolate Russia, Moscow will accommodate Beijing's rise in the near term but ultimately will balk before becoming junior partner to China—which would run counter to Russia's great power self-image.

Russian insecurity, disappointment, and distrust of the liberal global order are firmly rooted in the simultaneous enlargement of NATO and the European Union (EU) following the Cold War, motivating its actions abroad; its use of "gray zone" military tactics, which deliberately blur conditions of war and peace, is likely to continue. Russia's various moves in recent years, however—in Georgia, Ukraine, and Syria, and via support to far-right populist parties in Europe—raise three important questions:

Which of the principles of international order from the 20th century will Russia support in the 21st century?

How far will Russia go in championing a "Russian world," playing up the centrality of Russian civilization and the rejection of Western liberal values?

What, if any, challenges to the current political borders in Eurasia will Russia pose in defending its perceived sphere of influence?

Geopolitical Relevance of Region in Next Five Years: Revisionism, Again. Russia's aggressive foreign policy will be a source of considerable volatility in the next five years. Moscow almost certainly will continue to seek territorial buffer zones on its borders, including in the Arctic, and to protect sympathetic authoritarian governments, particularly along its periphery. This assertiveness will harden anti-Russian views in the Baltics and parts of Eastern Europe, heightening the risk of conflict. Moscow will cooperate internationally in ways that enhance Russia's geopolitical influence and encourage progress on issues of importance to the Kremlin, such as nuclear nonproliferation, while challenging norms and rules it perceives as inimical to its interests. Moscow believes it has little stake in the rules of the global economy and—even though a tepid economy will remain a source of strategic weakness—will take actions to weaken US and European influence over them. Moscow will test NATO and European resolve, seeking to undermine Western credibility; it will try to exploit splits between Europe's north and south and to drive a wedge between the United States and Europe.

- The **Putin government will continue to give priority to military spending** and force modernization, with an emphasis on strategic deterrence, even in the face of economic stagnation or recession.

- **Russia will continue to react to NATO** deterrence measures and an increased military presence—even if not permanent—in the Baltics and Central Europe. Moscow will also remain highly sensitive to US engagement in those regions, which Moscow sees as within its rightful sphere of influence.

- Russia's **robust cyber operations** almost certainly will pose an increasing threat to the West as it seeks to reduce dependence on Western technology and to improve its indirect and asymmetric warfare capabilities.

- Given the centrality of the United States to global affairs, Russia will also continue to devote resources to **efforts to shift US policies** in its own favor.

If Moscow's tactics falter, its geopolitical influence may steadily fade, and Russia may suffer domestic instability. On both counts, the adverse economic outlook—lower oil prices, Western sanctions, stagnant productivity, poor demographics, chronic brain drain migration problems, and inability to diversify into high-tech sectors—is likely to undercut Moscow's ambitions in the long term. Economic and political reform—the usual remedy for such problems—will not be forthcoming in Putin's Russia.

- A further decline in status might result in **more, rather than less, aggressive** international conduct, although **growing economic constraints** and a desire to avoid overextension ultimately could temper Putin's foreign policy capacity, if not his ambitions.

- Nevertheless, the **Russian population has shown resolve** in the face of harsh conditions and may not abandon Putin. To the extent that the Kremlin can continue to bolster the people's faith in Russia's greatness, large-scale revolt may be kept at bay.

Other Considerations: Eurasia. Like Russia, many Eurasian governments emphasize control over reform and suffer from poor economic performance and corruption. They are also highly vulnerable to Russian influence—including dependence on Russian remittances, propaganda, and military and cultural ties. Reliance on Moscow, brittle political institutions, high levels of corruption, and public repression raise the risk of Ukraine-style collapses in the region. In this context, three potentially transformative developments will become evident in the next five years:

- **Increased Chinese involvement in the region**, through investment, infrastructure development, and migration into Central Asia, as showcased in Beijing's One Belt, One Road initiative, will test Russia's willingness to accommodate China's great power ambitions. China's interests in the region will remain predominantly economic, but political and security objectives may become stronger if Beijing encounters intensifying domestic extremism. Russia—having little to offer economically other than raw materials, military technology, and migrant labor opportunities despite its Eurasian Economic Union initiative—will seek to deepen political and security integration in the region, potentially putting the countries at odds.

- **Resolution of the Ukraine conflict** would have repercussions across the region. A Western-oriented Ukraine reducing the systemic corruption that has plagued the country since its independence in 1991 and implementing reforms that produce at least modest growth would serve as a powerful counterexample to today's Russia. If Russia's intervention in the Donbas region led to economic and political failure in Ukraine, however, it might strengthen authoritarian systems across the region and weaken the resolve of those states looking to pursue a Western trajectory.

- Russia will continue to **seek to destabilize any Ukrainian government** that attempts to integrate itself into the West through the EU or NATO. Moscow will also continue to use a range of measures—from financial incentives for friendly governments to support for political parties and an active campaign of disinformation, through to military intervention—to support anti-Western forces in other states in the region.

- **Leadership transitions in Kazakhstan and Uzbekistan**—long functioning as anchors of stability in Central Asia—will cause concern in Moscow. The successions are unlikely to lead to dramatic changes in how these countries are ruled, but prolonged elite infighting could raise the potential for destabilizing crises, creating security vacuums that Islamic extremists would be tempted to exploit.

RUSSIA

2035 Population Projection:

135,674,000

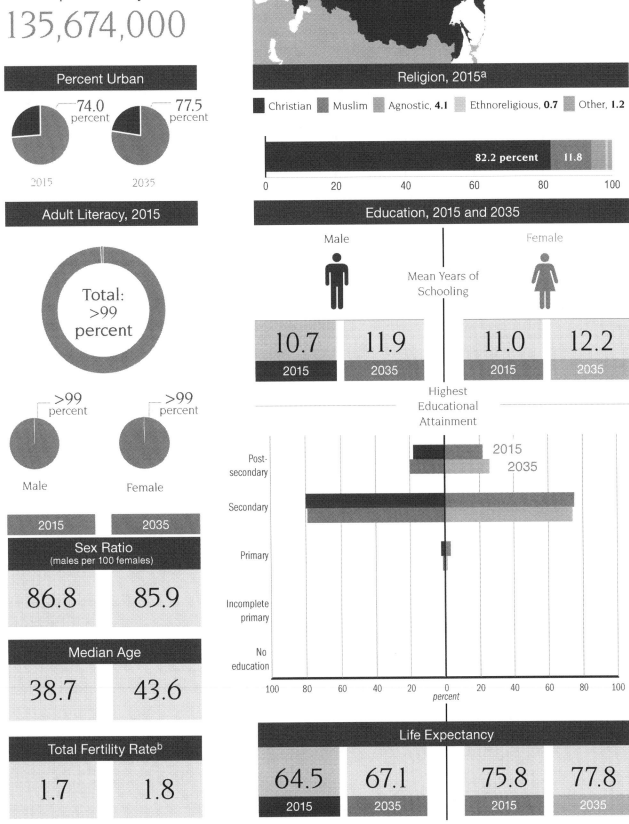

Percent Urban

74.0 percent — 2015

77.5 percent — 2035

Adult Literacy, 2015

Total: >99 percent

>99 percent — Male

>99 percent — Female

2015	2035
Sex Ratio (males per 100 females)	
86.8	85.9
Median Age	
38.7	43.6
Total Fertility Rate[b]	
1.7	1.8

Religion, 2015[a]

Christian | Muslim | Agnostic, **4.1** | Ethnoreligious, **0.7** | Other, **1.2**

82.2 percent | 11.8

0   20   40   60   80   100

Education, 2015 and 2035

Male | Female

Mean Years of Schooling

Male 2015	Male 2035	Female 2015	Female 2035
10.7	11.9	11.0	12.2

Highest Educational Attainment

2015
2035

Post-secondary
Secondary
Primary
Incomplete primary
No education

100 80 60 40 20 0 20 40 60 80 100
percent

Life Expectancy

2015	2035	2015	2035
64.5	67.1	75.8	77.8

[a]Estimates for religious affiliation are based on data from the World Religion Database and are rounded to the nearest one-tenth of a percent.

[b]Total Fertility Rate is the projected average number of children born to a woman if she lives to the end of her childbearing years.

Note: Demographic data is presented for countries estimated to have the largest population in each region in 2035.

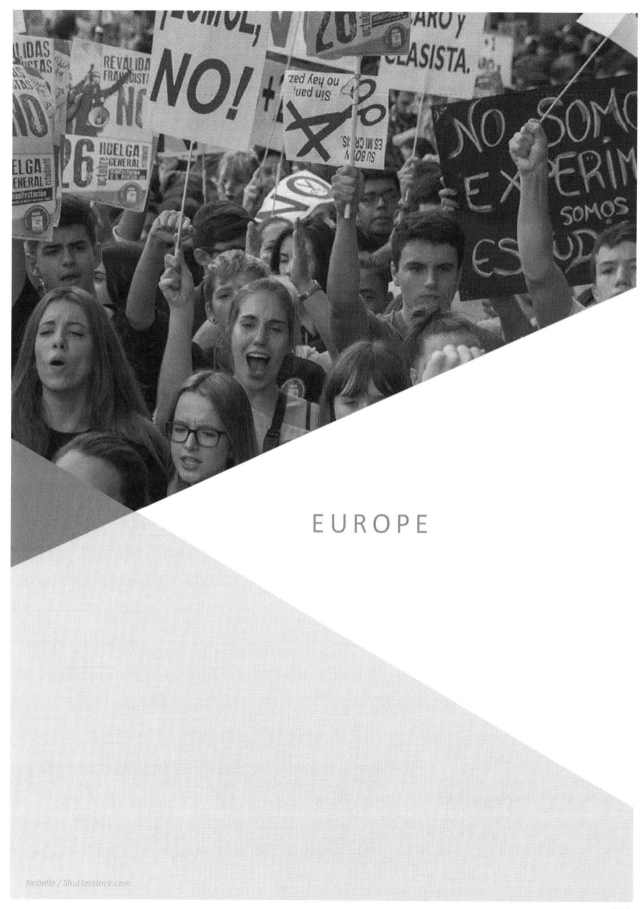

EUROPE

Europe

In the next five years, Europe will grapple with the potential unraveling of the European project while its post-World War II social order continues to be strained by rapid migration flows from its unstable, often threatening periphery and by economic pressures from a globalized economy that are increasing economic inequality. The regional organizations that shape Europe—the EU, the euro zone, and NATO, in particular—have maintained European influence on the global stage so far despite the region's declining shares of world GDP and population, but the EU's existential crisis, exemplified by the "Brexit" vote, is likely to continue through at least the next few years.

Although the EU helped governments create shared prosperity, economic security, and peace, the euro zone's lack of a fiscal union to match its single currency has left poorer states saddled with debt and diminished growth prospects since the financial crisis of 2008. Further, the EU has failed to create a sense that all citizens of Europe share a common fate, leaving it vulnerable to resurgent nationalism among its members in difficult economic times.

- **The future of the EU and the euro zone.** Political parties, national leaders, and EU officials will continue to disagree on the proper functions and powers of the EU, as well as the wisdom of the euro zone's current emphasis on maintaining budget discipline and current account balances without giving member states greater leeway to spur growth, much less bolder, pan-European solutions to growth differences and banking-sector problems. With policy constraints in place despite continued slow growth, EU and national governments will face weakening public support, particularly if the Union cannot adequately deal with incoming migration and terrorist challenges.

- **A threatening periphery.** The danger of a more belligerent Russia and the perceived threat of Islamic extremism and spillover from the Middle East and Africa will increasingly alarm publics while failing to generate support for a uniform response. Russia is threatening Europe directly through propaganda, disinformation, and financial support for anti-EU and anti-US parties, while ISIL has inspired and assisted foreign fighters, some of whom have returned to Europe and increased the threat of European terror attacks.

- **Demographic pressures.** An unstable periphery will continue to send considerable numbers of refugees and migrants to Europe, straining the ability of national governments and EU institutions to respond, causing tension between member states and with EU institutions and fueling support for xenophobic parties and groups. At the same time, the aging of existing European populations will create a growing need for new workers. EU institutions and national governments will continue to seek limits on migration and ways of better-integrating immigrants and their children.

- **Weakened national governments.** One of the cornerstones on which postwar Europe was built was the deal that gained popular support for a liberal international economic order in return for the social protections of the welfare state. This bargain fostered stability both in terms of economic growth and representative democracy. The increase in electoral volatility in the past 30 years in Europe and the region's weak recovery from the 2008 financial crisis are straining this bargain. New populist parties of both the right and the left are taking advantage of public dissatisfaction with slow growth, trimmed social benefits, opposition to immigration, and the decline in ideological distance between the established left and right.

Geopolitical Relevance of Region in Next Five Years: Uncertain Unity. Europe's status as a global player has rested with its unity, material capabilities, and the broad consistency in goals and geopolitical outlook shared by its member states, especially France, Germany, and the United Kingdom. For the coming five years at least, the need to restructure European relations in light of the UK's decision to leave the EU is likely to undermine the region's international clout and could weaken transatlantic cooperation. We expect further assertiveness from Russia and deliberate attempts to split the European project. While unlikely, Russian success in regaining political dominance in Kyiv or undermining stability in the Baltics would damage the credibility of the EU and NATO.

- The problem of an increasingly independent and **multidirectional foreign policy in Turkey** and its nondemocratic impulses, at least over the medium term, will add to the disintegrative currents in Europe and pose a threat to the coherence of NATO and NATO-EU cooperation.

- At the core of the European project has been the idea that Europe stands for peace, tolerance, democracy, and cultural diversity and that Europe can avoid the divisive battles that plagued its history only through unity. One reason that most EU member-state governments worked so hard to keep Greece in the euro in 2015 was their determination to prevent the unraveling of the European project. A range of issues pose a **serious threat to the future of the EU,** including the Brexit process and its fallout elsewhere in Europe, the failure of major EU member-states to implement needed economic reforms, the failure of the EU to spur growth across the region, its failure to coordinate refugee policies, and the growing nativism that is particularly virulent in some of its new member states. These stresses could usher in a nasty breakup that reinforced economic decline and even more democratic backsliding.

Other Considerations. The next five years could provide opportunities for regional governance. Brexit could spur the EU to redefine how it relates to the member states and the European public. If the Brexit vote led EU officials and member state leaders to advance policies that showed the benefits of cooperation, and if European leaders found an amicable exit for the UK that let London continue to work closely with its continental counterparts on international issues, Europe could prosper. Despite increased public dissatisfaction with European decision making, European leaders still show more ability to find common cause and craft common policies than leaders in any other region. They still have the opportunity to forge a more effective EU that better respects public sensibilities about national identity and decisionmaking, and the region's well-institutionalized democracies have structures and checks that may succeed in reducing the effects of populist or more extreme leaders.

- Despite **antidemocratic developments** in Hungary and Poland, institutional constraints have muted the impact of rightwing nativist or populist parties that have entered government in more established European democracies such as Austria and Finland. The development of strong judicial systems that practice substantive judicial review—introduced in much of Europe following World War II—remains incomplete in the newer democracies, but even in Hungary, there has been pushback to government policies seen as having overstepped accepted norms.

- **France and Germany remain committed** to working together despite their differing perspectives and policy preferences, as seen by the extremely close cooperation between German Chancellor Merkel and French President Hollande on the Greek bailout, EU policy toward Ukraine, and CT cooperation.

- It remains to be seen whether Merkel, having driven Europe's response to most of the crises of the past decade, will recover her political momentum after failing to win support—in Germany or in the EU—for a more welcoming approach to Syrian migrants. While other European countries have not been comfortable with Germany's role, it is hard to see another leader as capable of balancing the region's equities and responses.

GERMANY

2035 Population Projection:

78,403,000

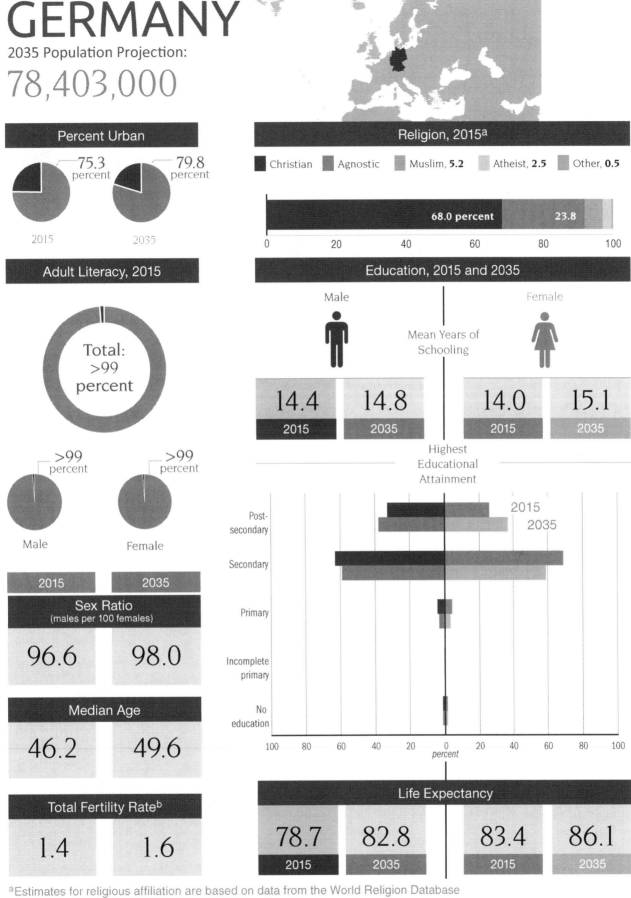

Percent Urban

75.3 percent — 2015

79.8 percent — 2035

Adult Literacy, 2015

Total: >99 percent

>99 percent — Male

>99 percent — Female

2015	2035

Sex Ratio
(males per 100 females)

96.6	98.0

Median Age

46.2	49.6

Total Fertility Rate[b]

1.4	1.6

Religion, 2015[a]

Christian	Agnostic	Muslim, **5.2**	Atheist, **2.5**	Other, **0.5**

68.0 percent   23.8

0   20   40   60   80   100

Education, 2015 and 2035

Male   Mean Years of Schooling   Female

14.4	14.8		14.0	15.1
2015	2035		2015	2035

Highest Educational Attainment

2015
2035

Post-secondary
Secondary
Primary
Incomplete primary
No education

100 80 60 40 20 0 20 40 60 80 100
percent

Life Expectancy

78.7	82.8		83.4	86.1
2015	2035		2015	2035

[a]Estimates for religious affiliation are based on data from the World Religion Database and are rounded to the nearest one-tenth of a percent.
[b]Total Fertility Rate is the projected average number of children born to a woman if she lives to the end of her childbearing years.
Note: Demographic data is presented for countries estimated to have the largest population in each region in 2035.

NORTH AMERICA

135

North America

The North American region will be tested by growing social and political pressures in the next five years, especially if economic growth remains lackluster and fails to generate broader prosperity. With economies ranging from the United States to Dominica, conditions and dynamics vary dramatically, but governments across the region are finding it harder to manage rising public demands for greater economic and social stability at a time when budget constraints and debts are limiting options. Public frustration is high throughout much of the region, because uncertainty about economic conditions and social changes is rising at the same time that trust in most governments is declining.

The health of the **US economy** will remain the prime variable for the region, given its large size and close links. The US recovery from the 2008 financial crisis has been slower and harder than after previous downturns, and most forecasts expect US economic growth to be modest—probably not strong enough to boost growth across the region—for the next several years. Economists are divided, however, over how long the current recovery might continue. Some, focusing on the current recovery's seven-year span, warn the US economy already is "overdue" for another recession based on historical averages, while others observe that periods of expansion have been longer—up to 10 years—in recent decades. Whenever the next US recession hits, it will reverberate through the region by reducing US demand for goods and the massive southward flow of remittances.

- Even in an increasingly diversified country like Mexico, **remittances from the United States** still account for around 2 percent of GDP, and they comprise as much as 20 percent of the economy in Haiti. Central America would be particularly vulnerable, with already struggling economies in Guatemala, El Salvador, Honduras, and Nicaragua deriving 10 to 20 percent of their GDP from remittances.

- A US economic downturn would also further close **a traditional safety valve for desperate people** who seek work in the United States as well as reduce the flow of remittances from the United States. The state of the US economy historically also has had a significant impact on Canadian growth patterns because of the large volume of bilateral trade.

Mexico's economic and social reforms also will probably have muted political impact within the country and region. President Pena Nieto has enacted wide-ranging reforms in key industries—such as oil, communications, and finance—as well as education in an effort to enhance Mexico's competitiveness, but growth has not increased significantly so far, and public support has soured amid corruption allegations, persistent violence, a weakening peso, and domestic crises such as the disappearance of 43 students at a demonstration in 2014. Major reforms, such as opening Mexico's oil industry to foreign investment, take time to bear fruit, but antigovernment protests could escalate if the disappointments remain more apparent than the benefits in the next several years.

- With presidential elections in 2018 and Pena Nieto limited to one term, voters may lean toward a more leftist opposition that pushes to roll back reforms and trade deals if reforms do not reduce Mexico's stark economic divide.

- Moreover, the success or failure of Mexico's high-profile reforms might affect the willingness of other countries in the region to take similar political risks.

If more protectionist sentiment takes root in the next several years, particularly in the United States and Mexico, the future of trade in the region could be in play. US domestic politics has raised doubt about the future of the Trans Pacific Partnership (TPP) trade deal, and one of the leading potential Mexican presidential candidates on the left for 2018 has blamed the North American Free Trade Agreement (NAFTA) for Mexican job losses. At the same time, however, the CAFTA-DR trade agreement between the US, Central America, and the Dominican Republic has generated less political controversy because of its more modest scope.

- Public opinion on trade varies widely across the region. Polls suggest popular concern about trade is significant in the United States—depending on how questions are phrased—while a small majority of Mexicans generally support NAFTA. A growing majority of Canadians have come to support NAFTA, although they appear less certain about the benefits of the TPP.

- In this atmosphere, an economic downturn in the region could drive some political leaders to take a harder line on trade to reassure publics, even though—as generally agreed among economists—technology and automation have been more important factors in job losses and flat wages and are likely to remain so over the coming years.

The issue of Caribbean, Central American, and Mexican immigration—and even travel—is likely to loom larger in the region in the next five years, even though the flow of workers from Mexico to the United States has dropped since the 2008 financial crisis, apparently due to the economic downturn and tighter border enforcement in the United States and more job opportunities and demographic changes in Mexico. If terrorism flares in the United States and Canada, yet tighter border restrictions could further limit movement within the region, with political, economic and social consequences.

- Strong **expressions of anti-immigrant sentiment** during the US election campaign have fueled public resentment in Mexico, which could feed into Mexico's presidential election in 2018. Moreover, the tighter the US border gets, the more Mexico is likely to increase its own efforts to gain better control of its southern border to discourage Central Americans from coming and staying in Mexico if they fail to get farther north.

- Meanwhile, the **further spread of the Zika virus** in the region over the next few years could discourage tourism, which some estimate provides around 5 percent of GDP in the Caribbean, around 7 percent of GDP in Mexico, and a large share of jobs in southern US states, such as Florida.

Concern about violence and social order will become increasingly salient for many countries in the region, though for different reasons. One prime driver of violence is the illicit drug trade. Violence is particularly rampant in northern Central America, as gangs and organized criminal groups have undermined basic governance.

- Prospects for improvement appear dim as long as governments lack the capacity to fight narcoterrorism or to provide such public goods as education, health services, infrastructure, gender equality, and the rule of law.

- El Salvador, Guatemala, and Honduras rank among the most violent countries in the world, as shown by their high murder rates for women, which have contributed to migrant flows northward, particularly of unaccompanied children in recent years.

- Some parts of Mexico have seen significant advances in economic development and governance, but other regions continue to struggle with pervasive poverty, corruption, and impunity that feed high levels of violence and social tension.

- In much of the region, activist civil society organizations can fuel social tension by increasing public awareness of elite corruption and mismanagement in their push for better governance. In August 2015, public revelations of high-level corruption in Guatemala sparked massive antigovernment protests, bringing down the President and Vice President, and civil society groups have helped mobilize major demonstrations in Honduras and Mexico, as well. Most of these protests have been peaceful but could turn violent as public frustration with political and economic elites grows, or if governments use heavyhanded suppression.

Geopolitical Relevance of Region in Next Five Years: Eyes on the United States. The arrival of a new US administration will draw intense scrutiny from across the region for any signs of change in the US global role. Given its extended engagement in Afghanistan and Iraq, highly polarized politics, and the domestic focus of the election campaign, outside observers wonder if Washington has the will and the means to continue exercising broader international leadership.

- While the US stance on trade has gotten the most attention, US allies also will be seeking assurance that Washington will honor security guarantees in the face of more assertive Chinese and Russian actions, and adversaries will be gauging their room for maneuver. North American security could become a greater concern if economic and political stresses in key states such as Mexico or Cuba spark destabilizing protests that result in changes in government or surges in migration.

Other Considerations. How public pressures for economic and political change are channeled will be a crucial issue in North America in the next several years. Modern communications have made it easier for frustrated citizens in the region to gain support and put pressure on elites, mobilize nongovernmental efforts, or compare the performance of different local governments, but the response still may not keep up with the demand.

- The capacity of social media and other forms of on-line advocacy to drive meaningful social and political change remains unclear, or at least varied across countries. For example, elites in Mexico and Central America have become increasingly aware of the risks of stark inequality and the publicity it can cause, but many observers doubt they are willing to forego their financial advantages to support reforms to improve competition, education, infrastructure, and social welfare benefits.

- Meanwhile, NGOs across the region have become more active in pushing for better government services—sometimes taking the initiative to provide services—but it is often difficult to scale these efforts to the scope of the challenge. In addition, wide variations in local and state government efforts allow for experimentation that may generate momentum for more successful approaches—or highlight the risks of poor governance.

In this environment, voters may be **driven by more-personalized politics** if they feel traditional parties and governments are not addressing their needs. Increased use of information technology has enabled some racial minority groups to highlight structural inequalities and injustices. This sensitive topic probably will continue to lead to complementary or contrary movements.

- Some citizens with the job skills and resources to work elsewhere **may vote with their feet**, expanding the brain drain from places like Mexico and Central America at a time when these countries most need strong human talent to strengthen their economies and political systems.

- Ultimately, frustrated **citizens may become more willing to take to the streets** to vent their anger if they judge conditions are worsening—with no prospect for improvement. Voters can express their views through elections, the spate of high-profile demonstrations in various countries around the world in the past several years suggests elites should not bank on public resignation.

UNITED STATES

2035 Population Projection:

365,266,000

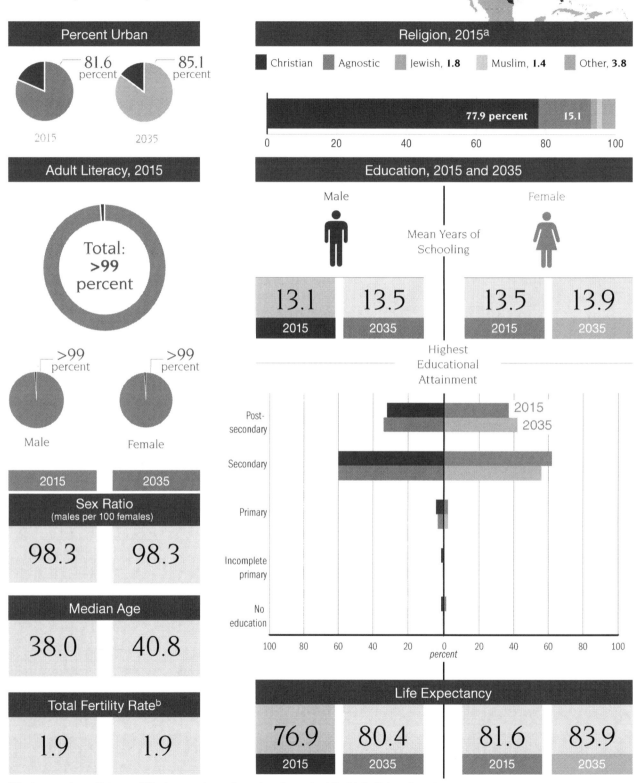

Percent Urban

81.6 percent — 2015

85.1 percent — 2035

Adult Literacy, 2015

Total: **>99** percent

>99 percent — Male

>99 percent — Female

2015	2035

Sex Ratio
(males per 100 females)

98.3	98.3

Median Age

38.0	40.8

Total Fertility Rate[b]

1.9	1.9

Religion, 2015[a]

- ■ Christian
- ■ Agnostic
- ■ Jewish, **1.8**
- ■ Muslim, **1.4**
- ■ Other, **3.8**

77.9 percent   15.1

0   20   40   60   80   100

Education, 2015 and 2035

Male   Female

Mean Years of Schooling

Male 2015	Male 2035	Female 2015	Female 2035
13.1	13.5	13.5	13.9

Highest Educational Attainment

2015
2035

Post-secondary
Secondary
Primary
Incomplete primary
No education

100 80 60 40 20 0 20 40 60 80 100
percent

Life Expectancy

76.9	80.4	81.6	83.9
2015	2035	2015	2035

[a]Estimates for religious affiliation are based on data from the World Religion Database and are rounded to the nearest one-tenth of a percent.
[b]Total Fertility Rate is the projected average number of children born to a woman if she lives to the end of her childbearing years.
Note: Demographic data is presented for countries estimated to have the largest population in each region in 2035.

SOUTH AMERICA

South America

In the next five years, South America will see more frequent changes in governments as a result of public dissatisfaction over economic mismanagement, widespread corruption, weak economic performance due to softer Chinese demand for commodities, and social stresses associated with new entrants to the middle class and the working poor. These conditions will also jeopardize the region's significant progress against poverty and inequality of the previous 20 years.

- An anti-incumbency wave is **reversing the leftward trend** that marked politics in parts of the continent in the past 10 years, most notably in defeats of leftists in the 2015 Argentine presidential election, the 2015 Venezuela parliamentary vote, and Brazilian President Rousseff's 2016 impeachment. Nonetheless, some incumbents facing rejection are seeking to protect their powers, which could lead to a period of intense political competition and possible democratic backsliding in some countries.

Paradoxically, some of the recent successes of the region's left are **increasing the appeal of market-friendly ideas** concerning rule of law and economic and social management. In the past dozen years, poverty and inequality have declined considerably in Latin America because of rising wages, greater access to schooling, and increased female employment. In 2003, 41.3 percent of the region's people lived below the poverty line, but by 2013 this figure had fallen to 24.3 percent. Latin America's middle class, defined as people with incomes of $10 to $50 per day, grew from 21.3 percent to 35.0 percent of the population during this period.

- A recent UN study, however, finds that poverty has begun to increase again—from an estimated 168 million impoverished in 2014 to 175 million in 2015—because of the region's economic slowdown. One of the chief causes for the slowdown is the dramatic drop in commodity prices, down 40 percent since their peak in 2011. Weak growth is likely to strain governments' budgets and depress already globally low rates of investment.

- The rise of evangelical Christianity in Brazil, and to a lesser degree elsewhere, will create **new political forces that stress the rule of law** and less government regulation, views that have lower-class support. In Brazil, the growing political strength of Evangelicals—roughly a fifth of the population—has shifted from an early alliance with leftist leaders to a more conservative agenda on issues such as abortion while seeking to address the needs of its poor and middle class members with a push for education. In the spring of 2016, the evangelical caucus, known as the "Bible block," helped drive the effort to impeach President Rousseff on corruption charges. However, charges of corruption against several Evangelical politicians in Brazil could damage their political clout.

Crime and corruption are likely to remain major political liabilities for incumbents whom the public blames for weakened employment prospects, while drug trafficking and organized crime geared toward northern markets will become more prominent. Both developments will raise security concerns and stoke public dissatisfaction that could topple governments perceived as ineffective against or enabling graft or criminal activity.

- Latin America is **one of the most violent regions in the world in terms of crime** and is responsible for nearly one-third of homicides worldwide, according to a UN study. Brazil and Venezuela have among the highest murder rates in the world.

- Crime will remain the top public concern. Opinion polls suggest that many citizens identify crime as the most serious problem facing their countries, but economic concerns will probably gain more prominence as countries manage slowing economies. Countries affected by large drug trafficking organizations may see an increase in violence as well as erosion of the quality of their institutions and the authority and legitimacy of their governments.

The general lack of structural reforms—in fields ranging from education and health care to infrastructure, productivity, and taxation of the informal economy—suggest that the region stumbles as the external economic environment becomes less favorable and competition for foreign investment stiffens. Successful resolution of Colombia's conflict would present a chance for development that might boost economic growth.

- Some fledgling but newly empowered and productive members of the working poor and **middle class bristle at supporting social welfare taxes** for those they perceive as lazy or corrupt.

- Increasing **economic and humanitarian pressure in Venezuela** could lead to a further crackdown by current President Maduro, but the loyalty of the military is uncertain, and there is a risk of humanitarian crisis that might send more refugees to neighboring countries and possibly the United States. Additional collapse in Venezuela probably would further discredit the leftist experiments of the past decade in Latin America and increase pressure to focus on improving economies.

- Health systems in the region are important **sources of political legitimacy and state-building**, arguably more than in other regions. Aging populations threaten the sustainability of health systems, and health care costs will dampen economic growth. The ongoing threats of the Zika virus and dengue fever put additional pressure on the region, especially the poorer populations.

Geopolitical Relevance of Region in Next Five Years: Political Economy. South America's relevance as a geopolitical actor will remain muted in the next five years but it—along with Africa—will bear the brunt of the drop in Chinese demand for commodities, continued low oil prices, and near-term environmental and climate challenges. Some commodity-dependent states will struggle to manage the global economic slowdown and will look to IMF programs and free trade to promote growth and employment. Brazil probably will join Argentina in turning toward better regional relations and increased regional trade.

- We expect Brazil and other countries to remain **influential voices on international climate change** policy, especially if citizens increasingly view the environment as something other than a source of financial profit. Countries bordering the Pacific are particularly affected by El Niño events, which alter rain patterns to cause heavy precipitation and flooding in some areas, drought in others, and climate models suggest that El Niño events will become larger. The 2015-16 El Niño, the largest on record by some measures, aggravated Brazil's recent drought, its worst in almost a century, affecting issues as diverse as Sao Paolo's drinking water supply, hydropower production, and Zika transmission. Nevertheless, greenhouse gas emissions by countries in the region are likely to remain significant, given middle class demand for cars in Brazil and its energy sector's belief that aggressive forestry can offset carbon emissions.

- South America's remaining left-leaning ALBA (Bolivarian Alliance for the People of our America) countries—Bolivia, Ecuador, and Venezuela—will **continue to court support from Beijing and Moscow**. China, in particular, has been generous with loans that strengthen the incumbents but have had mixed economic effects. Venezuela has long relied on Chinese financing to stay afloat, but Beijing has cut back on its largesse and is moving more closely to World Bank-like lending criteria that the ALBA countries are unlikely to meet. Large-scale instability and economic collapse in Venezuela looks likely, absent a change of government and major economic reform, and even these may not prove sufficient without substantial outside assistance.

- **Regional security threats will grow**, with the threat of large-scale instability in Venezuela, booming coca production in Colombia fueling crime in Central American and Mexico, and the persistence of drug trafficking and organized crime throughout the region. As illicit markets grow in many countries of the region, violence—and political and security institutions weakened by corruption—will become more pressing concerns. Latin American governments will press the United States and other developed countries to legalize drugs.

Other Considerations. The rightward turn in the region could be slowed or halted by corruption scandals in conservative governments. Other trends to watch are failures of governments— leftwing or rightwing—to narrow the socioeconomic gaps as economies slow. Such failures may lead to increasingly polarized societies, in which class, ethno-racial, and ideological cleavages largely reinforce each other. These inequalities could fuel the growth of indigenous and Afro-Latino movements in some Latin American countries in the years ahead.

The Zika epidemic that began in Brazil in 2015—declared a public health emergency by the World Health Organization—has radiated throughout the Americas, including clusters of infections in Puerto Rico and the southeastern US. Because Zika has been shown in some cases to damage neurological development during fetal gestation, the epidemic poses a potential new form of upheaval in women's health. Maternal fears about giving birth to microcephalic infants—worsened by the many continued unknowns about the virus's spread among populations—have provoked major changes in how people in the region travel, plan families, and conduct daily life. If Zika becomes permanently established throughout the Americas, the repercussions would intensify as governments seek to cope with and counter the epidemic's impact across generations.

BRAZIL

2035 Population Projection:

233,006,000

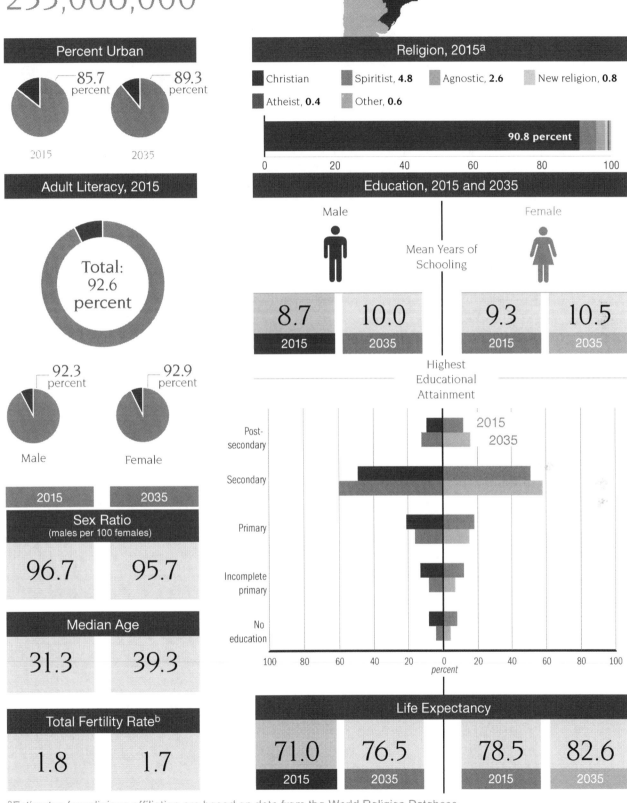

Percent Urban

85.7 percent — 2015

89.3 percent — 2035

Adult Literacy, 2015

Total: 92.6 percent

92.3 percent — Male

92.9 percent — Female

2015	2035
Sex Ratio (males per 100 females)	
96.7	95.7
Median Age	
31.3	39.3
Total Fertility Rate[b]	
1.8	1.7

Religion, 2015[a]

- Christian
- Spiritist, **4.8**
- Agnostic, **2.6**
- New religion, **0.8**
- Atheist, **0.4**
- Other, **0.6**

90.8 percent

0   20   40   60   80   100

Education, 2015 and 2035

Male   Female

Mean Years of Schooling

Male 2015	Male 2035	Female 2015	Female 2035
8.7	10.0	9.3	10.5

Highest Educational Attainment

2015
2035

Post-secondary
Secondary
Primary
Incomplete primary
No education

100 80 60 40 20 0 20 40 60 80 100
percent

Life Expectancy

2015	2035	2015	2035
71.0	76.5	78.5	82.6

[a]Estimates for religious affiliation are based on data from the World Religion Database and are rounded to the nearest one-tenth of a percent.
[b]Total Fertility Rate is the projected average number of children born to a woman if she lives to the end of her childbearing years.
Note: Demographic data is presented for countries estimated to have the largest population in each region in 2035.

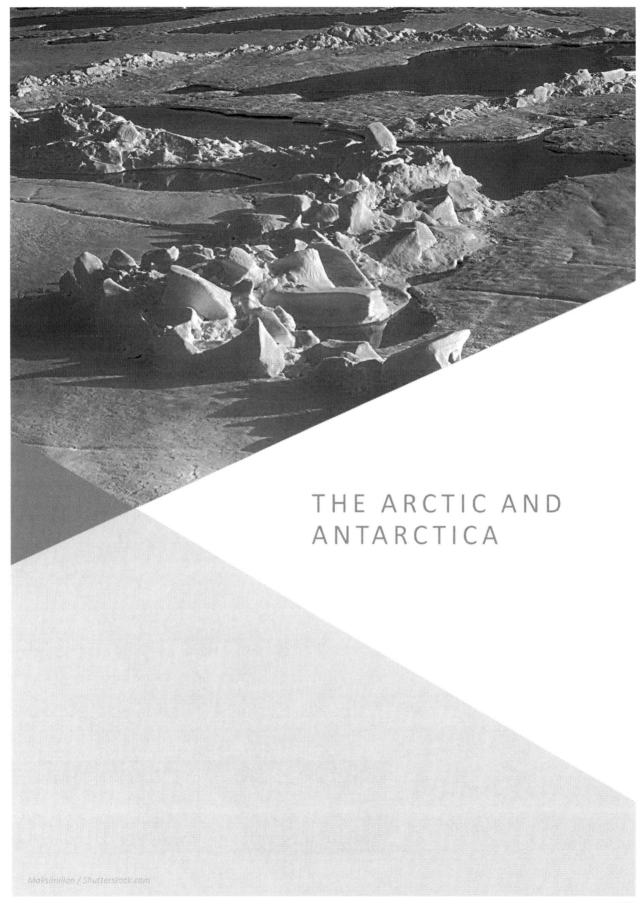

THE ARCTIC AND
ANTARCTICA

The Arctic and Antarctica

Environmental changes in the Arctic will shape the global climate and access to key transit lanes over the next five years. Warming twice as fast as the rest of the planet, the Arctic will continue to produce dramatic and newsworthy images that have become established earlywarning signs of the changing climate, such as stunning, high-resolution video of melting glaciers and thinning ice sheets and vivid photos of starving iconic mammals. However, other transformations under way are just as momentous, including the rapid acidification of Arctic Ocean waters, the decline in reflectivity that pushes solar heat back into space, and the temperature-induced ecological shifts that impact microbes and mammals alike. Beyond the physical changes that directly affect the 4 million people who live in the Arctic, linkages are increasingly evident between elevated Arctic temperatures and extreme weather events in mid-latitude continents, such as intense heatwaves in Russia, more severe winters in Europe, and high variability in Indian summer monsoons.

- **Shipping.** Fully ice-free summers probably remain a decade or more away, but an increasingly navigable Arctic makes the region a more salient economic and security issue. The melting of sea ice raises the possibility of drastically shorter commercial routes between major trading blocs, such as exports from China, Japan, and South Korea to Europe and North America. A more open Arctic, however, brings substantial hurdles—and potential calamities—as the unpredictability of ice, weather, and fog increases in already harsh conditions. In the next five years, pioneering efforts will outpace improvements in infrastructure needed for operation in the region, such as ship-to-shore communication nodes, transshipment facilities, refueling stations, and vessel tracking. Armed forces are typically the only national assets with the physical capabilities and monitoring equipment to operate in such an inhospitable environment, ensuring a military presence in the Arctic beyond the responsibilities of search-and-rescue and other contingencies.

- **Natural Resources.** Dangerous weather and sea ice will not dampen commercial or national interests in the Arctic's enormous natural resources. The largest unexplored area for petroleum remaining on Earth—which could contain well over 90 billion barrels of oil, 1,700 trillion cubic feet of natural gas, and 44 billion barrels of liquid natural gas—will draw continued interest in offshore drilling. Exploitation is unlikely to become economically profitable in the next five years, however—barring an unanticipated, sharp rebound in oil prices—and has been the subject of public protests. Likewise, onshore mineral development will remain largely theoretical, particularly in the absence of robust road and rail infrastructure. Warming waters increase access for commercial fishing, but environmental change and ocean acidification will have unpredictable effects on Arctic fish stocks.

Antarctica's warming has been slowed by the great depth and expanse of the Southern Ocean, with its massive thermal inertia relative to the continents ringing the Arctic. Furthermore, the several-kilometer-thick ice sheets at the South Pole are generally slower to respond than the several-meter-thick floating sea ice in the Arctic.

- However, the rapid disintegration of the Larsen B ice shelf in 2002 and the ongoing retreat of the Pine Island and Thwaites Glacier show how fast ice at the periphery of Antarctica can be lost as a result of ocean and atmospheric warning.

- Scientists have recently identified a rapidly developing crack in Larsen C—Antarctica's fourth-largest ice shelf—that could generate a breakaway piece of ice roughly the size of Delaware. Once predicted to destabilize over 50 years, some scientific estimates now project that Larsen C might fracture within five years.

- Loss of ice shelves and glacial retreat that expose the ice of Antarctica's interior to ocean water will accelerate sea level rises; West Antarctica alone has the potential to raise sea level by more than three meters worldwide. Whether this rise materializes over multiple millennia, centuries, or sooner remains an open question, however.

Beyond its role in doomsday sea level rise scenarios, Antarctica remains an important region geopolitically. The Antarctica Treaty of 1959—which froze the claims of 12 nations and established the continent as a scientific reserve—remains perhaps the most successful international treaty in modern history. However, an uptick in Russian and Chinese activities on the continent would fuel anxiety over possible violations of the treaty, especially among claimant states like Australia, New Zealand, and Norway.

- Controversial activities in the Southern Ocean, such as Japanese whaling and Chinese krill harvesting, will continue to spur diplomatic disputes within the Antarctic Treaty System.

Geopolitical Relevance of the Regions in Next Five Years: Avenues for Cooperation. Both the Antarctic and especially the Arctic have featured prominently in national security strategies, and diminishing sea ice is increasing economic opportunities in the region while raising Arctic nations' concerns about safety and the environment. Harsh weather and longer term economic stakes have encouraged cooperation among the countries bordering the Arctic, but economic and security concerns will raise the risk of increased competition between Arctic and non-Arctic nations over access to sea routes and resources. Sustained low oil prices, on the other hand, would reduce the attractiveness of potential Arctic energy resources.

- Russia will almost certainly continue to bolster its military presence along its northern coast to improve its perimeter defense and control of its exclusive economic zone (EEZ). It will also almost certainly continue to seek international support for its extended continental shelf claim and its right to manage ship traffic within its EEZ. If Russian-Western relations deteriorate, Moscow might become more willing to disavow established international processes or organizations in the Arctic and act unilaterally to protect these interests.

- **Arctic Council.** The Arctic Council, made up of the eight nations that have sovereign territory within the Arctic Circle—Canada, Denmark (by virtue of Greenland), Finland, Iceland, Norway, Russia, Sweden, and the United States—continues to grow in prominence. Arctic Council members are seeking to define their territorial boundaries in the Arctic Sea according to the UN convention on the Law of the Sea—which all members except the US have ratified. Since its creation in 1996, the Council has granted permanent participant status to six indigenous Arctic peoples' organizations and has given permanent observer status to China, France, Germany, India, Italy, Japan, the Netherlands, Poland, Singapore, South Korea, Spain, and the UK. The addition of observer nations that are thousands of miles from the Arctic reflects intensified global interest in the region, even though the Council's charter excludes security issues.

Other Considerations: Greenlandic Independence Efforts. The former Danish colony has gradually gained autonomy since the Home-Rule Act of 1979, and a majority of Greenland's residents favor full independence. Some prominent leaders have lobbied hard for independence by 2021, the 300th anniversary of Greenland's colonization by Denmark. Nuuk's reliance on critical Danish subsidies and the downturn in global oil prices have essentially quashed these notions for the immediate future, however. The population of just 57,000 will nonetheless have an increasingly stronger voice on the use of vast mineral resources on the world's largest island, also being transformed rapidly by climate change.

SPACE

Mechanik / Shutterstock.com

Space

Once the domain only of superpowers, space now hosts an expanding set of actors, whose number is likely to grow in the next five years. Although only 13 of the 70 governmental space agencies have actual launch capabilities, many nations participate in a wide array of space-based activities, from operating satellites to sending astronauts to the International Space Station aboard Russian or Chinese spacecraft. Missions are increasingly multinational and multisectoral, perhaps giving people a collective sense of ownership of space not felt in decades.

- **Multinational space exploration.** A growing number of nations now sponsor missions to contribute critical scientific knowledge about our solar system. With its Mars Orbiter Mission in 2014, India was the first nation to put a space probe in a Martian orbit on its first attempt. Later that year, after a 10-year journey through space, the European Space Agency's probe *Rosetta* reached Comet 67P/Churyumov-Gerasimenko and landed its module *Philae* on its surface, the first such achievement in human history. In 2015, the United States sponsored *Dawn*, the first spacecraft to explore the dwarf planets Vesta and Ceres, and provided the world with its first ever fly-by of Pluto and its moons with *New Horizons*. Planned missions in the next five years include Japan's land-and-return voyage to asteroid Ryugu, China's landing on the dark side of the moon, a joint EU-Japan mission to Mercury, the UAE's mission to put a probe in the Martian atmosphere, and NASA's James Webb Space Telescope, which could revolutionize all areas of astronomy.

- **Commercialization.** Space is no longer just for governments. Fueled partly by the allure of future profits as well as the void created by the dwindling budgets of space agencies like NASA, private companies such as Space-X, Blue Origin, and Virgin Galactic have mounted serious programs that could soon launch humans into space. Planetary Resources is a company that aims to mine asteroids, while Bigelow Aerospace promises inflatable space habitats. Although full realization of these industries is decades away, the next five years will bring early testing that teases at the potential for private individuals to reach space.

- **New Global Navigation Satellite Systems (GNSS).** The EU's Galileo satellite navigation system is expected to reach full operational capability by 2020, significantly advancing global positioning capabilities by operating with greater precision, more global coverage, and at higher latitudes. Galileo will join the US's GPS, Russia's GLONASS, China's BeiDou, and regional systems put in place by India and Japan. Devices that can simultaneously process signals from multiple GNSS constellations are likely to offer new capabilities—such as enhanced precision, indoor and z-axis positioning, and antijamming—to the more than 4 billion users worldwide who depend on space-based global positioning.

Space *(continued)*

- **Space debris**. More than 500,000 pieces of space debris are currently tracked as they orbit the Earth, some traveling as fast as 17,500 mph. Many millions of pieces are too small to be tracked but could be hazardous to critical satellites or other spacecraft. International action may soon be necessary to identify and fund the removal of debris most threatening to an expanding global space presence.

- **Space militarization**. As space becomes more congested, it is also becoming more contested. The immense strategic and commercial value of outer space assets ensures that nations will increasingly vie for access, use, and control of space. The deployment of antisatellite technologies designed to purposefully disable or destroy satellites could intensify global tension. A key question will be whether spacefaring countries, in particular China, Russia, and the United States, can agree to a code of conduct for outer space activity.

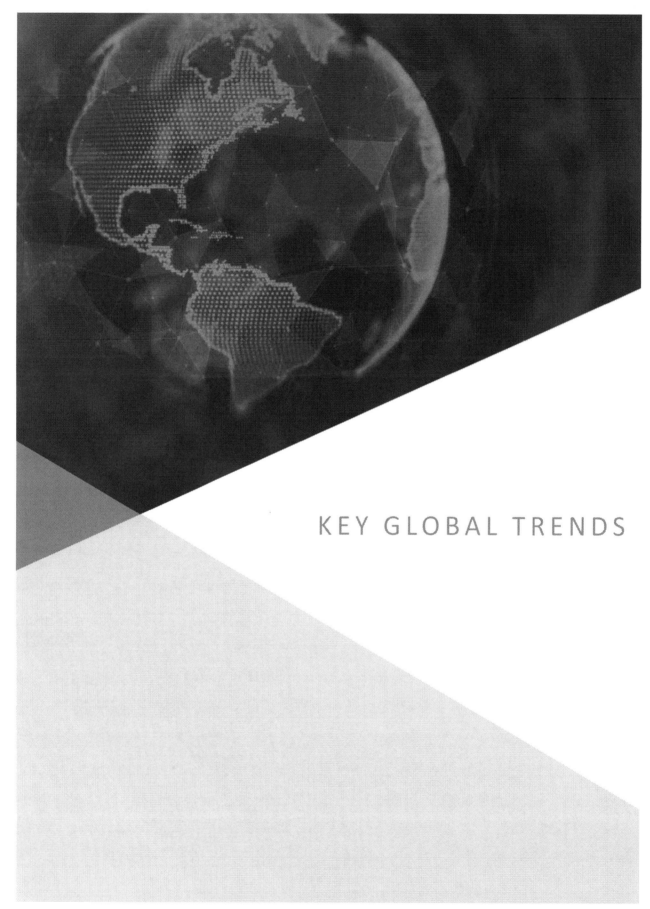

KEY GLOBAL TRENDS

Population Change by Region, 2015-35

The world's population will probably grow by about 20 percent between 2015 and 2035, according to UN projections. However, this growth will be unevenly distributed. The population of Africa, with a per capita income average of only about $5,000—despite including a number of dynamic, growing economies—will grow by nearly three-fifths; by contrast, the population of Europe, with an average income more than six times as large as Africa's, will actually decline without substantial inflows of migrants from other regions.

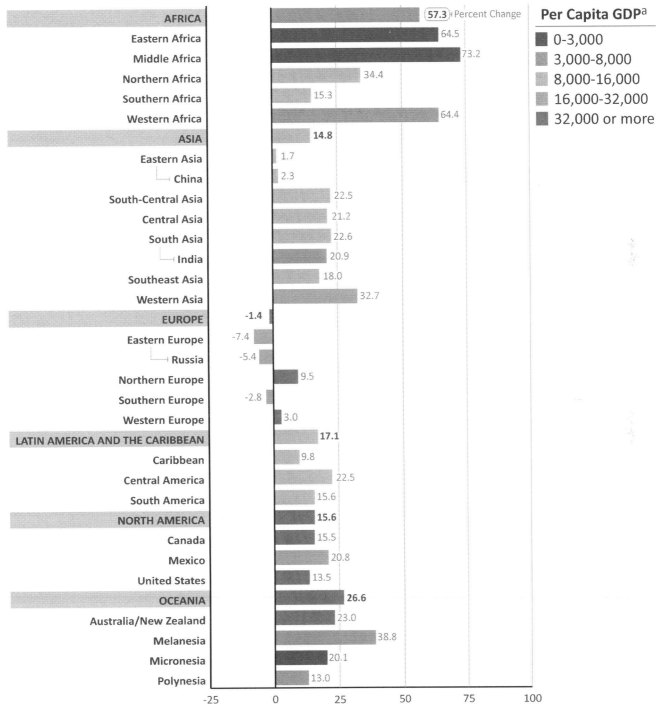

Region	Percent Change
AFRICA	**57.3**
Eastern Africa	64.5
Middle Africa	73.2
Northern Africa	34.4
Southern Africa	15.3
Western Africa	64.4
ASIA	**14.8**
Eastern Asia	1.7
China	2.3
South-Central Asia	22.5
Central Asia	21.2
South Asia	22.6
India	20.9
Southeast Asia	18.0
Western Asia	32.7
EUROPE	**-1.4**
Eastern Europe	-7.4
Russia	-5.4
Northern Europe	9.5
Southern Europe	-2.8
Western Europe	3.0
LATIN AMERICA AND THE CARIBBEAN	**17.1**
Caribbean	9.8
Central America	22.5
South America	15.6
NORTH AMERICA	**15.6**
Canada	15.5
Mexico	20.8
United States	13.5
OCEANIA	**26.6**
Australia/New Zealand	23.0
Melanesia	38.8
Micronesia	20.1
Polynesia	13.0

Per Capita GDP[a]
- 0-3,000
- 3,000-8,000
- 8,000-16,000
- 16,000-32,000
- 32,000 or more

[a]Per capita GDP for 2015 in purchasing power parity (PPP) dollars.
Sources: UN population data (median projection); International Monetary Fund.

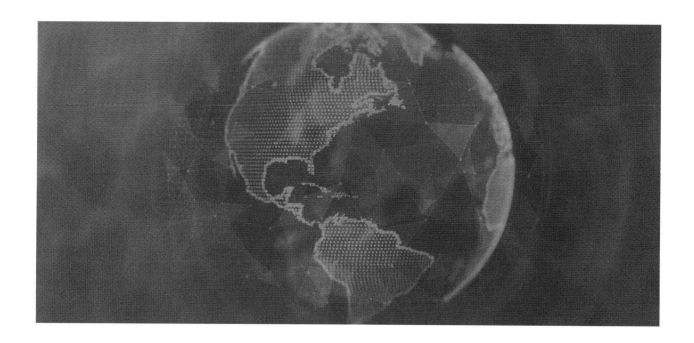

PEOPLE . . .

In 2035 the world's population will be larger, older and more urban than today, but change will progress unevenly across regions, with rapid growth in many promising but still-developing economies offset by stalled growth—or even shrinking populations—in many developed countries. These trends will challenge the former to provide infrastructure and opportunities for their growing populations and the latter to use technology to minimize their need for new workers and to smoothly integrate migrants from developing countries who seek improved prospects.

- By 2035, world population will have **increased by almost 20 percent to 8.8 billion**, while the global median age will have risen from 30 in 2015 to 34 years.

- By then, more **than three-fifths of the world's population will likely live in urban areas**, an approximate 7-percentage point increase from 2016.

Age Structure Changes of Key Countries, 2015-35

Age Structure (median Age)	Selected States					
	2015 PROJECTIONS			**2035 PROJECTIONS**		
YOUTHFUL (25 or less)	Niger	14.8	Kenya	18.9	Niger	15.7	Afghanistan	24.3
	Uganda	15.9	Iraq	19.3	Uganda	18.9	Ethiopia	24.3
	Democratic Rep. of the Congo	16.9	Yemen	19.3	Democratic Rep. of the Congo	19.4	Yemen	24.5
	Afghanistan	17.5	Pakistan	22.5	Nigeria	20.0		
	Nigeria	17.9	Egypt	24.7	Iraq	21.9		
	Ethiopia	18.6			Kenya	22.6		
INTERMEDIATE (26 to 35)	South Africa	25.7	Turkey	29.8	Pakistan	26.8	Venezuela	33.6
	India	26.6	Israel	30.3	Egypt	27.2	Mexico	35.1
	Mexico	27.4	Vietnam	30.4	South Africa	30.2		
	Venezuela	27.4	Tunisia	31.2	Israel	32.5		
	Indonesia	28.4	Brazil	31.3	India	32.8		
	Iran	29.5			Indonesia	33.2		
MATURE (36 TO 45)	China	37.0	Canada	40.6	Turkey	37.0	New Zealand	41.0
	Australia	37.5	South Korea	40.6	Tunisia	38.0	UK	42.7
	New Zealand	38.0	Cuba	41.2	Vietnam	39.0	France	43.3
	US	38.0	France	41.2	Brazil	39.3	Russia	43.6
	Russia	38.7	Spain	43.2	Australia	40.6	Canada	44.4
	Poland	39.6			US	40.8	China	45.7
	UK	40.0			Iran	40.9		
POST-MATURE (46 or more)	Germany	46.2			Cuba	48.0	Japan	52.4
	Japan	46.5			Poland	48.2		
					South Korea	49.4		
					Germany	49.6		
					Spain	51.5		

Source: UN Population Division, World Population Prospects, 2015 revision (median age data).

Areas of Concern

Five demographic trends will potentially underpin domestic instability and interstate political frictions during the next two decades: chronically youthful states; mass interstate/interregional migrations; transitions through demographic phases; advanced population aging; and majority-minority differential growth. The dynamics of each are outlined below, with examples of regions/states where the trend is likely to be most relevant within the next five years and during the next 20 years.

Chronically Youthful States. Age-structurally *youthful* states have been the most vulnerable to intra-state political violence, whether perpetrated by state or nonstate actors, and many have patronage-based governments ill-equipped to meet the demands of sustained high fertility, rapid urban growth—typically without sufficient fiscal means to plan and accommodate it—and an underemployed young-adult population, potentially contributing to instability.

- Youthful states suffering from protracted political violence and institutional dysfunction risk drawing intervention from regional and extra-regional powers, as seen during the past 40 years.

- In the regions where youthful states are clustered—and where the governments involved have been unable to contain or suppress insurgencies—armed violence has periodically spilled over origin-state borders into the region and well beyond.

The US Census Bureau's International Program Center (USCB-IPC) and the UN Population Division project that the current clusters of chronically youthful states—the Sahel region of Africa; Equatorial Africa; Iraq-Syria; Yemen, Somalia; and Afghanistan-Pakistan—will persist for the next five years—and nearly all will remain through 2035.

- The UN projections suggest that **Egypt will move out of the youthful category** by 2030 and **Pakistan** will follow by 2035, with **Yemen** projected to get closer to this category by 2040. However, past growth forecasts for all three countries were optimistically higher than they turned out to be—which may prove true again.

Mass Migration. Conflict-torn youthful-state clusters have frequently been the source of crisis-spurred migrations in recent decades, and their existence through 2035 suggests a continuation of political stress for population-receiving countries and the periodic disruption of more orderly—and more easily accommodated—flows of labor migrants and tourism to destination countries. Flows from conflict-torn youthful-state clusters will probably pose the greatest concern for migrant-receiving states, which must bear significant financial, social and political costs in having to accommodate and integrate new members of society—or deal with the stresses of poorly integrated populations.

- Even predictable flows of economic migrants can pose problems for source and destination countries. Migrant-source states face the loss of their most promising professionals and trained technicians, and beyond the above-mentioned integration costs, legitimate migrants evading or overwhelming receiving-state border controls—or traveling shared routes with unauthorized migrants—can help transform migration routes into conduits for contraband, trafficked individuals, and terrorist infiltration.

During the next five years, even relatively stable "front-line states" surrounding ongoing conflicts in the Middle East—including Turkey, Lebanon, and Jordan, with southern and central Europe as a second line of affected states—will have to deal with such stresses. The UNHCR warns that **the number of "protracted" refugee situations**—currently at 32 and with an average duration of 26 years—**has vastly increased** since the early 1990s. Their length makes it increasingly likely that the "temporary settlements" to accommodate refugees in front-line states will become permanent cities—but lacking the full complement of infrastructure, diversified economic activity, and governance institutions of well-planned and managed cities.

- During the next 20 years, without sufficient growth and development to maintain stability, the **Sahel youthful cluster could spark flows** that affect Algeria, Ghana, Kenya, Morocco, Senegal, and Tunisia, and conflicts in central equatorial Africa could send migrant to Botswana, Kenya, South Africa, and Tanzania. Iran would need to absorb more migrants if conflicts in the Iraq-Syria and Afghanistan-Pakistan clusters do not abate.

Large Working-Age Populations. States with relatively large working-age populations—called the "demographic window of opportunity"—typically enjoy improved maternal and child health, increased per-child educational investment and educational attainment, slowing workforce growth, and in some cases, the accumulation of household savings or assets to further support economic growth. China and South Korea, which recently left this window, vastly expanded human capital, created productive technology sectors, turned their cities into livable, functioning engines of growth, and amassed private and sovereign wealth.

- Since the 1970s, the demographic window has been associated with the **rise and stability of liberal democracies**, as seen in Brazil, Chile, South Korea, and Taiwan, during the late 1980s and 1990s, and more recently in Tunisia. This pattern suggests that in coming years, one or more of the major intermediate-phase countries—a group that includes Algeria, Colombia, Ecuador, Morocco, Myanmar, and Venezuela—could transition to greater democracy.

- Persistently high birthrates among the chronically youthful states mean that relatively few high-growth African countries will move into the intermediate category during the next five years, although several youthful clusters in Asia—including the five former Soviet republics in Central Asia—and in Latin America will make the transition, potentially setting the stage for strong economic performance in coming years.

Developed States' Population Aging. USCB-IPC and UN projections suggest that by 2035, countries with *"post-mature"* age structures will expand from only Japan and Germany today, to a group that comprises states in eastern, central and southern Europe, much of East Asia, and Cuba—with China nearly qualifying as well. These states will be to adjust—but maintain—the institutional frameworks developed during their structurally favorable periods, including social safety nets, liberal democracy, and global capitalism, so that they remain sustainable amid challenges that unfold in their advanced post-maturity stages.

- In all regions, the **decline in the prime military recruitment pool** will press more governments to consider smaller, technologically sophisticated militaries, use of for-hire soldiers, and broader military alliances.

Post-mature state governments are already trying to adjust; declines in young working-age populations in Europe, Japan and South Korea have led governments to subsidize efforts to boost per-worker productivity with measures such as decentralized networked workplaces, increased use of robotics, and support for life-long learning. Efforts to increase workforce participation include incentives to attract women and under-represented groups into the skilled workforce, and subsidized childcare to retain them. Governments have boosted part-time senior work and increased retirement ages to keep people working longer and reduce rolls of older dependents, with mixed success.

- In Europe during the next five years, **efforts to roll back retirement ages** and liberalize workplace rules are likely to continue to be met with stiff resistance. While immigration was once thought of as a stop gap form for support to maintain the welfare state, it is now politically "off the table" as a solution. Residents of East Asian "aging states," where benefits are typically less generous than in Europe, may be more willing to contribute more for pension and healthcare reforms, but they still expect government to ensure living standards.

- Countries where governments are **politically incapable of reining-in pension and healthcare benefits** will face difficult fiscal choices, potentially cutting education or other investment in their diminished youthful populations—and further undermining their economic prospects. Efforts to move from state-run, "pay-as-you-go" and employer-funded pensions to personal savings-based programs will alleviate pressure on government finances but will **leave individuals' retirements at risk** of losses from financial market volatility, potentially leading to calls for government intervention after financial crises.

Majority-Minority Differential Growth. In multi-ethnic states, gaps in population growth rates can aggravate social and political disparities between often better-educated, more-prosperous urbanized majority-group members, and ethnoreligious minorities that typically retain higher fertility rates or whose population growth is augmented by immigration. Limiting the political and economic participation and educational opportunities of minority groups—and encouraging their residential segregation—can widen the population-growth and prosperity gaps and worsen tension—called a *minority demographic security dilemma* by political demographers.

- These growth gaps often become **instruments of political rhetoric**—by both sides—with the differences exaggerated. This can have inter-generational impact, since large gaps can cause visibly apparent changes in ethnic composition among the youngest school-age populations, whose education is subsidized by the taxpaying majority and could be jeopardized if targeted by hostile politicians.

- Because of this political dimension, the **effects of ethnic-composition shifts** during the next twenty years are potentially greatest on electoral democracies, particularly when the political leadership of the dominant group works to stave off the group's loss of electoral power. Such shifts are occurring in Israel, where today's majority of secular and traditionally religious Jews are projected to decline in voting power over the next two decades in the face of rapid growth among Ultra-Orthodox Jews, National Religious Jews, and Palestinian Israelis.

- Similarly, in southeast Turkey the rapidly growing **Kurdish population could gain electoral power** as it becomes larger and more efficiently organized. Shifts are also occurring in the central Andes, as indigenous populations make up a growing share of the electorate.

Continued Urbanization. The world's urban population first exceeded the rural population about a decade ago, and it continues to grow through natural causes and migration while rural-population growth has been flat in recent years. Urbanization will shape global social and political dynamics, but its effects are likely to be uneven and depend on states' capacity to manage the political, economic, and social stresses that urban growth causes.

With proper planning, urbanization can provide the setting, the underlying population base, and momentum for sustainable growth by enabling governments, businesses and individuals to reduce transaction costs; more efficient public infrastructure and services; and greater knowledge generation and diffusion. By some estimates, the world's "megaregions"—networks of metropolitan areas that share environmental systems and topography, infrastructure, economic links, settlement, and land-use patterns—account for 66 percent of the world's economic activity and are the breeding ground for 85 percent of all technological and scientific innovation. Poorly-managed cities and urban centers, however, can serve as incubators for poverty, inequality, crime, pollution, and disease. Near-term decisions on infrastructure for developing megacities will determine their vulnerability to extreme events and climate change.

- Increased **urbanization enables new social and political movements** by concentrating social stresses without adequate capacity to deal with demands on infrastructure. In particular, urbanization without sufficient economic development and consideration of environmental sustainability contributes to poverty and poor living conditions. Such stresses have spurred calls for social change and resource redistribution that adds to volatility at the local political level and causes regional spillover if people move elsewhere.

- Even if city development is efficient, **urban areas will challenge city planners and governments**, including some in Europe, to fund adequate infrastructure, transportation, energy, clean water and air, stable food systems, and healthcare.

The Emerging Gender Imbalance

During the next 20 years, higher rates of education for women, access to birth control, and more equal participation in labor markets suggest birth rates will continue to decline, although biotechnology advances will make it more likely that children survive to adulthood. The male to female ratio of children born in many Middle Eastern, East Asian, and South Asian countries is likely to continue to rise. In recent decades, unbalanced sex ratios have grown in favor of males in countries, such as Albania, Armenia, Azerbaijan, China, Georgia, India, Montenegro, South Korea and Vietnam because of sex-selective abortion, female infanticide, and female selective neglect.

- During the next 20 years, large **parts of China and India are projected to have 10 to 20 percent more men than women**. The two countries are already seeing significant numbers of men without prospects for marriage, and the imbalances, which would take decades to correct, have been linked to abnormal levels of crime and violence, as well as human rights violations such as abduction and trafficking of girls and women for marriage or sexual exploitation.

- The spread of **gender imbalances** appears linked to the influence **patrilineal systems** play in providing security when government capacity dwindles. As this mindset gains greater traction, groups that abide by this ideology are likely to depress the perceived value of women's lives even further.

- Limited economic opportunity in the Arab world is causing many men to delay marriage because they cannot amass the funds to start a household in patrilineal societies where paying a bride price is obligatory. **Escalating bride-price and wedding costs** place a regressive tax on all young men in the society and become a potent source of grievance. Marriage market obstruction—whether from escalating costs, abnormal sex ratios, or high prevalence of polygyny—facilitates recruitment of young men into rebel and terrorist groups.

HOW PEOPLE LIVE . . .

Natural and human-induced changes in many of Earth's ecosystems during the coming decades are likely to weaken the planet's resilience and expose humans to new health, food, water, energy, and infrastructure vulnerabilities and demands. With changes in climate, weather will become less predictable and suitable for the status quo. The oceans' biodiversity will plummet as they become warmer and more acidic, fragile, and polluted. Human and animal health will face threats from heatwaves, cold snaps, and the altered dynamics of pathogen spread. These risks will be distributed unequally in time and geography but have the potential to harm most of the world's populations and ecosystems—severely in some cases, and catastrophically in others.

Environmental and climate changes will challenge systems in different dimensions; heat waves, for example, stress infrastructure, energy, human and animal health, and agriculture. Climate change—observed or anticipated—almost certainly will become an increasingly integral component of how people view their world, especially as populations are projected to swell in those areas most vulnerable to extreme weather events and sea-level rise, including coastal megacities and regions already suffering from water scarcity. Many of the ecological and environmental stresses from climate change—and the infectious diseases it will affect—will cut across state borders, making coordination among governments and international institutions crucial to effective responses. Policies and programs to mitigate and adapt to these challenges will spur opportunities for those well-positioned to benefit.

Major Trends

Changes in Earth Systems. Climate change, sea level rise, and ocean acidification are likely to amplify stresses already felt from population growth, urbanization, inadequate environmental protection, and the use of energy and past natural resources. Although new climate policies could reduce the rate of greenhouse gas emissions over time, past emissions already have locked in a significant rise in global mean temperature, which will in turn drive more frequent and intense extreme weather events, such as heatwaves, droughts, and floods. The steady run of record-setting weather and growing frequency of extreme events suggest to many scientists that climate change is hitting harder and sooner than the gradual change often projected. The intensity of the disruptions could vary widely, spawning unpleasant surprises, particularly given that an increasingly significant fraction of the planet's species already are at increased extinction risk.

- Forecasting changes with greater regional and time precision becomes increasingly uncertain, but the stresses will probably disrupt the most vulnerable—or unlucky—populations in countries at all levels of development.

- Storm surges, augmented by sea level rise, are likely to threaten many coastal systems and low-lying areas, and this environmental volatility almost certainly will disrupt food production patterns and water availability, fueling broader economic, political and social stresses. Changes in the Arctic will exceed those felt in the middle latitudes, and reductions in summer sea-ice will make the Arctic more accessible than any time in human history.

Human and Animal Health Under Pressure. Changing environmental conditions and increasing global connectivity will affect precipitation patterns, biodiversity, and the geographic distribution of pathogens and their hosts, which will in turn affect the viability and vitality of crops and agricultural systems; the emergence, transmission, and spread of human and animal infectious diseases; and potential medical and pharmacological discoveries. The direct impact by environmental stressors to human health from increased heat stress, floods, drought, and increased frequency of intense storms will force difficult decisions on how and where to live, particularly in low-income countries in sub-Saharan Africa and South Asia.

- **Indirect environmental threats to population health** will emerge in the form of food insecurity, under-nutrition, and air and water quality declines as a result of pollution. Troubling trends in communicable diseases—in particular, emerging zoonotic diseases, antimicrobial resistant (AMR) pathogens—and noncommunicable diseases (NCDs)—including heart disease, stroke, diabetes, and mental illness—may be the result of these effects,

- These concerns will be **further intensified by demographic and cultural trends**, such as aging societies in Europe and Asia; inadequate nutrition and sanitation in Africa and India, urbanization and development in uninhabited areas and the rise of megacities; and a widening inequality gap. Perversely, increased longevity—an almost-universal goal—will reduce food and water security in places that are only marginally capable of supporting their populations.

Unaddressed disease-control deficiencies in national and global health systems will make outbreaks more difficult to detect and manage, increasing the potential for epidemics far beyond their points of origin. Increasing contact between people and the easier spread of diseases mean that chronic infectious diseases that are already widespread—such as tuberculosis, HIV/AIDS, and hepatitis—will continue to pose heavy economic and human burdens on high-prevalence countries, despite the significant international resources that have been committed to combatting them. Many middle-income countries already struggle with the burden of increasing noncommunicable diseases on top of persistent infectious diseases.

Critical Human Systems at Risk. The increasing incidence of extreme weather events put all people at risk, although those concentrated in dense areas will be especially vulnerable. International organizations will be increasingly stretched to respond to the food, water, transportation, shelter, and health needs of those affected unless states and localities have made provisions to mitigate the risks, such as infrastructure improvements and early warning systems.

- **Soil and land degradation** during the next 20 years will diminish land available for food production, contributing to shortages and raising prices. Even more-affluent nations are at risk, to the extent that they rely on the highly efficient global agricultural trade that has developed under stable environmental conditions during peacetime.

- **Water shortages and pollution probably will undermine the economic performance** and health conditions of populations worldwide, including those of major developing countries. Economic output would suffer if countries do not have enough clean water to generate electrical power or to support manufacturing and resource extraction. Water problems—added to poverty, social tension, environmental degradation, ineffectual leadership, gender inequality, and weak political institutions—contribute to social disruptions that can prompt state failures.

Key Choices

How will political leaders and populations respond to a world less able to sustain life? Environmental and ecological degradation and climate change are likely to force governments and aid organizations at all levels to wrestle with how to divide their resources between crisis response—especially to the most vulnerable populations—and long-term investment to build more resilient and adaptive systems. Unprecedented weather events and ongoing desertification will hurt vulnerable populations in Africa, Asia, and the Middle East, with major droughts probably causing some water, food, and livestock systems to fail. More intense tropical storms will have a cumulative impact on infrastructure, health, and biodiversity in some coastal and low-lying areas that could overwhelm recovery and reconstruction efforts. Those struggling to survive such disruptions could, on the positive side, develop radical innovations for improvement or , more negatively, turn violent, migrate—if allowed by similarly struggling or less hospitable neighbors—or die.

- Some prominent voices will call for interventions involving **climate geoengineering**, although the governance and legal structures needed for these technologies to be deployed with minimal social disruption are almost certain to lag research and development.

- There are also likely to be calls to give the **victims of extreme levels of environmental degradation** some form of "asylum-like" right as refugees.

To what extent will individuals, governments, and private, civil, and international organizations employ new technologies to improve food, water, and energy security; air and ocean quality and biodiversity; human and animal health; and the resilience of transportation, information systems, and other critical infrastructure?

The inability to predict the timing or location of complex environmental and climatological events increases the need to develop information systems that would better enable officials to make near real-time assessment and policy decisions to minimize damages and casualties. Prevention is better than cure; the cost of building resilient infrastructure is generally much lower than disaster recovery, but mobilizing the political will and resources to take preventative action will be difficult without a dramatic crisis to realign priorities.

Even after a crisis, the will to prevent future harm is often overwhelmed by the breadth and complexity of investing in climate and public health research, monitoring and surveillance; financing climate-resilient health systems; developing a sustainable carbon budget; developing more energy-efficient buildings and transportation systems, applying "best practices" for industrial processes to reduce the risks to food, water, and health systems; improving water management through pricing allocations and "virtual water" trade; and investing in water-related sectors such as agriculture, power, and water treatment.

An increasingly important challenge for resource sustainability will be developing the capability to assess local population needs for power, fuel, and food in near real-time. Tracking the interactions between natural resources and people—and wildlife—would enable better understanding of resource needs, a key vulnerability in an era of increasingly scarce resources.

New investments in energy and technologies offer an important opportunity to reduce the risk of adverse climate change, although most of these will require substantial funding and years of effort to deliver benefits. These include clean-energy sources and enabling technologies, such as offshore wind energy, solar cells, distributed power generation, and energy storage; improvements in combustion sources such as biofuels and waste-to-energy; and mitigation through carbon-capture and sequestration.

- Reducing carbon output will **threaten entrenched economic interests** and disrupt longstanding communities built around hydrocarbon industries.

- Ocean energy, renewable synthetic fuels, next-generation nuclear power, methane hydrates, wireless energy transmission, and energy harvesting are promising but far from maturity. Industrialized biotechnology can contribute to the manufacturing and extraction sectors, food and health security, and defense.

Many new technologies hold great potential for addressing the complex challenges the world faces, but their impact will be blunted if available to only a few countries or elite segments of populations. Increased global connectivity makes populations more aware of new technologies and more eager to access them. Countries and regional and international organizations could be hamstrung by the differing rates at which national and international policies develop relative to those of technology developments.

- **Technological advances** in healthcare, synthetic biology and biotechnology, information, materials and manufacturing, and robotics are likely to improve disease prevention, surveillance, treatment, and management that will improve quality of life and lengthen lifespans.

- Automation could reduce pharmaceutical R&D costs by enabling computerized rational drug design and human-system modeling that reduce animal testing and failed products.

Advanced biotechnology alone cannot address a number of important public health threats, such as the rise of antimicrobial resistance (AMR). There is also a pressing need for relatively simple technologies that can be made affordable for a global population. To meet these needs, **business practices in generating new health technologies are likely to shift**. Pandemic and AMR research has already shifted toward public funds rather than private investment for product development; development funds are also likely to come from nontraditional sources, including other high-income countries, emerging economies, and philanthropic sources. In short, changes in innovation models will be as important as changes in the technologies themselves.

How much will individuals, governments, and private, civil, and international organizations partner in new ways to build resilience into critical human support systems? Making support providers more resilient will be critical to reducing the impact of climate-change related events—particularly in densely populated urban areas—and to improving the speed and quality of responses to those events. Many states and local governments will be unable to provide the capital needed for major infrastructure investments, making support from sources such as civil and international organizations, corporations, and individuals necessary for success. However, motivating donors and political interests—which may see little incentive to develop more-resilient, redundant infrastructure, rather than just more infrastructure—may prove difficult. An additional challenge will be to work with individuals, organizations such as researchers, NGOs, and corporations, states, and the international community to make technologies and capabilities available to both "haves" and "have nots."

HOW PEOPLE CREATE
AND INNOVATE . . .

Technology—from the wheel to the silicon chip—has greatly bent the arc of history, yet anticipating when, where and how technology will alter economic, social, political, and security dynamics is a hard game. Some high impact predictions—such as cold fusion—have not become realities long after first promised, while other changes have unfolded faster and farther than experts even imagined. For example, clustered regularly interspaced short palindromic repeats (CRISPR) gene-manipulation developments quickly transformed the biological sciences.

Technological development and deployment will be fast where the tools and techniques become widely accessible or are combined to achieve new breakthroughs. Advanced Information Communications Technologies (ICT), for example, are transforming everything from automobiles to manufacturing, and some technology experts argue that advances in biotechnologies and nanomaterials will have a similar catalytic effect during the coming decades. Combining new technologies will provide the greatest surprises and most exciting new capabilities, with some spawning developments in relatively unrelated areas. For example, biotechnologies and new materials technologies may spawn changes in energy technologies.

Major Trends

Advanced Information Communications Technologies (ICT)—Including Artificial Intelligence (AI), Automation, and Robotics. Development and deployment of ICT can improve labor productivity, business processes, and governance practices that support economic growth and political responsiveness. As a critical enabler, ICT will influence nearly every new and existing industry. The emerging Internet of Things (IoT) and artificial intelligence (AI) will ensure that analytics and Big Data processing enable new business insights, transforming industries and driving advanced machine-to-machine communication. People's use of some technologies, such as augmented/virtual reality (AR/VR), will have a transformative effect on society—particularly media, entertainment, and daily life.

- New ICT is likely to have a significant effect on the **financial sector**. Digital currencies; "blockchain" technology for transactions; and the predictive analytics enabled by AI and Big Data will reshape financial services, potentially affecting systemic stability, security of critical financial infrastructures, and cyber vulnerabilities.

- New ICT is also transforming **transportation and energy** consumption in profound ways. Applications that combine data analytics, algorithms and real-time geophysical information, such as Uber and Waze, can optimize traffic patterns, improve energy consumption, and reduce urban smog. These augment the benefits of semi-automated and self-driving vehicles, which can reduce traffic density and accident rates while producing huge economic gains.

Potential Issues: Increased data reliance—the common thread among these emerging information technology technologies—will require establishing clear limits and standards on data ownership, data privacy and protection, cross-border data flows, and cyber security that could become increasingly important points of domestic and international policy conflict. Some nations' attempts to stem the rapid spread of ICT technologies and control the flow of information might minimize labor dislocations and volatility, but would limit economic and social gains. Countries less ethically bound might deploy technologies that others oppose or loosen regulations to attract high technology firms and to build R&D capability.

States, businesses, activist groups, religious organizations, and citizens are all trying to manage information to their advantage, fueling an intense and evolving messaging competition that threatens to extend its reach into deeper and more sensitive areas of human cognition and emotion. The early days of social media fostered hopes that more and freer communication would usher in a new era of democratization, but authoritarian states have proven adept at controlling access to information to maintain social control and free-flowing information in open countries has fueled social divisions and political polarization. Social media also enable the rapid spread of dangerous misinformation; individuals disposed to believe it are more likely to accept the misinformation uncritically and pass it on to other, potentially naïve individuals.

- ICT may give rise to new occupations in fact-checking, error-reporting, privacy protection, and legal action against harassment. Standards of truth-telling in social media are increasingly ambiguous and negotiable—at the limit, every truth claim becomes a piece of propaganda without special epistemological status.

- It has taken decades or even centuries for people to develop somewhat shared standards by which to judge the veracity of claims, but technology has reframed many issues in interpersonal relations and is creating a new set of challenges for governments that want or need to establish 'credibility' for foreign policy or bargaining purposes.

Artificial intelligence (or enhanced autonomous systems) and **robotics** have the potential to increase the pace of technological change beyond any past experience, and some experts worry that the increasing pace of technological displacement may be outpacing the ability of economies, societies, and individuals to adapt. Historically, technological change has initially diminished but then later increased employment and living standards by enabling the emergence of new industries and sectors that create more and better jobs than the ones displaced. However, the increased pace of change is straining regulatory and education systems' capacity to adapt, leaving societies struggling to find workers with relevant skills and training.

- Autonomous vehicles, which will eliminate the need for truck, taxi, and other mass-transit drivers, are likely to be the most dramatic near-term example of technology displacement.

- New technologies and the opportunities they create will require specialized expertise and complex management skills that may not be widely available to displaced workers. As a result, ICT advances may aggravate the economic divide between those whose skills are in demand with orphaned abilities.

- New technologies will also increase public awareness of the growing inequality in opportunity and wealth. To mitigate the adverse effects of this awareness, programmers seek to develop sympathetic virtual worlds often referred to as "empathy engines," but social critics are concerned that misuse of ICT has already led to civil and social disengagement and that new developments like AR/VR will do likewise.

Biotechnologies and Advanced Human Health. Biotechnology, recently catalyzed by CRISPR[1] developments, is developing even faster than ICT and promises to improve the global food supply and human health. The application of biotechnology—to include gene editing—to food production, especially for lesser used crops, could boost agricultural productivity, expand growing ranges, and increase crop resistance to severe weather and plant diseases. Advancements in gene editing could also lead to potential breakthroughs in human health by eliminating malaria carrying mosquitosor altering genetic codes to cure diseases like cystic fibrosis. Reducing food insecurity and improving peoples' health in the developing world will be especially critical as climate change alters agriculture production.

Genetic engineering and other biotechnologies will aid disease prevention by enabling better diagnostics and treatments, helping to overcome antimicrobial resistance, and halting the spread of disease through early detection of new or emerging pathogens with pandemic outbreak potential. The eradication of

---

[1] CRISPR is the acronym for "Clustered Regularly Interspaced Short Palindromic Repeats," which refers to short segments of DNA, the molecule that carries genetic instructions for all living organisms. A few years ago, the discovery was made that one can apply CRISPR with a set of enzymes that accelerate or catalyze chemical reactions in order to modify specific DNA sequences. This capability is revolutionizing biological research, accelerating the rate at which biotech applications are developed to address medical, health, industrial, environmental, and agricultural challenges, while also posing significant ethical and security questions.

some genetic-based diseases and breakthroughs in genetic manipulation of the immune system would improve quality of life and global health and reduce healthcare costs.

- Nanomaterials are increasingly used for medical-device coatings, diagnostic contrast agents, sensing components in nanoscale diagnostics, and advanced drug delivery. Digital medicine and other new medical procedures will likely contribute to improved global health. Improved tools to characterize, control, and manipulate the structure and function of living matter at the nanoscale could inspire biology-based approaches for other technology development and new fabrication techniques.

- Advances in computation and high-throughput sequencing and culturing technologies will enable understanding and manipulation of the human microbiome that could lead to cures for autoimmune diseases like diabetes, rheumatoid arthritis, muscular dystrophy, multiple sclerosis, fibromyalgia, and perhaps some cancers. Certain microorganisms also could supplement treatments for depression, bipolar disorder, and other stress-related psychiatric disorders.

- Optical monitoring of neurons and optogenetic modulation of neural activity promise to help neuroscientists observe brains in action, with the aim to prevent or curing diseases like dementia, Parkinsonism, and schizophrenia. The procedures could also yield insights into the construction of brain-like systems for artificial intelligence.

Potential Issues: Many parts of the world still consider genetically modified (GM) food unsafe or inadequately tested and will not accept its development or deployment, which will erode its potential to expand food supplies, lower prices, or increase the nutritional benefits in foods. Some genetic technologies, like "gene drives" that can potentially alter the genome of whole species, may be difficult to contain if deployed, and species-level genetic manipulation—to render mosquitos incapable of carrying malaria or other virulent pathogens, for example,—may have unforeseen consequences. Regardless of their potential benefits, such technologies will inevitably attract domestic and international political opposition.

- By 2035 rapid, "step" changes in human longevity may be plausible, but improving the length and quality of life could increase financial costs to societies, especially where aging populations already burden government budgets. These costs could be potentially offset, however, by healthcare savings from breakthroughs in treating genetic-based diseases and advanced genomic therapies.

- Debates over the morality and efficacy of intellectual property rights regimes for life-and-death medical issues and broader technological issues are likely to become more contentious internationally.

- Technological advances to treat diseases or enhance human capabilities, such as human augmentation, are likely to raise divisive political debates over access—assuming that most early techniques will only be available to higher income people. Altering fundamental human capabilities to enhanced mental capacity or physical strength could prompt strident domestic and international battles over the ethics and implications of altering the human gene pool

- Advances in biotechnology, including automation and the development of standardized tools and "programming languages"—for synthetic biology—will give individuals the potential to fabricate virulent micro-organisms for bioterrorist attacks.

Energy: Advances in energy technologies and concerns about climate change will set the stage for disruptive changes in energy use, including expanded use of wind, solar, wave, waste-streams, or nuclear fusion for electrical power generation and the use of improved mobile- and fixed-energy storage technologies. "Green" energy systems—competitive with fossil fuels—are already being deployed, and the future will see more carbon- and noncarbon-based technologies. Innovations—such as small-scale distributed energy systems that do not require connection to a power grid, can include renewable energy sources, and can integrate power for homes and transport/farm equipment—are likely to transform current models for energy production and distribution by freeing citizens from reliance on state-provided energy. Distributed, networked systems for energy generation and storage could improve the resilience of power systems and critical energy infrastructure systems to natural disasters, which would be particularly valuable in areas vulnerable to climate change and severe weather events.

Potential Issues: During the next 20 years, the combination of fossil fuels, nuclear, and renewable sources can meet global energy demand, however, the large–scale, commercially successful deployment of nonfossil fuel **energy technologies** is plausible. This would reduce the value of fossil resources reserves for energy-supplier states dependent on energy revenue to fund their budget and provide for their citizens, many may find it hard to reorient their economies. The commercial impact will also be substantial for oil and gas companies, some of the world's largest firms. Without major improvements in low-cost batteries or other forms of energy storage, new energy sources will continue to require substantial infrastructure, potentially slowing their adoption by poorer countries and limiting their mobility and flexibility.

Climate Intervention: Technologies to enable geoengineering—large-scale manipulation of the Earth's climate—are in their infancy and largely live only in computer models. Effective geoengineering would probably require a range of technologies. One set, called solar radiation management, aims to cool the planet by limiting the amount of solar radiation reaching the Earth, possibly by injecting aerosols into the stratosphere, chemically brightening marine clouds, or installing space-mirrors in orbit. A more expensive—and likely longer to deploy—group of technologies focuses on removing carbon dioxide from the atmosphere through direct air capture, ocean iron fertilization, and afforestation, which is the creation of forests in areas previously lacking tree cover. Carbon capture and sequestration, or CCS, is a known technology that seeks to capture carbon dioxide at the point of emission and store it underground. Afforestation also is a known technology, and scientists have conducted limited ocean iron fertilization tests.

Potential Issues: Increasing climate disruptions will boost interest in geoengineering interventions well before the scientific community understands the impact and unintended consequences of such efforts. With continued research, the advanced industrial countries might be able to develop the technology for solar radiation management quickly and at a cost far smaller than the damages anticipated from climate change. Without time to assess, however, the research probably cannot evaluate the trade-offs associated with the distribution of surface solar radiation, variations in temperature patterns, and changes in rainfall and storm systems—or determine the appropriate international regulation of global temperatures.

- A critical shortcoming of geoengineering strategies is that they do not counter all of the effects of an increase in atmospheric carbon dioxide, such as unabated ocean acidification. Carbon-capture technologies also have economic and physical limitations that suggest their implementation would be expensive, slow, and ultimately ineffective if carbon escapes back into the atmosphere.

- Atmospheric carbon-removal technologies will require significant research and a break-through in nonfossil fuel energy sources.

- The unilateral deployment of geoengineering technologies—even in small-scale tests—would almost certainly aggravate geopolitical tension. The intentional unilateral manipulation of the entire global ecosystem will likely alter how people think about their relations to the natural world and to each other.

Advanced Materials and Manufacturing: Materials and manufacturing developments are directly or indirectly the core enablers of most technology advancements. The uses of nanomaterials and metamaterials are likely to expand given the novel properties of these materials. More electronics, and health, energy, transportation, construction, and consumer goods already have these materials than most people realize. Nanomaterials' ability to exhibit enhanced mechanical and electrical characteristics, as well as unique optical properties, suggest they will outperform conventional materials in many applications and revolutionize most industrial sectors.

Other advanced synthetic materials innovation will alter commodity markets if they prove useful in manufacturing and their relative cost declines. High strength composites and plastics can replace conventional metals and create new markets. Developed countries will have an initial economic advantage in producing and using these materials, but they will become more widely accessible over time. Additive manufacturing, or 3D printing, is becoming increasingly accessible, and will be used for things not even conceived of today. 4D printing—the construction of objects that can change their form or function over time or in reaction to the environment—will also provide an economic edge to developers of commercially viable applications.

Potential Issues: Advanced materials could disrupt the economies of some commodities-dependent exporting countries, while providing a competitive edge to developed and developing countries that develop the capacity to produce and use the new materials. New materials, such as nanomaterials, are often developed faster than their health and environmental effects can be assessed, and public concerns about the possible unknown side effects will hold back commercialization of some. Regulations to protect against such effects could inhibit the use or spread of these materials, particularly in fields such as medicine and personal-care products.

Advances in manufacturing, particularly the development of 3D-printing from novelty to a routine part of precision production will influence global trade relations by increasing the role of local production at the expense of more-diffuse supply chains. As a result, global labor arbitrage will have diminishing returns, as the margin saved through locating manufacturing in distant factories shrinks relative to the amount saved by using an efficient factory in an area with a lower cost of transportation. Advanced manufacturing technologies will add to the considerable cost pressure on low-cost manufacturers and their employees, and the technologies could create a new worldwide divide, between those who have resources and benefit from new techniques and those who do not. This bifurcation might redraw the traditional north-south divisions into new divisions based upon resource and technology availability. 3D manufacturers, however, will still need access to raw materials, electricity and infrastructure, as well as the intellectual property rights to what they produce.

Space-based technologies. Heightened commercial interest in space and space-enabled services will improve efficiency and create new industrial applications with civil and military purposes. China is undertaking plans for a permanent manned presence in space similar to the International Space Station, and entrepreneurs plan for manned flights to Mars. Satellite systems—smaller, smarter, and cheaper than in the past—will bring new capabilities in remote sensing, communications, environmental monitoring, and global positioning. Low-altitude satellites could bring internet access to the two-thirds of the population that do not currently have online connectivity. Higher bandwidth will enable and increase availability of cloud-based services, telemedicine, and online education.

Potential Issues: Significant increases in data from remote sensors and spaced-based communications will challenge personal privacy and actors' abilities to hide their actions. Some states will seek to block or control data from space to protect their perceived core national interest. Geopolitical tension will erupt over the use of highly sensitive remote sensors—once reserved to only a few states—and open transmission of data.

Key Choices

Expert opinion remains divided on new technologies' impact on productivity and growth of measurable economic output. Some experts argue that the world is on the cusp of a technology-driven productivity revolution, while others believe new technologies will not have a much smaller impact than the second industrial revolution, from the 1870s to the early twentieth century. These skeptics argue the new digital technologies have had a minimal impact on transportation and energy so far and have failed to genuinely transform measured economic output for many decades.

Technology will unleash an array of positive and negative effects. As one expert wryly observes: "technology is the greatest cause for my optimism about the future...and my greatest cause for pessimism." History shows the impact of technology varies significantly depending on the user, the purpose, and the local context: geography, economics, infrastructure, culture, security and politics. Each technological advance bears a cost—sometimes in natural resources, sometimes in social cohesion, and sometimes in hard-to-predict ways.

The ability to set international standards and protocols, define ethical limits for research, and protect intellectual property rights will devolve to states with technical leadership. Actions taken in the near term to preserve technical leadership will be especially critical for technologies that improve human health, change biological systems, and expand information and automation systems. Multilateral engagement early in the development cycle will reduce the risk of international tension as deployment approaches, but may be insufficient to avoid clashes as states pursue technologies and regulatory frameworks that work to their benefit.

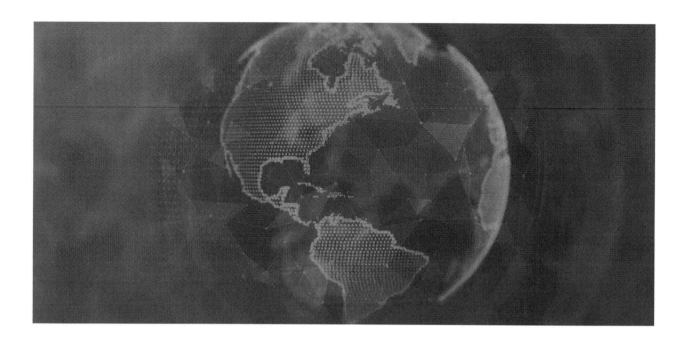

HOW PEOPLE PROSPER . . .

Global Economies Under Stress

New and unexpected tests during the coming decades are likely to increase global economic and financial stress, instability, and uncertainty. Global growth will be driven more by the largest developing economies, especially India and China, whose economies will expand faster than advanced economies even if their pace slows from current levels. Greater globalization is not certain, however, and is vulnerable to geopolitical tension. Even with strong global growth, skepticism about the benefits of further integration and support for protectionism is likely to increase if the wealthiest economies continue to struggle to return to "normal" growth and income inequality rises across a range of countries.

- **Key sources of economic growth flagging.** Two of the world's largest economies—China and the EU—are undergoing major transitions, with China the biggest wild card. Demographic trends that led to growing workforces—and helped boost both output and demand—in the post-World War II period have reversed for most of the world's major economies. Many developing countries appear reluctant to pursue difficult economic reforms that would boost their growth rates over the longer term.

- **Global economic integration in play.** Momentum for further global trade liberalization is weakening after 70 years of progress, and a growing popular consensus against free trade could trigger spasms of protectionist sentiment and escalate into a broader retreat from integration.

- **The productivity challenge.** The productivity gains of the past 150 years have owed much to technology advances. Use of new technologies in the economy is impossible to predict—and they may prove pivotal—but may fall short of the immense impact of electrification or the internal-combustion engine on economic output. New technologies will also introduce major social, political, and economic disruptions as they require different business processes and education to provide workers the skills needed to make use of them.

Major Trends

Sources of Economic Growth Flagging. The global economy faces serious stresses as two of the world's three largest economies—China and the EU—undergo significant transitions, with China the biggest wild card as it shifts from an investment-driven to consumer- and service-based economy. This historic transformation, which is still not on a clear trajectory eight years after the global financial crisis, reflects the waning of an era dominated by China's rural-to-urban migration and industrialization that drove the country's building boom, raised living standards, and produced capital surpluses that help fund borrowing worldwide. China's population will age rapidly because of decades of Beijing's "one-child policy," and its growth will be constrained by domestic overcapacity, high debt, and a vulnerable banking system. The rest of the world, particularly developing countries, will have to adjust to a China that is no longer a center of ever-growing commodity demand but is instead a more-balanced trading partner. Efforts by Beijing to forestall the inevitable difficulty and cost of this transition—as seen with Beijing's latest round of officially-encouraged bank lending to state-owned enterprises (SOEs) in early 2016—will prolong the transition period, widen imbalances, and increase losses from the unproductive, debt-financed investments made.

Managing the transition and minimizing dislocation will be crucial. A dramatic slowdown that causes ordinary citizens to doubt Beijing's ability to improve living standards could undermine social stability and the Chinese Communist Party's hold on power, leaving Beijing unable to rely solely on its authority—even with increasingly centralized power—and aggressive social control to maintain stability.

- **Beijing probably can cushion the transition** by boosting spending and encouraging state-owned banks to finance projects to minimize the impact on the broader economy as investment declines—particularly on the part of large, inefficient SOEs. Improving retirement and healthcare benefits could boost private consumption and help speed the process.

- During its transition, **China will be at risk of sharper, short-term economic shocks** that emanate from external or domestic causes, such as a financial crisis affecting China's largest trading partners or a domestic misstep that erodes public confidence.

A substantial disruption in China, the world's second-largest economy, could cause a global slump and erode growth prospects for many of the country's economic partners.

- **The end of China's urbanization-industrialization boom** and its decelerating economic growth have already undermined market assessments of the prospects for global demand for commodities, contributing to sagging prices and reducing revenue for states that depend on oil and mineral exports. Further slowdown would tighten the squeeze on Russia, Saudi Arabia, Iran and other key countries.

- **A successful transition would be a boon to the rest of the world.** Strong Chinese consumer demand would offer the promise of new customers for a broad range of goods, from low value-added goods from other developing economies to luxury goods and cutting-edge personal technology gadgets.

European economies also are in transition—with many still trying to regain positive momentum since the Great Recession of 2008—as they struggle to manage high debt levels that provide less room for fiscal stimulus to appease aging populations and restive middle classes, and ease sharp divisions over economic policy. Their evolution—or lack thereof—could affect momentum for economic liberalization and perceptions of Western global leadership.

- **Europe's economic future is tied to strains over its political future**, and uncertainty about the Britain's political and financial relations with the EU will probably dampen investment and growth through the medium term. In addition, the EU's ability to use free trade agreements to promote growth has been constrained by the precedent set when the European Commission decided national parliaments needed to approve the recently signed Comprehensive Economic Trade Agreement (CETA) with Canada—in response to German pressure and perceived EU overstepping expressed in the Brexit vote. Finally, the Schengen Agreement, which abolished passport and other border controls among the 26 EU states, is being undermined by controls set up by many member states trying to curb large-scale refugee cross-border movements.

- **Uneven growth rates in the EU** and debt challenges in Greece, Spain, and Italy are dividing the Union, and the EU's inability to craft monetary and fiscal policies that foster growth throughout its territory could be its undoing. The rise of nativist and antiglobalization voices in the EU undermines global support for free trade and economic liberalism.

The world will also closely watch to see if US growth rebounds to historically more-typical levels, to confirm or repudiate the viability of US economic policies. Many countries appear more eager than a decade ago for US leadership on vexing economic and security challenges, but most are prepared to hedge their bets if they doubt Washington's will or capacity to focus externally.

- Expectations have faded of strong bipartisan support to propel the Trans-Pacific Partnership and the Transatlantic Trade and Investment Partnership into being.

Developing countries lack the capacity to "fill the gap" in global growth amid the major economies' weakness. Most have taken steps to integrate into the global economy, but many are reluctant during a period of economic and political uncertainty to take harder—but necessary—steps to boost growth by reducing the role of state-owned enterprises, cutting back consumer subsidies that distort markets, implementing legal and governance reforms to encourage foreign investment, and liberalizing labor markets, including mitigating high levels of gender inequality.

- **India probably has the greatest potential** to boost global growth because of its size and the success of its technology sector, but it would have to improve its energy, transportation and manufacturing infrastructure to sustain high rates of growth. Infrastructure has improved in some locales but not in wide swaths of the country. Unlike China, India will benefit from 10 million new working-age residents per year during the coming decades, yet harnessing such a massive labor pool increase in ways that increase productivity and boost output has proven difficult. The global success of India's technology sector, in contrast with its lackluster manufacturing success, underscores the imbalances between the country's relatively strong higher education and its poor basic education, which would need to be improved to generate higher employment.

- **Optimism about Africa's growth potential** has largely tracked commodity price swings in recent years, but it has been muted by uncertainty over generational political transitions in several countries and its cities' ability to absorb the continent's massive population surge. Demographers forecast that Africa will provide most of the growth in the world's working-age (15-64) population over the next two decades, which could either be an economic boon or a cause of major instability if governments cannot create economies that can harness the productive potential of these mostly urban job-seekers.

Political leaders and publics throughout the developing world appear worried about the reliability of any model for stable development, although public confidence in their countries' prospects is stronger than in the richer countries. The best path for them to follow to that prosperity is unclear for many. In this environment, countries seem to know they must engage with the global economy to reap benefits, but they fear disruptive forces and shocks will make it harder to gain stability and prosperity.

- Financial crises, an increased sense of vulnerability among the middle class, growing inequality, and political polarization have tarnished the Western model in the eyes of some.

- Beijing's state-capitalist approach is also showing serious signs of strain as China's growth slows, its financial and housing markets appear fragile, inefficient state enterprises sag under heavy debt, pollution worsens, and Communist Party ideology loses traction with the public.

The Challenge of Financial Adaptation

The financial sector has been one of the most adaptive over the years in creating new mechanisms to manage evolving markets, but even these networks are showing key limitations. In particular, the "non-system" patchwork of accepted practices, markets, and regulations around global currencies has empowered governments to use monetary and exchange rate policies as tools of global economic competition—even as the WTO prohibits efforts to affect competitiveness in trade. This tension is currently barely contained within the G-20 framework and could explode or give way to a new push for governance around currency relations.

Noteworthy successes in financial cooperation include establishment of the Basel Committee on Banking Supervision 40 years ago to help Central Bankers from more than 20 countries coordinate standards and communication. The Financial Action Task Force combat money laundering and the Global Forum on Transparency and Exchange of Information tackles tax evasion, although gains are continually challenged by new illicit tactics in an escalating "arms race."

However, differences among major power and the declining ability of the United States to forge consensus may undermine attempts by regulatory institutions to secure agreements on—and ensure implementation of—emerging financial sector challenges, potentially setting the stage for a more fragmentary financial landscape.

Global Economic Integration at Risk. The historic, steady increase in economic integration during the past several decades is meeting with greater resistance, with a growing number of political leaders and movements pushing back against free trade and more open labor markets. After seven decades of major global and regional trade deals, most countries involved already have low barriers to trade in nonagricultural goods, and there is **little remaining room for major gains** in narrowly defined trade liberalization. There is limited appetite for universal WTO global deals in agriculture and services trade, where domestic political resistance to liberalization is strongest in most countries. As a result, contemporary trade negotiations have focused on ancillary issues, especially investment policy, and countries have looked to hybrid agreements—more-comprehensive regional "coalitions of the willing," with the TPP and TTIP as prime examples.

- Financial market volatility, the erosion of the middle class, and greater awareness of inequality **feed the view that trade liberalization has gone too far.** Given that some of the loudest criticism of free trade comes from within the United States—a longstanding leader in pushing for more-open markets—other countries will be watching US leaders closely for signs of an economic retrenchment. Trade skepticism in the United States threatens an agricultural deal, while sharp trans-Atlantic differences will be hard to reconcile on a range of regulatory issues on services.

- The WTO sees **the risk of "creeping protectionism"** in some countries' steps to restrict trade and opposition to new free trade agreements such as the TPP. More-restrictive regulations or more-overt efforts to use currency policy to boost export-competitiveness could create a dangerous competitive cycle, with countries not wanting to be the last to counter such moves and leave their economies vulnerable.

The Productivity Challenge. With global productivity gains and workforce growth flattening in the largest economies, finding new ways to boost productivity will become more important—and more difficult to maintain—during the coming decades. The productivity challenge will be especially acute during a period when working-age population growth will slow in the United State and shrink in Europe, China, Japan and Russia, potentially eroding economic output. The same age cohort will be grow significantly in developing regions of Africa and South Asia, but leaders there will be hard-pressed to rapidly scale up their economies.

- **Technology has been a crucial driver of productivity gains,** and a source of anxiety for workers who perceive they are at risk of being displaced. Continued technological advances will be vital to maintaining economic growth for countries facing flat or shrinking workforces, but future technology-driven productivity gains in advanced countries may be modest or take longer to realize. Productivity in these economies has sagged or stagnated during the past several decades, even with major infusions of new information technology, possibly because the infusions have most affected activities done at no, or only indirect, cost to users or have helped eliminate for-cost business, such as social media, other on-line activities, gaming, and personal communications. However, poorer countries, where modern ICT is less ubiquitous, are likely to enjoy substantial productivity gains as hitherto underserved residents gain communication access.

- **Productivity in all countries could also be increased** through a broad range of more fundamental steps, such as improving education and training, infrastructure, research and development, and regulations and management practices, but these will require funding, expertise, and lead-time that may prove difficult for many developing—and even developed—countries to marshal.

Technology's Impact on Jobs: Fears Despite a Positive History

Recent ominous forecasts about the potential for new robotic technology to eliminate large numbers of jobs have echoed writings of economists and the anxieties of at-risk workers since industrialization began in the 19th Century. One study projects that automation and artificial intelligence could replace 45 percent of the activities people are now paid to perform, including relatively high-paid workers like financial managers, physicians and senior executives. The rate of advances may lead to short-term dislocations in some sectors, but fears of widespread displacement have proven unfounded. Nonetheless, the fears may lead some government leaders and publics to call for slowing the use of new technology to protect jobs, potentially slowing gains.

Key Choices

Economic Integration. Governments probably will be tempted to revert to protectionist measures as real, perceived, or anticipated challenges to their economies stir public fear and uncertainty. Holding the line on economic integration almost certainly will become politically difficult, and taking new steps to open and reform markets will take even greater courage. Hard choices will center on trying to forge policies that help retrain and sustain people displaced by market disruptions, particularly as tight budgets and rising debt limit fiscal options.

Technology. How countries manage the commercialization of new technology will bear directly on their economic success and social stability. Major technological breakthroughs will give companies significant leverage in seeking favorable business conditions in countries, and governments (and consumers) will have to decide how quickly they adopt new technology and how they cope with the repercussions.

Labor Force Participation. For most countries, the greatest opportunity for boosting economic output will be increasing the share of residents participating in the workforce—particularly for societies that have low female employment and large numbers of rural citizens not engaged in the formal economy. Longstanding cultural norms are likely to complicate moves to tap into an increasingly important talent pool by stirring social tension, but rising global economic competition will raise the cost of inaction. Graying developed countries could also make gains by boosting participation rates of able-bodied older workers as fixed retirement ages and increasing life expectancies mean longer nonworking lives for typical workers, but curtailing pension benefits to workers will face political opposition, even if it helps ease fiscal pressures.

HOW PEOPLE THINK . . .

Ideas and identities define who we are, reflecting individual beliefs about oneself and one's role in the world. Beliefs provide moral guidance and a lens through which to understand and navigate the future. They define who belongs to a community, group, society, state, culture, and civilization—and, critically, who does not. Although resilient, ideas and identities are not static. Discrete ideas and identities interact with one another—challenging or reinforcing beliefs about which values matter most and how people should be treated. Both are also influenced by economic, political, social, technological, and other developments. Expanding Internet access is likely to increase the salience of global and transnational identities and ideologies—such as religion or ethnic identities in some quarters, as well as secularism and liberalism in others.

People react more strongly to negative ideas than to positive. Although life expectancy, livelihoods, security, and overall health and wellbeing have improved for most people around the world during the past few decades, most people remain gloomy about the future. Across the globe a sense of alienation and injustice is fostered, based on real and perceived inequalities, lack of opportunities, and discrimination. Generations of economists have noted the plusses and minuses of technological and economic developments that have changed the way people work. Social theorists have highlighted the sense of worth and identity most people derive from work, and the lack of satisfaction—dating to Karl Marx's "alienation," if not earlier—that can result when people feel insufficiently engaged by their work.

- Recognizing that most people need to feel good about their production may help explain growing signs of rejection of the "globalized" economy, facilitated by improved connectivity that fosters on-line communities and constituencies.

- Even with greater access to more material benefits and technological entertainment and distractions, people may experience a loss of meaning and crave ideas that provide them with a sense of worth. As automation proceeds, one might expect such issues to come to fore in some advanced industrial societies.

- Everywhere, information and communication technology enables people to connect and develop communities with whom they can share frustrations and anxiety. However, these same technologies can foster polarization and lower the organizational costs of recruitment and collective action.

It is not clear that economic ideologies, such as socialism and neoliberalism, which had dominated much of the 20th Century until challenged by the collapse of communism and the 2008 financial crisis, will remain relevant in a world in which both low-growth and high levels of inequality dominate political agendas. Other forms of political thought remain viable alternatives —in particular, nationalism, political liberalism, and religiously-based political thought.

Looking forward, deepening connectivity and the increasing speed of communication will cause ideas and identities to evolve more quickly. Diasporas will play an increasing role in the shaping of ideas. Extreme views will more easily find likeminded followers. Especially as Internet access expands in the developing world, shared experiences and identities will likely increase the salience of global and transnational bonds—such as religion or ethnic identities in some quarters, as well as secularism and liberalism in others.

Old ideas and identities will continue to prove resilient. Nationalism will be prominent in those parts of the world where states or national communities seek to shore up their claims to power in specific geographies—especially as alternative ideas and identities become accessible through Internet connectivity and pose threats to national interests. Such dynamics will play directly into the geopolitical competition between Western liberalism and authoritarian nationalism in China and Russia. Conversely, nativism and populism will also rise in the West in response to mass immigration, growing economic inequality, and declining middle-class standards of living.

- Technology, the expansion of women's participation in economic and political life, environmental changes, urbanization, migration, and disagreements over the interpretation of religious and other cultural norms will shape each of these trends in the next 20 years. Whether these drivers encourage exclusive or inclusive attitudes and actions is a key uncertainty.

Major Trends

Transnational Identities Will Become More Powerful. During the next 20 years, information and ideas will move easily across borders. Advances in information technologies—whether in the 15ᵗʰ century with the printing press and Gutenberg Bible, or in 1989 with the invention of the World Wide Web— usually facilitate the spread of religious ideas, in part because religions transcend borders and state authority. Migration and displacement has had similar effects. Religion has long proven a particularly potent source of tension, and we anticipate that frictions within and between religious groups and between religious and secular communities will increase in many parts of the world. The spread of information, propagation of ideas, and awareness of conflicting religious beliefs and interpretations contributed in important ways to the religious wars of the 16ᵗʰ and 17ᵗʰ century and to Islamic and other religiously claimed terrorism of today. The widespread accessibility of information technologies also provides a platform for extreme voices to find followers, support, and sympathizers in cyber space. Such dynamics are likely to intensify as Internet access deepens in the developing world and as new information technologies like Virtual Reality allow for more seemingly intense and personal experiences and interactions across time and space.

The role of religions. More than 80 percent of the world is religiously affiliated and high fertility rates in the developing world are increasing that proportion, according to the Pew research center. As some religious groups push more actively for governments to incorporate religion and its values into law and norms, social and political tension is likely to flare, whether the religious represent the majority or an active minority. These developments will also incite fears among secular and religious minorities in these countries, potentially fueling exit or rebellion. Many communities with growing religious affiliation—including in the Middle East and Africa—will expect their governments to incorporate religion and its principles into legislation and government policies. They often see secularism and disaffiliation as Western ideas that reject God and the value of faith and undermine social coherence.

- New avenues of religious influence will become geopolitically consequential in areas where traditional secular intermediary organizations—such as trade unions—weaken and other ideological options, such as liberalism, prove unsatisfactory as substitutes. Many religious organizations—including Catholic Relief Services, Compassion International, and World Vision— are already essential to the delivery of basic public services, humanitarian aid and development.

- The Catholic Church, with 1.25 billion followers, provides global leadership on issues ranging from peace and conflict to environmental stewardship. Recently, the Church has addressed issues as diffuse as non-fetal stem cell research and nutrition and food security. However, established religious organizations—similar to public institutions—will be increasingly scrutinized given the modern communications environment.

- Competition within and between religious groups is likely to intensify over defining and controlling the faith—much as battles to control political parties have become more personalized and divisive. In these disputes, radical minority religious activists will often push out moderate voices because dramatic action and anger tend to generate attention and mobilize dissatisfaction better than calls for compromise. Charismatic and extremist leaders can gain disruptive capabilities, although violent and extremist groups that lack technocratic skill will struggle to provide governance. Most religious people will not actively support extremism, but passive support or implicit acceptance of extremists will worsen tension between groups, and violent leaders will be acknowledged as actors on the world stage. Religious divisions will be amplified when regional rivals or other outside patrons support competing sides. Examples include Iran's support for Alawites in Syria and Sunni regimes such as Qatar, Saudi Arabia, and Turkey backing their coreligionists.

The role of secularism. One possible response to intensifying religious violence could be a turn toward secularism or away from religious affiliation in general. Worldwide, those identifying themselves as religiously "unaffiliated" represent the third-largest grouping after Christians and Muslims, and polls suggest that the number of people not affiliated with religion, although not the percentage, is likely to grow worldwide—especially in the Asia-Pacific, Europe and North America.

- Even states with high levels of integration between religious and government structures could see moderate growth in disaffiliation and secular ideas. Opinion polls show a rise in Saudi Arabian citizens who identified as atheists. Tunisia's ruling Ennahda party recently announced its will identify as Muslim Democrats rather than Islamist, citing in part a sensitivity to the connotations of the latter term.

Geopolitical Competition Will Take a Stronger Ideological Turn. *Liberalism is likely to remain the benchmark model for economies and politics over the coming decades, but it will face stronger competition and demands from publics to address its shortfalls.* Western ideals of individual freedom and democratic action will exert enormous global influence, judging by the aspirations of migrants and dissidents worldwide who are drawn to these principles. Many developing countries will strive for modernization more or less along Western lines, but the allure of liberalism has taken some strong hits over the years as political polarization, financial volatility, and economic inequality in western countries have stoked populism and caused doubts about the price of political and economic openness. Governments having trouble meeting the needs of their citizens will be strongly tempted to turn to nationalism or nativism to transfer blame to external enemies and distract from problems at home, while publics fearful of loss of jobs to immigrants or economic hardship, are likely to be increasingly receptive to more exclusive ideologies and identities.

- The longstanding effects of the crushing of the Arab Spring uprisings include the de-legitimization of the institutions and norms of democracy and degradation of organized institutions for channeling political opposition. Some disenchanted and traumatized former protesters, many of whom believe the West controls world events and is responsible for their plight, will look for alternatives to the liberal ideals they once supported.

- Meanwhile, China's recent economic success and the emergence of other non-Western powers will encourage some countries to consider alternatives to the Western liberal model to achieve their goals of a strong, stable, and modern society, even though China's harsh repression, shocking levels of pollution, and rising public frustration have long been known. Evidence that China's government retains control of the country's economy and can maintain growth—particularly as Beijing attempts a difficult economic rebalancing—will bolster its appeal as a model.

- Russia's uptick in nationalism focuses on ethnic, religious, and linguistic bonds instead of state citizenship, manifested by its invasion of parts of Ukraine, branding of opposition as 'foreign agents,' and legislation banning "homosexual propaganda." Some regional experts attribute these actions to President Putin's efforts to create a common sense of purpose in response to loss of power on the world stage and domestic struggles. Putin lauds Russian culture as the last bulwark of conservative Christian values against European decadence, saying Russia, with its great history, literature, and culture, will resist the tide of multiculturalism. Russian nationalist aggression is likely to increase under Putin, which will provoke sometimes violent nationalist responses among its neighbors—like in Ukraine and Georgia—and spark feelings of disenfranchisement among ethnic minorities.

Exclusionary Ideas and Identities in Democracies Threaten Liberalism. Without a return to secure and more-evenly-distributed living standards, economic and social pressures are likely to fuel nativism and populism in the West, risking a narrowing of political communities and exclusionary policies. A weakening of the rule of law, political tolerance, and political freedoms in the United States and Western Europe—the traditional strongholds of democracy—could delegitimize democratic ideas around the world. Just as the world is watching the United States and Europe grapple with divisive politics and often uncivil rhetoric in debates over immigration, racial justice, refugees, and the merits of globalization, the world will look to see how India tames its Hindu nationalist impulses, and how Israel balances its ultra-orthodox extremes. Such dynamics could result in democratic backsliding—as in Hungary and Poland—or a move toward authoritarianism, like in Turkey. Without a strong response from other stable democracies, this trend is likely to accelerate.

- Anti-immigrant and xenophobic politics among Western democracies will challenge established parties and complicate their ability to maintain popular appeal and implement inclusive policies that meet the needs of their increasingly diverse populations. The national and international visibility of divisive populist parties and social movements—and the tendencies of incumbent governments to seek to preempt them with exclusionary policies—could increasingly undermine the global prestige of the Western democracies and their credibility in standing up for liberal values.

- Racial tension is also likely to play a large role in politics in both developed and developing countries. With the emergence of information and communication technologies, structural disparities in protection for different groups are becoming more apparent, and perceived violence perpetuated by the state and law enforcement against minority groups is especially likely to incite protest and tension.

Key Choices

Developments in technology, growing gender equality, and urbanization—each manifestations of modernity—will shape the future of family, religion, secularism, nationalism, and especially liberalism. Each of these poses moral, legal, social, and political challenges that are likely to be navigated according to existing cultural norms that vary by country. Among the most consequential choices will be how diverse belief communities, societies, and states choose to deal with technology's potential to manipulate human biology and the environment. This is likely to generate intense disagreement over what is morally acceptable, and fundamentally challenge traditional definitions of what defines human beings, human groups, and definitions of "self" and "other." Developments in technology that enable more people to voice opinions will also serve to highlight differences over societal notions of gender inclusion, urbanization, and changing political participation.

Technology and Life. How people think about the very nature of life and how people love and hate is likely to be challenged by major technological advances in understanding and efforts to manipulate human anatomy, which will spark strong divisions between people, country and regions. These developments will spur debates within and between belief communities, potentially leading to even starker distinctions between the religious and secular worlds. Conflicting pressures on balancing privacy and security interests will have far-reaching consequences for governance, economic competitiveness, and social cohesion. Key choices in technology will become increasingly political and ideological.

- **Human enhancements.** Technological advances in communications, biology, cognitive science, and pharmacology will increasingly blur the line between natural and enhanced human performance for even basic functions such as memory, vision, hearing, attention, and strength. Many people probably will embrace such technical enhancements as critical to getting ahead in an increasingly competitive world, but some are likely to resist on moral or ethical grounds—because they are "unnatural," or not available to the poor. Differential access to such technologies will reinforce the divide between haves and have-nots.

- **Genetic engineering.** Health experts forecast that biotechnology research could yield breakthroughs against some cancers and other diseases, but expensive and limited early iterations of such methods probably would spark heated disagreements on access to healthcare if the techniques mean the difference between life and death. Biotechnology is also propelling a broader trend toward personalized medicine, with customized approaches keyed to an individual's biological and genetic makeup that hold high promise in transforming diagnosis, intervention, and prevention. Again, the ability of the wealthy to harness these technologies for elective procedures will contrast starkly with the developing world's struggle to control diseases that already have known cures. Finally, advances in genome manipulation may create the potential for "designer babies," human embryos that reflect a set of pre-selected characteristics based on social preferences—which will call attention to ideas about race and what constitutes an 'ideal' person.

- **End-of-life decisions.** As lifespans lengthen, millions more people worldwide will reach 80, 90, or even 100 years of age and beyond. In the United States, a significant portion of healthcare spending occurs in the last six months of life. In developing and emerging economies alike, caring for so many senior citizens could overwhelm personal and public budgets and health systems with current retirement ages and benefits.

  - Biotechnologies that extend life may also be made available to enhance the comfort of living, reduce pain, and extend basic human functions in ways that promote individual independence and reduce caregiver burdens. Housing and public facilities will be designed to incorporate technologies that reduce the risk of falls and facilitate daily tasks for the elderly. Trends that encourage home care create more options for elderly who choose die at home rather than in a hospital.

  - The demand for capabilities to improve humane choices in confronting death and dying will grow worldwide, including advances in hospice care that mitigates the pain and suffering of the terminally ill and provides psychological support to reduce fear and enable dying with dignity.

- **Privacy and security.** As monitoring and sensing devices become more affordable, ubiquitous and integrated, the line between what is technically possible and what is legally and socially acceptable will be tested. Tools that determine identity and location could radically alter how work and criminal behavior is tracked, or algorithms that highlight patterns of behavior could be used to "predict" individuals' health issues, criminal activity, educational potential, or job aptitude.

  - The widespread use of drones in civilian life will also alter the possibilities for privacy and could potentially be harnessed by criminal groups, undermining a sense of security. Such technologies can also be used to stifle freedoms in authoritarian states.

  - Global governance of common-pool resources such as public health, water, food and other key resources will inevitably challenge current ideas of privacy, control and power.

- **Political participation.** Social media has radically lowered the transaction costs of mobilizing populations, but some social scientists worry that virtual activism will replace more concrete political participation—including voting—diluting the quality of the political process. Worse, some worry that that new technologies fracture and polarize populations; social media, in particular, typically passes information and ideas through narrow, existing networks to members who self-select, rather than traditional forms of media, which project ideas to a broader audience. This selective dissemination and receipt of information contributes to reinforcement and confirmation bias, segregation, and polarization.

Education. Education will be one of the most determinative factors of success for countries and individuals because it determines options for occupations, wages, innovation, and development. Rapid advances in science, technology, engineering, and mathematics, fields in which a large portion of future jobs will reside, require continuous maintenance of skills. As millions of youth seek education to match employment opportunities—and millions of adults look for continuing education and career training in rapidly evolving fields—alternative models are likely to emerge from a variety of sources. Large-scale improvements in education access for women and girls will be determinative in improving women's rights and changing expectations for gender roles.

- Many states provide basic education to their citizens, but with politically determined—or censored—curricula. Some regimes use public schools as a way to spread progovernment propaganda and instill a sense of patriotism. Russia recently expanded efforts to spread pro-Moscow sentiment by building Russian language and cultural centers on campuses of elite universities in the United Kingdom.

- Companies have an interest in maintaining a highly skilled and current workforce to keep pace with changing technology, and employers seeking to be competitive will include education in benefits packages or require continued education as a condition for employment. The role of technology in the education process itself will also rise. Massive Open Online Classes (MOOCs) are increasingly being used by elite universities and influential companies to train students and employees on a variety of subjects, and AI technologies will make individually customized learning programs routine.

Gender. Demographic and economic forces are likely to make women's roles and opportunities a more salient and contentious issue in nearly all countries. Women will increasingly be included in formal work sectors, public and private leadership, and security planning. Gender roles and expectations will increasingly be recognized as crucial to economic and security planning. The trend toward greater equality will continue—if only for economic productivity—but progress will be slow and accompanied by domestic violence and backsliding in some areas where women's empowerment is not yet socialized. Some communities will probably revert to patriarchal value structures in the face of insecurity.

- In the West, businesses are likely to moderately narrow pay and opportunity gaps for women to overcome slowing productivity through inclusion. Increased visibility of women participating in social, governmental, and economic institutions around the world will provide models for communities where women are not as visible outside traditional gender roles.

- Increased support for reconciling productive work with reproductive work will open new opportunities for women, as will the movement towards recognizing unpaid family caregiving as a significant labor contribution to society. These developments will both drive and be driven by public policy and institutions.

- Improved technology and infrastructure will ease the daily burdens associated with traditional women's roles, freeing women for formal sector work and education. However, climate change and associated challenges such as epidemics will affect women profoundly, given their traditional responsibilities for family care work, as would cuts by fiscally pressed governments to social safety-net programs that force elderly or other vulnerable groups to rely on family for support. States' implementation of welfare programs and health care will have profound consequences for women's participation in labor markets.

- Religious or cultural norms limiting the role of women in the economy are likely to come under pressure—from women seeking greater opportunities for social advancement and the economic need to expand the labor pool to boost productivity. Issues of family and personal-status law—which directly affect relations between men and women—are likely to be social flashpoints.

Urbanization. First-generation city dwellers tend to be more religious than the broader population, turning to faith communities for support in the absence of extended family. This is a dynamic that for Africa and Asia—the most rapidly urbanizing parts of the world—will represent both an opportunity for deepening organized religion and a potential source of religious tension. Cities also tend to be more diverse, bringing people into contact with one another across cultural lines, potentially becoming a source of conflict. Rapid city growth will strain infrastructure to support more people, while growing inequality and greater awareness of it within the confines of a city setting are likely to increase social frictions as well.

- In and around growing cities, religious groups are likely to provide support by "taking care of their own" during times of economic volatility and weak governance, which could alleviate some public needs, but could raise tension with governments and other citizens over authorities and norms. If religious groups demonstrate they are more effective than the state in meeting basic social needs and providing a sense of identity, justice and moral guidance, their membership and influence are likely to grow—sowing unease and potential resistance by those outside the group. In religiously plural societies such as Lebanon, this could become a source of further conflict.

- Urbanization will mix populations together, sharpening competition for jobs and resources and potentially increasing xenophobia against new groups in the short term—but typically promoting integration and acceptance in the long term. Cities can create peculiar combinations of tolerance and intolerance for diversity. Commingling groups can improve familiarity and tolerance, but working across cultural lines also has the potential to change perceptions of liberalism, including acceptance of human rights norms. Academic literature suggests migration can transfer norms on human rights issues when people move to a society with increased attention to human rights—leading those people to view standards in their home country as unacceptable. These views on what is acceptable behavior are often transferred back home even if migrants do not physically return.

- Rapid urbanization also will probably spur political mobilization by boosting resentment for the status quo in cities and spawning new social and political movements, as they long have done.

- Meanwhile, governments will reassess how to deal with minority demands for more rights and influence if those groups can raise the political costs of excluding them, or if political parties need to appeal across cultural lines for support. In countries with small minorities, ruling governments have had little incentive to cater to groups outside their core constituency. Governments also may be tempted to direct ire toward minorities to whip up their base. However, as minority groups grow or become more skilled at exerting influence—through political, social, economic, or violent means—government leaders will find it more difficult to calibrate the line between resisting or accommodating minority demands.

How leaders and media portray diversity and adapt policies to incorporate changing populations will greatly influence how inclusive or exclusive identities will become during the next 20 years. Influential groups, including the young and religious organizations, have the potential to shape the wider population. According to polls and studies, younger populations tend to be more exposed to diverse groups and think diversity is natural, including connectivity and ties to people who are not geographically close. Generations growing into maturity and political activity during the next 20 years are likely to redefine definitions of communities.

- Studies have shown that public perceptions and media portrayal of violence has a greater influence on fear than the actual risk or threat. Because of highly publicized terrorist attacks in places that have not recently seen violent conflict, international discrimination against Muslims and others from the Middle East and North Africa—who are largely perceived to be Muslim, whether they are or not—will continue in most non-Muslim majority countries.

- A fundamental aspect of a culture is its view of the proper relationship between men and women; this issue is likely to catalyze social conflict when groups with differing views on women's status are combined.

Competing silos of information and perspectives of truth and fact among proliferating influential actors are poised to complicate governments' ability to generate compromise. A combination of factors, including growing distrust of formal institutions and the proliferation and polarization of media outlets, are driving some academics and political observers to describe the current era as one of 'post-truth" or "post-factual" politics. This results in part from the growing number of individuals and agencies providing information to consumers. Whether this atmosphere continues, or people and political groups adjust to growing flows of communication and trend back toward more-balanced perspectives, will be crucial in coming years.

- As a result of this "post-factual" trend, individuals appear more likely to base their political views more on feelings than on fact and to seek out information that supports their opinions. Conflicting information actually reinforces views that the new information is from a biased or hostile source and further polarizes groups.

- To interpret the deluge of details, people turn to leaders who think like they do and trust them to interpret the 'truth.' According to the most recent Edelman Trust Barometer survey, a sizeable trust gap is widening between college-educated consumers of news and the mass population; the survey showed respondents are increasingly reliant on a "person like yourself," and that these like-minded people are more trusted than CEOs or government officials.

- A Pew study from 2014 showed that the highest percentage of trust for any single news agency among US persons polled was only 54 percent. Instead, individuals gravitate to social media to obtain news and to respond to events.

HOW PEOPLE GOVERN . . .

Governments will face increasing difficulties in providing security and prosperity, which prompt questions on whether historical bargains negotiated between society and their government will hold. This uncertainty and the broad decline in trust in government could make it hard for established systems to meet public expectations and deal with problems that transcend national boundaries.

- Trust in government during the past decade varies among countries but has generally declined. In a 2015 OECD study using Gallup polling, confidence in national governments across all OECD countries declined 3.3 percentage points, from 45.2 to 41.8 percent during 2007-2014; with declines of more than 25 percentage points in Slovenia, Finland, and Spain—but increases of more than 20 points in Germany, Israel, and Iceland. According to a Gallup Poll survey released in September 2016, only 42 percent of Americans have a "great deal" or "fair amount" of trust in the country's political leaders—a drop of about 20 points since 2004 and a new low for Gallup trends.

- These dynamics are shaping government structures that have endured since World War II. Democracy is under stress in many parts of the world, with some academics pointing to a possible decline in support. While the number of democracies has remained stable during the past 10 years, global migration and economic stagnation—along with technology that empowers individuals as well as extremist groups—has weakened some previously stable democracies, such as Hungary and Poland. Many states are finding liberal and democratic institutions at odds with their desire to sustain control, and academics argue that several large, illiberal democracies will be unstable and face significant internal challenges. There are signs of polarization and decay even in long-established liberal democracies like the United Kingdom and the United States.

- For their part, China and Russia have shown they can use new technologies to double down on their control of opposition expressions and have used new technologies to exercise more sophisticated forms of repression as well. Russia has increasingly sought to undermine democracy, liberalism, and human rights through intensive propaganda and making common cause with other authoritarian regimes. In 2015, the Kremlin passed a law prohibiting the work of 'undesirable' foreign organizations, which is widely seen as a tool for cracking down on dissent.

Major Trends

Economic Change and Perceptions of Injustice Prompt Questions About Capacity. Slower rates and shifting sources of economic growth, increasing income inequality, and the perception of "losing out" to global competition will spark public demands to improve and protect living standards. This frustration with "globalization" is likely to build, as many of the factors causing wage growth to slow are also making it harder for governments to provide broad-based prosperity, such as intensifying competition among low-cost producers of low value-added manufactures, the emergence of technologies that disrupt and transform industries and sectors vital to many countries' economies, and swings in global financial and commodity markets.

- Absent different policy choices, this volatility is likely to widen inequality between winners and losers—individual workers and countries alike—by contributing to a "winner take all" dynamic in many sectors, and further sharpen clashes over the role of the state in ensuring living standards and promoting prosperity. Some governments investing in human capital and infrastructure to promote growth may find they are forced to impose fiscal austerity measures because they are saddled with additional debt until the initiatives bear fruit.

- Economic instability will erode governments' ability to deliver on promises of social welfare. In the developed world—where populations are expected to age and life expectancies will increase—we can anticipate a rise in health care costs while business profits and tax revenues shrink and government debt levels remain high. Public anger over the government's inability to protect constituents' interests probably will be aggravated as wealth, technology and social networks enable affluent citizens to opt out of many public goods, such as education and health care, undermining a sense of shared fortunes.

- Slower rates of economic growth and falling commodity prices are hitting middle classes that only recently emerged from poverty in Asia and Latin America. The global forces that enabled their prosperity during the past several decades are now fueling their anxieties by threatening to undo recent gains, as firms continue to pursue cheaper labor and greater use of automation, disrupting industries and labor markets in the affected countries. The result is a public that believes government is not serving their needs, which has contributed to high-profile mass protests in recent years in countries with newly expanded middle classes, such as Brazil and Turkey.

Similarly, perceptions of injustice stemming from mismanagement and sclerotic bureaucracies will fuel societies' search for alternatives to the status quo. Corruption and impunity remain predominant concerns across the world; according to Transparency International, 68 percent of countries worldwide—including some G20 states—have serious corruption problems. Corruption is particularly acute in some of the demographically youthful states that are poised to face the greatest employment challenges. Transparency International's Middle East and North Africa Corruption Survey found that 50 million adults in that region have to pay bribes to receive basic services. In these surveys, public officials and politicians are perceived as far more corrupt than religious leaders, potentially contributing to the tension between governments and religious groups that offer competing services and support.

- The view that established political actors fail to coordinate to resolve political and social concerns sharpens the perception that the existing forms of governance are inadequate. Academic studies suggest this coordination failure can aggravate persistent governance challenges. A review of local institutions in Afghanistan showed that a multiplicity of institutions with no clear hierarchy fueled competition among elites and hampered the quality of governance.

This flagging capacity to carry out even basic governance functions and the inability to develop mutually constructive relations with society threaten to add to the world's group of fragile states. In a 2013 report, the OECD highlights that, in addition to facilitating legal business, the effects of globalization also enable growth of illicit activity—such as transnational and organized crime—that risk weakening those states least capable of dealing with this challenges. In 2015, the OECD identified 50 countries and territories—home to one fifth of the world's people—as being fragile or in conflict. The OECD underscores that fragility occurs not just across states, but also within them, raising the prospect of growing areas of "alternately governed spaces," and posing a serious challenge to reestablishing central authority in many weaker states.

Dissatisfaction and Expectations Gap. Frustration with government performance in the areas of security, education, and employment is likely to fuel public discontent and provide a foundation for greater political instability. In some cases, the frustration stems from a deterioration of lifestyles and standards of living—or a sense that standards of living are not keeping pace with those of other countries—as populations are buffeted by the effects of globalization. In other instances, increasingly wealthy, well-educated, and well-informed publics expect more from their governments at a time when the problems that governments must address—including climate change, terrorism, and increased migration—are increasingly complex and costly. The diffusion of power through technological, economic and social change also is making it more difficult for governments to implement effective policies by creating more potential veto players on issues, reinforcing a gap in expectations. Economic and social change is weakening traditional intermediary organizations, such as political parties, that once aggregated interests and represented them to the state, as public demands for direct participation clash with the multi-layered nature of the modern state.

- Governments will have to deal with an increasing number of actors—NGOs, corporations, and other entities—that can directly appeal to citizens and build their own coalitions, particularly online. A broad weakening of political parties and the ability of individuals and groups to use money and media to communicate directly with the public and mobilize support—if not necessarily sustain it—will personalize politics, making electoral outcomes and the policymaking process less predictable.

- Governments must also deal with technological changes and the growing leverage of individual players in financial markets, which can cause major, rapid disruptions across national boundaries, as occurred in the great recession. Financial experts warn these vulnerabilities will grow as speculators seek new instruments that provide short-term profit and take advantage of gaps in regulation or develop new capabilities—using big-data analytics or automated trading using artificial intelligence—to capitalize on existing markets and instruments. On the other hand, technology will enable states and subnational entities with the leadership, public trust and infrastructure to better provide more efficient and transparent services, to challenge corruption, and to increase their ability to regulate activities.

- Waning public tolerance for crime and corruption will fuel pressure on governments to reform or lose power. Wide variation in how governments respond to such pressure will persist, with some moving to greater transparency and responsiveness, while others retreat to authoritarianism and less accountability. New access to detailed information on government operations and news of other governments forced out of office are likely to raise public expectations of government behavior.

Political entrepreneurs can tap this reservoir of frustration to shape new forms of political participation. Populist sentiment that is couched in the language of anti-corruption has become a staple of politics in South Asia. Political parties in India and Pakistan have witnessed a surge in "reform" politics, mass movements fueled by disgust with the established political elites and mainstream parties.

- Surveys show overwhelming majorities of populations in Eurasia reject the legitimacy of their governing institutions and show little trust in parliaments, presidents, police, judges, and other elites. Similarly, according to Pew, concerns about corruption and inequality are top concerns of citizens in China.

Enter Non-State Actors. The division of labor among service providers is evolving as governments increasingly compete with business and other nonstate actors poised to assume the functions of government. Many of these entities are not new but might find increased opportunity as confidence in national administrations declines:

- **Corporations.** Globalization has broadened multinationals' reach, providing some with the opportunity to engage in public-private partnerships to provide services. Corporations, sometimes with governments, have chosen to address persistent social and environmental causes, assessing that responding to a public need will improve their standing and their financial performance. Coca Cola and USAID have partnered to support water treatment in Tanzania and other countries.

- **Religious-based entities.** Faith-based organizations historically have provided development and aid provision. Some NGOs note that their donors are more willing to contribute to them when governments are faltering.

- **Cities and their mayors.** As urbanization progresses and megacities develop, cities' influence—and that of their leaders—will increase. During the past several years, leaders of the world's largest cities have developed the C40—a collaborative network focused on addressing climate change. In 2014, the group held a widely publicized climate meeting in South Africa; their next in Mexico City in December 2016 will bring together C40 mayors from all over the world and hundreds of urban and sustainability leaders to advance urban solutions to climate change.

- **Criminal and terrorist organizations.** The proliferation of nefarious actors and virtual criminal networks that prey on digital-security gaps and exploit differences in national laws for profit will be a growing challenge for even strong states, as seen by the criminal groups' use of Facebook to connect with refugees and control migrant paths to Europe. In addition, terrorist organizations—most notably ISIL—have sought to provide governance to advance their cause and attract adherents.

Increasing Variation in Governance. During the next 20 years, governance will increasingly vary between and within states, in the forms that states take and their level of success, in response to differences in degree of urbanization, economic growth, basic social norms such as gender equality, and migration. The division of authority between national, regional, and local governments is likely to shift as some cities and regions become more important than existing administrative divisions.

- The number of states that mix democratic and autocratic elements is on the rise, with no apparent trend toward stable democracies. Some studies suggest these blended states are prone to instability. Many societies will suffer from chronically weak and unstable political institutions. The range of countries' degree of existing institutionalization and public political trust will mean substantial differences in states' ability to absorb political or environment shocks.

- Even within regions, variation in the quality of governance will increase. In Europe, the relatively high level of political trust in the Nordics allows those governments to use information technology to better provide services, while governments lacking the public's trust, such as Italy, will be hampered from taking such actions. Weak Central American states are foundering, while more-mature institutions in countries such as Chile or Uruguay can effectively cushion the impact of economic difficulties. Africa will also see increasing differentiation between the many failed or failing states and nations like Ghana or Kenya that are more likely to enact reforms.

- Successful states and subnational entities will use public-private partnerships, which can be transformative even if they do not guarantee greater democracy or accountability. Developing countries are increasingly open to such partnerships to jump-start construction of new infrastructure and to disseminate information to rural areas that the state could not easily serve. Reliance on parastatals, as in Singapore will probably gain renewed appeal as a model to emulate amid post-2008 skepticism that economic growth is best left to private bodies and a loosely regulated market.

- The center of gravity of government, particularly in the developing world, is likely to shift from the center to cities, and the regions where they are located—as localities seek to control their fiscal resources and exercise consensual decisionmaking with skilled bureaucracies, often by harnessing private expertise as well, according to a recent Brooking Institution report. Cities are emerging as key actors in advancing policies to mitigate climate change and are networking across national boundaries to do so.

Key Choices

The ability of developing states to progress economically and establish stable political systems will depend on how much governments and others invest in human capital and improved public service delivery. Investment in human capital, training, and organizational design will determine how fast capacity is built, or if it is built at all.

- It is unclear whether decentralization in the developed and developing world will shift power to cities that are frontrunners in innovation and public-private partnership—such as Lagos—and whether corporations will step in to perform formerly government functions. Some recent assessments suggest corporate firms that invest in areas traditionally thought of as the responsibility of the state, such as health care and renewable resources, provide stakeholders with greater returns, which suggests corporate roles could expand into these and other sectors.

- The degree to which states look to non-Western models of development remains unclear. Ultimately, government performance, especially on the economy, will determine citizens' assessment of its success. If citizens do not see an improvement in their well-being, they will lose confidence in their ruling elites—and will have modern communication and community-forming capabilities to express it. To that end, if Beijing can surmount China's economic challenges, escape the middle-income trap, and use technology to sway—or defuse—public opinion, other nations will probably try to follow its path.

Advanced industrial democracies and emerging powers also face key choices in how to respond to inequality, increasing debt burdens, and perceptions of less effective governance. The ability of leaders to manage these stresses will be severely tested because governments will find it hard to rebuild credibility with publics and maintain elite support at a time when hard choices are likely to alter the mix of winners and losers. With publics appearing more willing to take to the streets, political leaders may have less room to implement difficult policies and less time to show results. In this environment, leadership continuity could be rare, whether in industrial democracies or advanced autocracies like Russia and China, where power is bound to a single leader, increasing the potential for instability when an abrupt turnover in power does occur.

- Governments and leaders will probably adopt different strategies to address the challenges of slow growth and economic inequality. Turbulent times can produce transformative leaders who build new coalitions that reshape relations between governments and the public, but they may have few options for dealing with the durable technological factors that are slowing growth and generating inequality.

- Governments will also face difficult choices that come with aging populations and gender inequality. Leaders will have to balance the need for adjustments in welfare systems—long regarded as politically untouchable—with demands to invest in human capital and other initiatives to ensure greater opportunities and protections for women and other groups. Decisions that will have long-term repercussions for food security, health, child welfare, and environmental security.

International Institutions: Major Trends

Existing international institutions—especially the UN system of agencies—will struggle to adapt to the expanding range of actors and complexity of new issues that reach deeper into national sovereignty sensitivities and have a greater impact on domestic life than in the recent past, when international agreements could be negotiated by elites. As traditional organizations like the UN struggle to evolve, demands will rise for peacekeepers, humanitarian assistance, a forum for combatting climate change, and other shared concerns. A mix of forums that incorporate more nonstate actors, regional institutions, and informal consultation will emerge to address transnational issues underserved by traditional approaches. The creation of the Asian Infrastructure Investment Bank (AIIB) to pick up programming not supported by the World Bank is an example of one such regional approach.

A Rise in Veto Power. A lack of shared vision among major powers and competition among aspiring ones will impede major reforms in the international system. While everyone agrees that the UN Security Council (UNSC) must be reformed, there is little prospect for consensus among states on what that reform should look like, suggesting such change, while acknowledged by states to be needed, and while not impossible, will be slow in arriving if it does occur within the next two decades.

Some aspects of the international system will become more relevant as states begin to experience stress and governance difficulties in managing environmental and economic change, or internal conflict.

Demand for Multilateral Assistance To Grow. A cluster of environmental and demographic factors—global warming, energy shortages, unauthorized migration, resource scarcities, epidemics, ocean acidification, and bulging youth and aging populations—will increase strains on national governance efforts, especially where government competencies are fragile. As states face challenges to their domestic legitimacy, the need for multilateral resources to fill gaps in governments' capability will increase. Fragile national governments may require a range of multilateral assistance, including emergency IMF loans; UN peacekeeping; election assistance; international judicial investigations; technical assistance and policy advice; humanitarian aid; and guidance for containing or eradicating disease.

A Broader Mix of Development Instruments To Assist. At the same time that demands for multilateral approaches to assistance are growing among fragile states and those seeking to help them, a broader mix of instruments will be available, including loans and financing for middle income countries, which increasingly will bear the brunt of many humanitarian challenges. A true diversity is now rooted in the development community, with venture capitalists working with aid agency chiefs; corporate executives conferring with foreign policy advisers; and technologists consulting NGO leaders. This mix of diversity and experience will lead to experimentation—and both successes and failures—in an effort to better meet future needs. However, the biggest donor states, such as China and the United States, will provide most of their aid through bilateral channels.

No Alternative to Multilateralism on the Horizon

Although many formal intergovernmental institutions, such as the UN, will increasingly engage in new forms of partnership, these changes are unlikely to challenge the one-state-one-vote model of multilateralism during the next 20 years. The sovereign state has shown itself to be remarkably resilient as the cornerstone of international decisionmaking. Despite the changes of the past 500 years, the state has largely remained the key element of political order and is likely to continue to be dominant.

- The world will face international crises across a broad range of issues and theaters—some technical, and some societal—but it is unlikely that the next two decades will bring an inflection point resulting in a radically different approach to international governance. Nor is any state now championing a radically different alternative, despite the fact that nonstate entities, such as the Islamic State in Iraq and the Levant (ISIL) or the Baha'i faith—with the former attempting to impose a world caliphate through violent means, and the latter using peaceful activism to promote equality and a democratically-elected world government—are trying to do so. Although alternative models such as these have some support in certain parts of the world, the broad diversity of individual state interests will continue to prevent an alternate system from taking root at the global level, much as it currently inhibits UNSC expansion.

- To be clear, we expect the term "World Government" to remain seldom spoken aloud, even though two of what might be considered four "branches' of such governance have been augmented in recent years—international courts and the rising bureaucracy of agencies like the World Trade Organization. Notably, these are the two entities that vest legal standing in nations and, to some degree, in corporations and NGOs, rather than in private persons. As yet, no major or substantial movement has gathered to press for the two missing branches—executive and a legislature—in part because those would require standing elections on the part of global citizens. For now, at least, this appears to be a "concept too far" and nations are content to leave things that way.

- The UN of 2035, in terms of peace and security institutions, will probably look a lot like it does in 2016, even though its tools and agenda will evolve. The constitutional barriers to Charter amendment are high and, for all the complaints about the real inequities in the architecture of the UNSC, small states and aspiring powers have an enormous stake in maintaining the system and keeping the major military powers engaged in it.

- The majority of states will continue to value the UN and other multilateral institutions because of their ability to bestow legitimacy on a global, state-led agenda. Smaller states are also aware that multilateral institutions serve to protect their interests; without rules, major and regional powers would have more coercive power.

No Alternative to Multilateralism on the Horizon *(continued)*

- The role of international institutions will also be reinforced by the mutual embrace of these institutions by regional and subnational entities, international NGOs, philanthropic capitalists, multinational corporations, and individuals, which will ensure a certain continued centrality. Policy reforms and accommodations will occur when warranted, just as IMF voting practices have been reformed, and states with growing influence will renegotiate their roles.

- In pursuit of consequential action, multilateral institutions will deepen their engagement with companies, civil society organizations, local government offices and other authorities.

Harder Problems Ahead

Looking forward, the UN and its system of agencies will be less helpful in developing new standards for behavior on emerging issues, such as artificial intelligence, genome editing, or human enhancement, because of the diverging values and interests among states, private actors, and scientific and technological communities; because of the large knowledge gaps across technical and policy communities; and because technological change will continue to far outpace the ability of states, agencies, and international organizations to set standards, policies, regulations, and norms. All of these factors will serve as a brake on collective agenda setting. The challenge of future international governance will lie in the crossdisciplinary impact of these technologies and other challenges ahead, suggesting that coordination and strategic understanding of synergies across a range of issue areas—not depth in just one of them—is going to be needed for effective international governance to proceed.

- **Artificial intelligence, genome editing, and human enhancement.** Developments in artificial intelligence, genome editing, and human enhancement are examples of issues that are likely to pose some of the most contentious values questions in the coming decades by automating critical legal and security decisions affecting people's lives and stretching the concept of what it means to be human. Developments in these technological areas will affect relations between states and between a state and its population. Given the potential promise and peril of these technologies, debate among states, private companies, publics, and religious actors at the global, regional, state, and local level will intensify. Proponents argue that major advances in these areas will cure diseases, reduce hunger, and increase longevity, but critics warn that such technologies risk permanently altering the human race—either accidentally or intentionally—and possibly leading to individual or group extinctions. Policies, laws, and treaties to manage such technologies will lag, because of the speed and distributed nature of their development.

Technological developments in cyber and space will also raise new normative challenges. We have only modest understanding as to what states, publics, and private actors will want to see as norms in these domains during the next two decades, but it is clear that private commercial actors will play a bigger role in shaping normative development across them.

- **Cyber.** Cyber attacks—encompassing the exfiltration, exploitation, and destruction of information—are likely to be more widely employed to advance state interests and punish adversaries during the next two decades, creating new challenges for the law on armed conflict and principles related to noninterference in a state's internal affairs.

- **Space.** With more states and commercial firms stepping up their capabilities in space, traditional international approaches to govern these activities will be challenged, and developed countries will see their military and intelligence advantage ebb. Expanding use of space including from developing countries and private companies increase the importance of the international community retaining the ability to ensure safe operation in a more congested environment. But new technological capabilities will not be the only crossdisciplinary struggles. Many longstanding issues will increasingly appear together as elements of broader, complicated problems.

- **Ocean warming.** Ocean warming will cause fish to migrate to cooler waters and create resource challenges and local economic stress.

- **Climate.** Climate change will threaten agricultural output and increase fragility in rapidly growing poor countries.

- **Trade agreements.** Trade and economic agreements will require consensus on complex and contentious issues, such as genetically modified organisms, intellectual property rights, health and environmental standards, biodiversity, and labor standards, suggesting that global policy formulation will increasingly have meaningful domestic implications.

Coordination and synergy will be difficult for the UN when facets of a single issue are handled by different parts of the system.

- **Atrocity prevention.** Efforts to address atrocity prevention are scattered throughout the UN human rights and security bureaucracy. The UN is limited in its ability to address mass atrocities committed by nonstate actors, primarily because such situations often involve the absence of state authority and therefore lack a "valid" interlocutor. Tackling the problems associated with reinforcing sovereignty and governance are often essential to tackling the atrocities problem.

- **Countering terrorism.** On the criminal justice front, the International Criminal Court has difficulty exercising jurisdiction over active terror groups: most prosecutions are focused on state actors or militia groups, rather than "terrorist organizations," in part because officials differ on how to define such a group. Despite these impediments, the ICC is likely to serve as a forum through which terror issues are debated and countered.

- **Human mobility.** The international mobility of people—primarily migrants, refugees, and internally displaced persons—is likely to stress state governance as population movements grow in scale, reach, and complexity, and as growing demographic disparities, economic inequality, and the effects of environmental change among countries keep numbers of displaced and migrating people high. Environmental scientists' estimates of future environment-induced movement vary widely, from 25 million persons to 1 billion by 2050, with 200 million the most widely cited number. Debate over these numbers is heated: some migration experts argue they underestimate human resilience, the ability of people to endure hardships, and the share of future populations who will not be able to move. What is clear is that human movement is likely to increase substantially, prompting calls—similar to today's—for a review of state obligations to such populations.

An "a la carte" World

The increasing complexity of old and new challenges alike is generating new requirements for collective problem solving. How states approach issues is changing because of the increasing complexity of challenges, and because a greater number of states are needed to secure collective action at a time when there is a lack of consensus—particularly among major powers—on what the global goals should be.

Nevertheless, some remarkable recent landmark agreements suggest progress will continue to be possible in coming years:

- In June 2015, the General Assembly endorsed the Sendai Framework for Disaster Risk Reduction.

- In July 2015, UN member states adopted the Addis Ababa Action Agenda on financing for development.

- In September 2015, the UN General Assembly adopted the 2030 Agenda for Sustainable Development.

- In December 2015, the Twenty-First Conference of the Parties to the UN Framework Convention on Climate Change concluded with an agreement by 195 countries to strive to keep the global temperature rise below two degrees Celsius.

- And in 2016, the International Organization for Migration joined the UN.

A lack of overall shared strategic understanding continues, however, which has resulted in a prevailing mode of international cooperation that is problem-centered, ad hoc, and issue-specific rather than anticipatory, cross-disciplinary, or universal in scope. States, corporations, and activists line up behind their specific causes, and this ad hoc approach in the long term can potentially cause a loss of coherence and direction among international bodies—the UN and others—that make up the international system. The advantage, however, is that voluntary, informal approaches can help create trust, common language, and shared goals—benefits that can eventually lead to support for, or a rebalance, in agreement at an international level. Whether the current institutions can be effective in the future, or whether new institutions or parallel mechanisms are formed, will depend largely on how governments interact with a variety of actors and whether current institutions and major powers can help states negotiate mature bargains on core national interests that recognize the interests of others.

- **A greater number of states are necessary to secure collective, global action.** The number of states that matter—that is, states without whose cooperation a global problem cannot be adequately addressed—has grown. The aftermath of the 2008-09 financial crisis and the subsequent emergence of the G20 as a key group exemplify how a broader range of countries can lead to effective problem solving. The group, which had been in existence for almost 10 years before the 2008 global financial crisis, became the principal forum for global economic-crisis management, not because of a desire by major powers to be more inclusive, but because no state or small group of states could solve the impending problems alone. The UN Framework Convention on Climate Change is another example where, as a consequence of progress, more states—representing a diverse range of interests—need to act collectively to reach stated goals.

- **A growing number of actors are now solving and creating problems.** An increase in the number of private, regional, and subnational actors meaningfully involved in aid delivery, development and other economic issues, and human rights is likely to occur. This trend may diminish the role of state provision in these areas, but it could bolster overall goals put forward by international institutions. However, such networks cut in both directions: a more-interconnected "uncivilized" world—including groups as varied as ISIL and Anonymous—will challenge the fundamental basis of the system. And populism and xenophobia might grow, but new technologies may protect and possibly empower those who seek to enlarge the international human rights regime.

- **States are forum-building to create "shared" understanding on controversial issues.** States are building and participating in regional institutions, multi-stakeholder forums, and informal consultation processes to give greater visibility and voice to their interests and to solicit support for their views.

  - In formal settings, China and Russia have built new arrangements to assert what they see as their rightful dominance in their respective regions. China, for example, will promote the AIIB, and Russia, the Eurasian Union, as platforms for regional economic influence.

  - China and Russia together, with aspiring powers, Brazil, India, and South Africa, have also built a nonbinding summit platform known as the BRICS, to give themselves a transnational platform from which to promote their views. Mexico, Indonesia, South Korea, Turkey and Australia have also created a similar platform, MIKTA, based on shared values and interests.

  - These structures are emerging not because aspiring powers have new ideas about how to address global challenges or because they seek to change global rules and norms, but so they can project power—and because sometimes it is easier to get things done in smaller groups. However, these aspiring powers will continue to invest in traditional institutions—even as they create new ones—if only in recognition of the strength of today's system.

  - Efforts to change the state hierarchy in existing institutions will continue, in an attempt to gain privileges. Structures that might seek to reorient the state hierarchy of power include the BRICS-led New Development Bank and the China-led AIIB (to complement the World Bank and IMF), the Universal Credit Rating Group (to complement the private-sector Moody's and S&P ratings agencies), China Union Pay (to complement Mastercard and Visa), and CIPS (to complement the SWIFT payment-processing network).

- **Multi-stakeholder multilateralism will complement state efforts.** Government officials will dominate—but not monopolize—multilateral cooperation in the future. National regulators and technical experts will inform governance by engaging their counterparts abroad. This is already happening in the effort to ensure the safety and reliability of medicine in an age of complex supply chains. The US Food and Drug Administration, recognizing its own limitations, spearheaded the creation of an informal, "global coalition of medicine regulators," to close drug-safety gaps worldwide, particularly with major producers like China and India. And a good model for how private authority might be involved in future global governance is the International Accounting Standards Board (IASB), which develops accounting standards for the 27 countries of the European Union, and about 90 other countries by drawing technical experts from large accounting firms who are organized by an independent foundation chartered in Delaware.

Key Choices

One way to address the future constellation of challenges is for national political leaders to generate strategic guidance calling for interdisciplinary relations across institutions. In finance, some actors are already experimenting with such a model. By better understanding the synergies embedded in multisectoral agendas, such as the Sustainable Development Goals, both states and institutions can better advise and support positive outcomes. Political leaders will be key as only heads of state have the authority to press crossministerial agendas within their states. Such an approach will be a necessary counterbalance to what is now a very siloed international system.

- A new, more broadly defined, more widely conceived definition of national interest, based on the concept of mutuality, might induce states to find far greater unity in deliberations at the international level. With the growing number of existential challenges facing humanity, "collective interest" could become "national interest."

However, the following developments remain uncertain:

- **Whether adequate resources will be available to enable coalitions of states and international organizations to address and lead programmatically on common challenges.** This will depend in part on governments treating international commitments with the same importance as national demands—rather than viewing them as competing priorities—mobilizing coalitions to support these priorities, and enjoying their public's trust. It also depends on the role large-scale private partnerships and foundations take on—including organizations such as the Gates Foundation, the Global Alliance for Vaccines and Immunization (GAVI), the Global Fund to Fight Aids, Tuberculosis and Malaria, and the Global Education Fund—in developing an approach to funding and delivering critical programs on the ground.

- **Whether the monitoring and compliance tools of international organizations will serve as confidence-building measures to reduce geopolitical tension.** This will depend on state willingness to accept election monitors, weapon inspections, and other compliance agreements outlined in international agreements. For example, the UN mission to eliminate Syria's chemical weapons program was marked by extraordinary international cooperation and represented the first time an entire arsenal of a category of weapons of mass destruction has been removed from a country experiencing internal armed conflict.

- **To what degree elites will be effective in guiding institutions and states through global transitions, and in promoting a strategic vision on crucial issues such as mitigating climate change and navigating global commons.** Leadership among international institutions will need to promote a long-term perspective and a global mentality—and be decisive in the short term—to overcome the temptation toward insularity and muddling through.

- **To what extent private actors will involve themselves in international rule making, enforcement, or dispute resolution—areas traditionally the responsibility of a state or public authority.** National and international laws are established and enforced differently in various state legal systems, but most—if not all—involve state authority. Rule-making, enforcement, and dispute resolution by private actors, however, is becoming more common. For example, the eBay/PayPal resolution center works in 16 different languages and solves roughly 60 million disagreements between buyers and sellers each year. Deepening internet penetration allows self-policing among online communities, which can now shame those whose behavior does not conform to the norms of the group. These mechanisms are not accessed and used to the same degree by societies across the world, but they do represent behavior that contributes to governance, and over time will provide a broader array of venues in which people might choose to act.

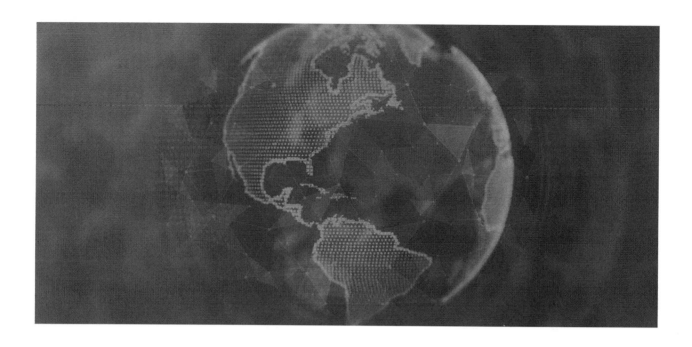

HOW PEOPLE FIGHT . . .

The risk of conflict, including inter-state conflict, will increase during the next two decades because of diverging interests among major powers, ongoing terrorist threats, continued instability in weak states, and the spread of lethal and disruptive technologies. The last 20 years' trend of decreasing numbers and intensities of conflicts appears to be reversing: current conflict levels are increasing and battle-related deaths and other human costs of conflict are up sharply, according to published institutional reports. Furthermore, the character of conflict is changing because of technology advances, new strategies, and the evolving global geopolitical context—challenging previous concepts of warfare. **Together these developments point to future conflicts that are more diffuse, diverse, and disruptive.**

- **"Diffuse" because the greater accessibility to instruments of war will enable a variety of actors, including states, nonstate and substate entities (terrorist groups, criminal networks, insurgent forces, mercenaries, and private corporations), and motivated individuals, to engage in conflict.** One example of the diffusion of conflict is the growth in the numbers of private military-security firms and organizations that provide personnel who complement and substitute for state militaries in conflict zones and potentially as peacekeeping forces. Conflicts will become more complex and the traditional distinctions between combatants and noncombatants less meaningful as the range of participants expands.

- **"Diverse" because the means of conflict will vary across a wider spectrum—ranging from "nonmilitary" capabilities, such as economic coercion, cyber attacks, and information operations, to advanced conventional weapons and weapons of mass destruction (WMD)—and occur in multiple domains, to include space and cyberspace.** The diversity of the potential forms of conflict that might arise will increasingly challenge the ability of governments to prepare effectively for the range of possible contingencies.

- **"Disruptive"** because of an increasing emphasis by states and terrorist groups, on disrupting critical infrastructure, societal cohesion, and government functions rather than on defeating enemy forces on the battlefield through traditional military means. Adversaries will almost certainly seek to exploit greater connectivity in societies and the ubiquitous nature of cyberspace to create disruption. Terrorists, for example, will continue to exploit social and other forms of media to spread fear and enhance the disruptive impact of their attacks on the psyche of the targeted societies.

Major Trends

Four overall trends are likely to exemplify the changing character of conflict during the next two decades regarding how people will fight:

The blurring of peacetime and wartime. Future conflicts will increasingly undermine concepts of war and peace as separate, distinct conditions. The presence of nuclear and advanced conventional weapons will contribute to deterring full-scale war among major powers, but lower levels of security competition will continue and may even increase. Such conflicts will feature the use of strong-arm diplomacy, cyber intrusions, media manipulation, covert operations and sabotage, political subversion, economic and psychological coercion, proxies and surrogates, and other indirect applications of military power.

- The goal of these approaches is to stay below the threshold of triggering a full-scale war by employing mostly noncombat tools, often backed by posturing of military power, to achieve political objectives over time. This trend is already occurring: China's and Russia's actions—in the South China Sea and Ukraine respectively—are contemporary examples of this approach.

- While such approaches to conflict are not new, states like China and Russia view these methods as an increasingly integral part of future conflicts compared to traditional military capabilities. Technology advances, such as cyber tools and social media, are also enabling new means for conducting conflicts and sowing instability, below the level of full-scale war. These capabilities also will often obfuscate the source of attacks impeding effective responses.

These strategies, combined with a continuing risk of periodic terrorist attacks, will probably lead to persistent, economic, political, and security competition—occurring in the "gray zone" between peacetime and full-scale war—as the new normal for the security environment during the coming decades.

- States' employment of "gray zone" approaches seek to avoid general war but will probably increase the risk of inadvertent escalation, through miscalculation, accident, or misinterpretation of adversary "red lines."

- States and nonstate entities alike will employ "nonmilitary" tools, such as information networks and multimedia capabilities, to exploit faith-based ideologies, nationalism, and other forms of identity politics to legitimize their cause, inspire followers, and motivate like-minded individuals to take actions. China, for example, views media, legal, and psychological forms of warfare—the "three warfares"—as important to ensuring international and domestic support for future Chinese military operations and for weakening an enemy's resolve, according to Chinese military writings.

Nonstate groups capable of creating greater disruption. The spread of disruptive and lethal technologies and weapons will enhance the ability of nonstate and substate groups—such as terrorists, insurgents, activists, or criminal gangs—to challenge state authority. Such groups, motivated by religious fervor, political ideology, or greed, are likely to become more adept at imposing costs and undermining state governance. For example, activist groups, such as Anonymous, are likely to employ increasingly disruptive cyber attacks against government infrastructure to draw attention to their cause. Nonstate groups will also wield greater firepower. Terrorist groups, like Hizballah and ISIL, or insurgents in Ukraine are examples of nonstate and substate groups that have gained access to sophisticated weaponry during the last decade.

- This trend is likely to continue because of the ongoing proliferation of commercial technologies and weapons and the support from states that seek to use such groups as proxies in advancing their own interests. The proliferation of increasingly lethal and effective, advanced, man-portable weapons and technologies, such as antitank guided missiles, surface-to-air missiles, unmanned drones, and encrypted communications systems, will enhance the threats posed by terrorist and insurgent forces. Access to weaponry, such as precision-guided rockets and drones, will provide such forces new strike assets to attack key infrastructures, forward operating bases, and diplomatic facilities.

Such groups also will probably exploit commercial technologies—such as additive manufacturing, autonomous control systems, computer processors, and sensors—to create tailored weapons and "intelligent" improvised explosive devices, complicating the development of countermeasures. These groups will often seek to enhance their effectiveness and survivability by operating in urban environments.

- The spread of lethal and disruptive technologies will provide opportunities for insurgents, terrorists, and weak militaries to conduct "irregular" forms of warfare more effectively. The use of satellite navigation systems and mobile communications will enable more effective, coordinated, small-unit attacks and dispersed operations to impose casualties and wear down an opponent's resources and political resolve while avoiding large-scale, direct engagements with superior military forces.

- A potential implication of an increasing privatization of violence and diversity of actors is the emergence of many small, but interconnected conflicts that overwhelm the ability of governments and international institutions to manage.

Increasing capabilities for stand-off and remote attacks. The proliferation of cyber capabilities, precision-guided weapons, robotic systems, long-range strike assets and unmanned-armed, air, land, sea, and submarine vehicles will shift warfare from direct clashes of opposing armies to more standoff and remote operations, especially in the initial phases of conflict. Precision weapons and unmanned systems have been a mainstay of the US arsenal, but the continuing proliferation of these capabilities increases the potential of both sides possessing these capabilities in a future conflict. Long-range, precision-guided, conventional ballistic and cruise missiles, unmanned vehicles, and air defense systems will enable advanced militaries to threaten rival forces seeking access to the air and maritime commons surrounding their territory. The development of scramjet engines and hypersonic vehicles will also significantly increase the speed at which targets are engaged. For example, developing long-range precision strike capabilities—including missiles, hypersonic vehicles, and manned strike assets—are critical to China's strategy of increasing the risks to US naval and expeditionary forces operating in the western Pacific, according to US military experts.

In addition to countering foreign military intervention, long-range, standoff capabilities might enable some states to assert control over key maritime chokepoints and to establish local spheres of influence. Cyber attacks against critical infrastructures and information networks also will permit actors to impose costs directly on rivals from a distance, bypassing superior enemy military forces. Russian officials, for example, have noted publicly that initial attacks in future wars might be made through information networks to destroy critically important infrastructure and disrupt an enemy's political and military command and control.

- The increasing automation of strike systems, including unmanned, armed drones, and the spread of truly autonomous weapon systems potentially lowers the threshold for initiating conflict, because fewer lives would be at risk. Adversaries also might employ massed "swarms" of unmanned systems to overwhelm defenses.

- The proliferation of long-range, precision-guided weapons will probably promote cost-imposing strategies involving strikes on critical infrastructures, such as those related to a state's energy production, communications, diplomatic facilities, economy, and security.

- A future crisis involving militaries similarly equipped with long-range, precision-guided conventional weapons risks being unstable, because both sides would have an incentive to strike first, before their own systems are attacked. In addition, command, control, and targeting infrastructure—including satellites that provide navigation and targeting information—would probably become targets of attacks for forces seeking to disrupt an enemy's strike capabilities. Russia and China continue to pursue weapons systems capable of destroying satellites on orbit, placing US and others' satellites at greater risk in the future.

- Terrorist groups will almost certainly engage in a "poor man's" version of long-range strike by recruiting and inspiring like-minded individuals to carry out terrorist acts in the homelands of other countries.

- Cyber attacks against private sector networks and infrastructure could induce a response that draws corporations into future conflicts. This trend, combined with opportunistic cyber attacks by individuals and nonstate groups, will muddle the distinction between state-sanctioned and private actions. Protecting critical infrastructure, such as crucial energy, communication, and health systems, will become an increasingly important national security challenge.

New concerns about nuclear and other WMD. During the next two decades, the threat posed by nuclear and other forms of WMD will almost certainly remain and will probably increase as a result of technology advances and increasing asymmetry between rival military forces. Current nuclear states will almost certainly continue to maintain, if not modernize, their nuclear forces out to 2035. Russia, for example, will almost certainly remain committed to nuclear weapons as a deterrent, a counter to stronger conventional military forces, and its ticket to superpower status. Russian military doctrine purportedly includes the limited use of nuclear weapons in a situation where Russia's vital interests are at stake to "deescalate" a conflict by demonstrating that continued conventional conflict risks escalating the crisis to a large-scale nuclear exchange.

- Similarly, Pakistan has introduced short-range, "battlefield" nuclear weapons that it has threatened to use against Indian conventional incursions, which lower the threshold for nuclear use. Nuclear "saber-rattling" by North Korea—including its development of ICBMs—and the possibility that Iran might renege on its commitments under the Joint Comprehensive Plan of Action and the Non-Proliferation Treaty and develop nuclear weapons also will probably remain concerns during the next two decades.

- In addition, the proliferation of advanced technologies, especially biotechnologies, will potentially reduce the barriers to entry to WMD for some new actors. Internal collapse of weak states could open a path for terrorist WMD use resulting from unauthorized seizures of weapons.

- At-sea deployments of nuclear weapons by India, Pakistan, and perhaps China would nuclearize the Indian Ocean during the next two decades. These countries would view these developments as enhancing their strategic deterrence, but the presence of multiple nuclear powers with uncertain doctrine for managing at sea incidents between nuclear-armed vessels increases the risk of miscalculation and inadvertent escalation.

- The technical barriers to developing biological agents into weapons of societal disruption or terror probably will shrink as the costs of manufacturing decreases, DNA sequencing and synthesis improves, and genetic-editing technology become more accessible on a global basis.

- Some states are likely to continue to value chemical agents as a deterrent and for tactical use on the battlefield. The ease of manufacturing some chemical weapons will make their potential use of by terrorist or insurgent groups a concern.

Key Choices

The implications of how people fight in the future will depend heavily on the emerging geopolitical context and decisions made by major actors that increase or mitigate risks of conflict and escalation. Although US relative advantages are decreasing in some areas, the United States will almost certainly retain key security and military advantages compared to other states as a result of the country's economic strength, favorable demographic profile, geographical position, technology edge, openness to information, and alliance systems, providing Washington opportunities to shape the emerging security environment. However, other states and nonstate groups will continue to view the US military as an object of competition—as well as for emulation—in developing their own concepts and capabilities for future war. Furthermore, key uncertainties remain about the future likelihood of major war, its costs, and potential for escalation. These uncertainties also suggest potential opportunities for the United States and its partners to mitigate worst outcomes through confidence-building measures, increasing resilience, and promoting international agreements to restrict the development and use of the most unstable escalatory capabilities.

How global and regional players respond to future geopolitical developments and security challenges, such as transnational terrorism, sectarian violence, intrastate conflict, and weak states will significantly shape inter-state competition and the potential for wider conflict during the next two decades. China, Iran, and Russia will probably seek greater influence over their neighboring regions and will want the United States and other countries to refrain from interfering with their interests, a situation likely to perpetuate the ongoing geopolitical and security competition occurring around the periphery of Asia and in the Middle East, to include the major sea lanes. Tension between major and regional powers also could increase in response to the global redistribution of economic and military power and the rise of nationalism in state politics. The diversity of security threats and the potential for future, multiple, simultaneous regional contingencies risk overwhelming the capacity of the US military to manage, emphasizing the continuing need for competent military allies and multilateral approaches.

- The choices that major powers make in response to increasing competition will determine the likelihood of future conflicts. Constraints that inhibit full-scale war among major powers, such as nuclear deterrence and economic interdependence, will probably remain. However, changes in the character of conflict will probably introduce greater risk for miscalculation that would increase the likelihood of major-power conflict, unless competing states undertake mitigating confidence-building measures.

- The continuing threat of transnational terrorism and state use of "gray zone" strategies would probably increase the incidents of external powers intervening in future intrastate conflicts and engaging in proxy wars. Cooperation among major powers and international institutions in resolving intrastate conflicts could bring much needed stability. However, the involvement of a diversity of actors with competing objectives risks prolonging and expanding local conflicts, creating broader instability.

The proliferation of long-range strike systems and cyber attack capabilities and more sophisticated terrorist and insurgent operations suggests a trend toward increasingly costly but less decisive conflicts. The strategies of major powers and nonstate groups that emphasize disrupting critical infrastructures, societies, government functions, and leadership decisionmaking will exacerbate this trend and increase the risk of future conflicts expanding to include homeland attacks. The character of future conflicts would change significantly if an unexpected advantage in cyber attack capabilities creates the ability to cripple advanced, information-dependent military systems found in most modern militaries.

- Future conflicts will probably be fought in multiple domains beyond traditional air, land, sea, and undersea domains to include computer networks, the electromagnetic spectrum, social media, outer space, and the environment—as adversaries seek competitive advantages and new means of imposing costs. Future conflicts in the environmental domain, for example, are likely to involve controlling access to water supplies or intentionally creating environmental damage to impose economic costs on rivals.

- Efforts to enhance resilience, by increasing the security and redundancy of critical infrastructure and networks, deploying defensive systems, and enhancing societal emergency preparedness levels, for example, would decrease the ability of adversaries to impose crippling costs.

Advances in military capabilities, such as unmanned, automated weapon systems and high-speed, long-range strike systems, which reduce response times, are likely to create new, but uncertain, escalation dynamics in times of crisis. Furthermore, the rapid pace of technology developments—in areas such as cyber, genetics, information systems, computer processing, nanotechnologies, directed-energy, and autonomous, robotic systems—increases the potential for surprise in future conflicts.

- Conflicts with an asymmetry of interests and capabilities among the combatants are probably most ripe for deliberate or inadvertent escalation, as some states might choose to threaten escalation against a superior conventional force—including WMD use—to deter a military intervention or to compel a cease-fire.

The Changing Character of Warfare

TRADITIONAL FORMS OF WARFARE	EMERGING FORMS OF WARFARE
Use of military force	Increasing use of nonmilitary and covert means
Targeting of enemy forces	Targeting of enemy perceptions, society
Direct clash of militaries	Remote strikes using standoff precision weapons, robotic systems, and information attacks
Destruction of military personnel and weaponry	Destruction of critically important military and civilian infrastucture
Deterrence by fear of retaliation	Deterrence by fear of escalation
Winning by defeating the enemy on the battlefield	Winning by distrupting the support systems (political, economic, information, etc.) on which the enemy military depends

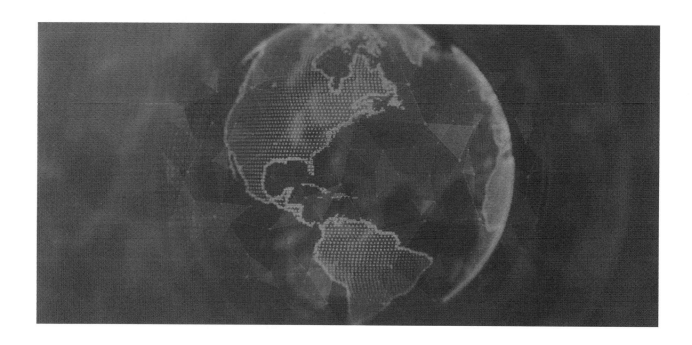

TERRORISM

The means for states, nonstate, and substate actors to impose harm are diversifying, as are the motivations for doing so. These trends will further blur the lines between different forms of violence; governments will continue to debate which actions constitute "terrorism" versus "war," "insurgency" or "criminal acts." These developments suggest that how we fight terrorism will probably continue to evolve.

The trends shaping the future of terrorism during the next five years and beyond will depend heavily on how two ongoing developments are resolved. First, the resolution or continuation of the many intra- and inter-state conflicts currently under way—most important, the Syrian civil war, but also conflict in Afghanistan, Iraq, Libya and the Sahel, Somalia, Yemen, and elsewhere—will determine the intensity and geography of future violence. The spread of ungoverned space, particularly during the past five years, created an environment conducive to extremism and encouraged the enlistment of thousands of volunteers eager to fight. Until some semblance of security is established, militancy will continue to breed.

Second, today's foreign fighters unless identified, deradicalized, and reintegrated back into society are likely to become the recruiting pool for tomorrow's violent nonstate actors. Similarly, disaffected migrants, without better integration, education, and economic opportunity, could become an ideal recruiting pool for violent extremist groups.

- States or regions where governments lack the capacity or will to maintain security or provide political and economic stability, correspond with areas that experience high degrees of violence and where extremism flourishes. A lack of stability and responsive governance—especially in Africa, the Middle East, and South Asia—will continue to create conditions conducive to terrorism.

Extreme minority interpretations of religion will probably remain the most frequently cited justification for terrorism—certainly five years from now and, likely, also 20 years into the future. Three drivers are notable: 1) the likely continuing breakdown of state structures in much of the Middle East and the proxy war between Iran and Saudi Arabia fueling Shia-Sunni sectarianism; 2) tension between and within various forms of militants citing religion, and a continued perception of Western hegemony; and 3) retention of the "far enemy" ideology among extremist movements.

Although the location of religiously driven terrorism will fluctuate, the schism between Shia and Sunni, and between extremist Sunnis and who they regard as "nonbelievers" seem likely to worsen in the short term and are unlikely to abate by 2035. Violence becomes more likely when a powerful ideology like Salafi-jihadism, whether ISIL's or al-Qa'ida's, in a region undergoing vast and rapid political change combines with generations of autocratic government, gender inequality, and economic disparities.

A combination of psychological and situational factors will drive participation in terrorism and help terrorist groups attract resources and maintain cohesion. The relative weight of motivating factors for recruits and supporters is highly individualistic and situational, making it difficult to generalize. Nevertheless, some of the most important drivers of individual participation will be:

- **Disenfranchisement, repression, and humiliation** can drive people to seek power and control through violence. Some level of alienation, arising from disconnection from the sociocultural mainstream, inability to participate in the political process, coping with diminished opportunity for marriage, or inability to attain one's perceived "deserved" economic benefits and status from society will remain consistent sources of grievance-driven violence. Such frustrations can affect any walk of life; the pool of potential terrorists is not limited by social class, economic status, or educational background. Additionally, perceived grievances against a common group, or ethnic and kinship bonds—to include peer, social or familial networks—will motivate retaliation or violence against alleged perpetrators. Individual desire for adventure, fame, and belonging will contribute to individual terrorist participation.

- The "denationalizing"—the loss of connection with their community of origin of young people in European cities, combined with the lack of effective incentives to assume a European national identity, will continue to generate potential recruits for extremist organizations.

- Ethnic and religious tension beyond today's hotspots will cause eruptions of nationalist and communal violence and terrorism, such as between Chechens and Russians, the Malay and Thais in Thailand, Muslims and Buddhists in Burma, and Christians and Muslims in Central Africa. Such developments create conflict zones for transnational terror movements to exploit.

- Environmental change related to degraded soils, water resources, biodiversity and increased frequency of extreme and unusual weather, particularly the impact of climate change, is likely to amplify pressure on fragile and failing states to provide sufficient food and water to stressed populations. The interactions between chronic and acute stresses in local and regional food, water, and energy systems has led to failure of some governments—especially in the Middle East and Central and South Asia—to meet popular demands or address perceptions of unequal distribution of scarce resources, which might prompt future violent behavior by populations seeking redress.

Technology will introduce a new set of tradeoffs, facilitating terrorist communications, recruitment, logistics, and lethality, but also giving authorities more sophisticated techniques to identify and characterize threats. Technology will enable nonstate actors to mask and obfuscate their activities and identities and will be key to their ability to talk to one another, recruit new members, and disseminate messages. Advancements in technology also raise the stakes for a high-impact, low-likelihood terrorist WMD scenario and enable the proliferation of more lethal, conventional weaponry to terrorist groups

- Technology will enable further decentralization of threats to devolve from the relatively organized and directed al-Qa'ida to an atomized jihadist militancy. This trend will pose challenges to counterterrorism efforts and change the nature of future terrorist plots and strategies.

Previous waves of terrorism have peaked and declined over the course of multiple generations. The current religiously motivated wave of terrorism—which, arguably has dominated global terrorism since the mid-1990s—is different from previous waves in terms of motivation, reach, mobilization, and justification and will probably last considerably longer. Current religious conflicts are intensifying rather than abating, as the Sunni–Shia schism and ISIL's rise are increasing extremism and polarization worldwide. Just as Usama bin Ladin's contemporaries who went to Afghanistan became the core of al-Qa'ida a decade or more later, the current generation of youth now being radicalized by ISIL (and other various extremist groups) are likely to dominate the Sunni extremist scene for the next 20 years.

- Despite the current intensification of terrorism, it is possible that significant reductions in the Middle East and North Africa could occur if states are able to address terrorism's underlying drivers. The ability of governments to institute political and economic reforms that address many grievances and perceptions of disenfranchisement also would contribute to discrediting extremist ideologies as the only means for achieving reform.

- In the future, gender will probably play an increasing role in counterterrorism, especially related to countering narratives promoting violence as a prerequisite to political reform. Several international nongovernmental organizations are working on the issue. The McKinsey Institute's study on mothers and wives, for example, concluded that women—and mothers in particular—possess the unique ability to recognize early warning signs of radicalization in their children enabling them to play a key role in curtailing violent extremism. Empowering women to express their perspectives within their households and their societies is a key counterterrorism investment. However, framing women exclusively as peaceful will cause policymakers to miss important opportunities for information gathering and prevention tools. Women also play an active role in promoting, recruiting, and committing violence. On 4 September 2016 French police discovered an abandoned car full of explosives parked near Notre Dame Cathedral in Paris. Discovery of the car led to the disruption of a female terrorist cell with ties to ISIL.

- Ideas about gender roles and masculinity are also likely to influence counterterrorism as information technology and the sharing of ideas broaden perceptions of acceptable 'masculine' behaviors. Studies show that violence is sometimes linked to feelings of injured masculinity;

when men cannot fulfill traditional roles of husbands, fathers, or providers, they may turn to violence to demonstrate their masculine power or ability to defend their people and values. Encouraging modification of concepts of gender norms, which has been undertaken by several NGOs, may also help ameliorate the link between masculinity and violence at all levels.

Made in the USA
Columbia, SC
30 June 2017